Blue Money

Janet Capron

A Mostly True Memoir

The Unnamed Press
Los Angeles, CA

The Unnamed Press
P.O. Box 411272
Los Angeles, CA 90041

Published in North America by The Unnamed Press.

1 3 5 7 9 10 8 6 4 2

ISBN: 978-1944700263

Library of Congress Control Number: 2017940509

This book is distributed by Publishers Group West

Cover Photograph by Leland Bobbé
Cover design & typeset by Jaya Nicely

This book is a work of creative nonfiction.
Names, identifying details, and places have been changed.

In loving memory of my mother

Author's Note

I grew up on Park Avenue with my mother and a series of live-in maids. My grandfather, a retired liberal newspaper publisher and quixotic champion of the workingman, supported us in style. I mention my grandfather not only to show the source of my mother's and my good fortune but also to help the reader understand my fall from grace. I translated his lifelong fight for the underdog to mean I should become the underdog. I went to a good private school and to camp in the summer, and spent Easter vacations at my grandparents' winter home in Palm Beach. But I was destined to join, for more than a decade, the ranks of the marginal and despised.

By the time I got to a progressive women's college in the mid-sixties, I was drunk almost every day and barely functioning. The dean of students seemed genuinely sorry when she had to ask me to leave. I started to rebel more pointedly after that, experimenting with drugs in addition to booze and exploring radical feminism, all of which took me to the threshold of the time of this book—the summer of 1971.

Blue Money is a memoir written in the guise of fiction. Everyone's name has been changed except my own. While the book is drawn directly from my life on the streets of New York City in the seventies, a few characters are composites and timelines may not be entirely accurate.

In spite of these novelistic details, all of *Blue Money*, at its heart, is true.

Well, you search in your bag
Light up a fag
Think it's a drag, but you're so glad
To be alive, honey
Live, honey

Say, when this is all over
You'll be in clover
We'll go out and spend
All of your blue money

Say, when this is all over
We'll be in clover
We'll go out and spend
All your blue money

Blue money
Juice money
Loose money
Juice money
Loose money, honey
What kind of money, honey
Juice money
Loose money
Blue money

Van Morrison

Blue Money

PART I

Initiation

The doorman tipped his hat. That was strange. I was seven blocks south on Park Avenue, seven short city blocks from my mother's house, my childhood home. I thought it was odd, too, that I was wearing the old, low-cut black crepe cocktail dress with little capped sleeves my mother had bought for me at Miss Bergdorf's more than five years ago on my eighteenth birthday. The length of my dress came just to the knee, no longer fashionable in 1971, but I didn't mind. I told myself I looked like one of those gamines in a black-and-white New Wave movie. I was glad to be who I was that evening in mid-August: no coat, no wrap of any kind, no gloves obviously, no stockings even. Just lots of pink lipstick. Anyway, the doorman deferred to me here as my own doorman Joe—seven blocks north, on the same side of the avenue, too, the east side—had never done. "Take that ball around the corner, gowan now, get." Joe had more important things to do than mind kids was I'm sure how he saw it. He was still there, over twenty years. Well, Joe certainly never tipped his hat to me, and I would have been shocked if he had. Now, here I was, about to turn my first trick—I was a whore, or about to become one any minute—and the doorman, who had been instructed in advance to let me up—who, in fact, conveyed hookers to 17D on a regular basis—was treating me as if I were a lady.

My tongue was sticking to the roof of my dry mouth, and the palms of my hands were damp. I was actually shivering, and not from the air-conditioning. I was crazy with nerves, in a stage-fright frenzy. Even so, the exquisite symmetry, the beautiful irony, didn't entirely escape me, not even in the final moments when the elevator operator and I ascended to the seventeenth floor in the noiseless, velvet, vacuum plush of the Otis, a grand car with a gold carved-wood ceiling, and the elevator operator kept his hand on the old-fashioned lever as if he were running something, as if he were guiding this upward-bound Jules Verne capsule through open space to its destination.

These male servants valued discretion to such an extent that, I was sure, all knowledge of the foul goings-on of their tenants would die with them. I was high on a few Dexamyls, ups, and so, a captive of my own inflamed imagination, I began to entertain a wild thought. As I rode up in the elevator, I made the sudden discovery there was an ongoing conspiracy of men, older than the Masons, older than religion, that closes around the whore, hides and even honors her.

As I considered this, I stared at four doors in the dimly lit corridor and wondered which one was marked "D." I found a mirror on the wall and ran my fingers through my short hair. I took out my compact and powdered my nose. I sucked in my cheeks and pursed my pink lips and posed in front of the mirror to remind myself I was pretty. Unfortunately, as soon as I stopped looking, I forgot again. Meanwhile, I kept thinking about how I was about to step outside of society into the unknown.

Suddenly I remembered Lillian Maurice. While I was still in grade school, my libertine mother, Maggie, and I invented Lillian Maurice, who lived in the most extreme luxury. Whenever we passed a store on Madison Avenue that struck us as particularly grand, such as a lingerie shop featuring feathered silk negligees, we would say, "Almost good enough for Lillian Maurice." Our exalted character lived in a social vacuum without a husband or children, exactly as a kept woman would. Apart from the roguish example of Lillian Maurice, I didn't have much to go on. I was beginning to warm to the theory that a lot of men really don't like getting it for nothing. They want to pay for it one way or the other. But I was afraid I might find it difficult to sell that which, up until now, I'd always been so eager to part with for nothing.

The john's sumptuous apartment was a standout even for me, who had spent a lot of time growing up around my grandparents and their rich friends on Fifth Avenue. The decor could hardly have been called understated—too much oak paneling and Wrenaissance mahogany for that—but the living room was elegant, furnished sparingly with good Georgian pieces. The surface of the high-top desk, open to reveal nothing but a Montblanc pen resting on a blank sheet of linen stationery, seemed to be suffocating under a thick coat of wax, as if it had been too frequently polished by a maid with nothing else left to do. Two green-and-white-striped silk upholstered chairs stood on either side of the fireplace, and a luxurious sofa covered in the same material had been situated equidistant between them. I thought I spied an original Beardsley to the left of the (original) mantelpiece. The apartment was sensual and guarded at once, a masculine confection of a home, perfumed with a lingering trace of sweet Maduro cigar smoke and cognac.

He had greeted me at the front door in evening slippers and a floor-length paisley silk dressing gown thrown over trousers and shirt, the studs removed, his sleeves hanging loose. His wrists were too delicate, I thought. He offered me a drink, which I accepted, of course, scotch on the rocks. We sank first into his ripe sofa, side by side, like old friends. He was a gaunt man with high cheekbones, and his eyes flashed with a forced intensity when he spoke. I reassured myself he wasn't scary looking; in spite of the backdrop, in spite of me and why I was there, I told myself he just looked spiritual, ascetic even. I took him to be about fifteen to twenty years older than I was.

He said with his perfect diction that he liked my hair, "Very gamine."

It was short, the Jean Seberg look, a novelty in those days, left over from my recent submersion in a sect of radical feminists. Just about a week before, I had decided to forsake that calling for this one.

I was trying not to smile too much, because I knew I had the warm, spontaneous grin of an ingenuous fool. I had a young, expressive face, the kind that registers every wisp of emotion like a sunny day at the seashore that passes instantly into shadow each time the smallest cloud approaches, and I was afraid my face would betray me now.

I tried to act cool, but acting cool is difficult to do when you're not. After a few more light stabs at small talk, I couldn't bear it any longer. I blurted out that this was my first time, my first professional engagement. I felt compelled to confess because no one had told me what to do. Corinne, the madam whose job it should have been, had only said, "This trick is a cinch—the perfect introduction—nothing to it. You'll see."

But what was expected of me? Surely I was there to provide something that ordinary nice girls wouldn't, or couldn't, at the very least an attitude: friendly, chirpy, distant. Instead, I sat frozen in the depths of his sofa like a timid virgin. I needed to be guided through it. I apologized. I was apologizing for my freshness and innocence in the same way I now feel obliged to apologize to men for my experience.

Naturally, Maitland, the worldly john, beamed. He actually flushed pink with delight and maybe also with a soupçon of delicious shame. He did exactly as I had hoped, leading me by the hand through the living room and down the hall to his dark bedroom. More polished wood in here, and tapestry throw pillows, too.

He tossed the pillows on a straight-backed chair and lay back on his bed underneath the white silk canopy. Then he pulled me on top of him and flipped me over and kissed me. Oh, I knew that was wrong. Whores aren't supposed to kiss. I wriggled out from under him and he laughed.

"Good instincts," he said. "I suppose you want your money now, too."

Corinne's only explicit instruction had been to *always, always* get the money up front. That was the single commandment of hooking then. Maitland handed me two one-hundred-dollar bills. I stuck the money in my little black brocade evening purse, which was also left over from my childhood days of privilege.

Immediately, I felt suffused with glowing calm. Money was power; it freed me. I was free of the man, of men. I could take him or leave him, or anyone now. I was in control. This stranger had just paid me two hundred dollars in advance for doing practically nothing. The idea excited me. I stood there offering my high little breasts that were poking against the scratchy crepe. In my mind, I had become the object of unacknowledged worship.

'No wonder they go out and work for us,' I thought.

Not that I was even subliminally interested in finding a breadwinner. This was 1971, remember, and the nuclear-family scam had just recently been exposed. A housewife was merely a whore who was selling instead of renting herself, so the pundits had declared. I took this popular notion to heart. I decided I would rather make my way freely and directly. I wanted to get paid up front and be up front, as in the currently popular expression "be up front with me." Be honest.

Anyway, I was never trained in my fancy dilettantes' college to do anything, nor could I remember any discussions at home about how I might eventually make my own way. Oh, I heard a lot of vague, impractical talk about how I should "amount to something," and it is true that there was no shortage of career women around my mother's house, even back in the fifties, but collectively, the usually divorced career women served as a cautionary tale. It made a lasting impression when they got tight and cried like little children who were being punished. I remember watching transfixed from my secret vantage point behind the living room door as the black dirt of their mascara ran down their faces. They were extremely unhappy because they were without men. They looked everywhere for men. That was not going to happen to me.

Once I put down my little purse, suddenly, like an actor onstage who hears herself speaking the lines, I knew what to do. I slipped out of my dress, letting it fall to the floor. I stood naked except for my bikini underpants. I imagined that I towered over him, my john, who was lying back on the bed watching me with amusement. With the casual authority of a distracted mother engaged in her mindless routine, I opened his dressing gown, unbuttoned his shirt, tugged off his slippers, and unzipped his fly. After he yanked off his pants, he reached for me and pushed me back on the bed. There I pretended to surrender my power. He was wearing a touch of cologne, a restrained scent of sandalwood mixed with a pungent male smell like sea spray that I had not noticed before, until, on top of me, his pores opened.

It was not unpleasant under there, canopied by his clean, spare flesh. It wasn't uncomfortable or difficult. If you took the act we were performing out of context, nothing could have been more benign, I thought.

He fumbled with the rubber, a Day-Glo grape color it was. Then he put himself inside me. Before he could get off one stroke, he came. It was over. At first, I was flattered: 'Am I that hot?' I asked myself.

"Now you know," he said as we lay there in some kind of parody of the intimate aftermath. "I'm a premature ejaculator. I tried for years with women, but they won't put up with it."

I was being taken over to the far side where women are "other," initiated into the genderless center, the neutral world of men.

Maitland needed to explain his affliction, perhaps especially because I was new, in other words, full of compassion. Or is it that ladies of the evening are, as legend would have it, full of compassion? Anyway, by now I wasn't really listening to what he was so earnestly whispering to me. My heart had started pounding too loudly once it was over. Somewhere in there, though, I did hear him say, "Finally, after my last girlfriend left me, I got too lonely to stand it. That's when I hit on this solution."

He turned on his side and propped his narrow head on one bony hand like a monk, an anhedonist monk, no longer seeking the things of this earth, and he looked right at me with his mechanically bright eyes. I didn't ask him why he never tried to fix it. What for? Anyway, maybe he had. That he still needed and wanted this, that he was willing to pay a stranger for the brief contact, for the nudity, for the humble semblance of heterosexuality, touched me. So I kissed him. He didn't respond. As I pulled away, I caught in those open eyes the look of absolute resignation you would expect to see on a dying man's face.

The tall doorman was down on one knee, feeding a doggie candy to a bouncy, fluffy Lhasa apso straining at the end of its leash. When the man saw me approach, he jumped up and fairly ran to the big glass door to open it for me. Once again, he tipped his hat. This time, I thought I detected a slight exaggeration of style, an obsequiousness that bordered on a leer.

But who could tell? I had been surrounded by doormen and elevator men, servants in uniform, all my life, and their ways, their devotion to duty, their strange enthusiasm for the job, remained inscrutable to me. I continued down the avenue, August in New York, the air close and *intime* the way I like it, the doormen, all dressed in summer-weight gray or sky-blue uniforms, nodding as I passed, a few of whom I recognized. They stood outside in the twinkling night like familiar trees, landmarks from my childhood.

Of course, not all servants are so proudly humble. Maids are traditionally begrudging. Governesses temper their affection with a no-nonsense approach. Chauffeurs act like union men who have been hijacked off the assembly line, or mercenaries between wars. Cooks lord it over everybody else. Laundresses, usually the only black member of an all-white cast, at least at my grandparents' house, slink in and out the back door like noiseless visitations.

And what pose does the whore assume? Lazy. That's the trick. It aroused me just thinking about it. I remembered the joke my Edwardian grandfather used to tell in mixed company, and in front of me, about the man who goes into a whorehouse. He picks a woman out of the crowd, and she takes him upstairs to her room. Over the bed hangs a Vassar diploma.

"Is that yours?" he asks.

"Yup," she says.

"But I don't get it. What would a girl like you be doing in a place like this?"

"Just lucky I guess."

Once outside, I felt giddy with relief, dissolute and free. I turned left and headed east to Corinne's house, a large one-bedroom corner apartment overlooking the East River. Corinne was about fifteen years my senior, and although she had renamed herself after a French heroine in an old Charles Boyer movie, she was really a slightly overripe Irish American woman. I knew her from the bar scene. We both fooled around with Michael McClaren, the pied piper of women, sometimes separately and sometimes together. She was tall, auburn haired, and luscious in a damp way that suggested perversion. Like so many whores I would meet, she didn't get into it only for the money. If you asked her she'd say it was the money, but Corinne belonged to the not-so-rare breed that did it just as much for the sake of pleasure. Corinne dedicated herself to pleasure. She believed in it in the same way Republicans believe in free enterprise. In her spare time, she screwed professional athletes: big-name stars on football teams, basketball teams, and the occasional good-natured baseball player, too. Corinne was a jock groupie.

When she opened her door, she was dragging a telephone cord behind her, the receiver tucked in her ear. She raised her forefinger as if to say, "One minute," and then returned to the sofa, draped over with swatches of satin, where she plopped herself down in her flowing caftan and continued to speak.

"Is that how you want it, honey, long and slow? You want me to tell you what I'm going to do? Yes? First I'm going to run my tongue up and down, up and down that big, hard shaft. Then I'm going to put it in my mouth one inch at a time until the head of your great, big cock is rubbing up against the back of my throat...You want to hear more? I'm going to suck it, sweetheart, suck it and suck it. Oh so good..."

But her voice betrayed no enthusiasm. Instead, she barely modulated her tone, speaking in measured cadences, in the dead-level affectless calm of an overseas telephone operator.

I sat down in one of the satin-covered easy chairs, its material slipping and sliding around underneath me like unruly morning-after bedsheets, and waited for Corinne to finish priming her john.

"Yes, darling, I'm dying for it, yes, yes, all wet, oh, I'm so wet. Till tomorrow at six o'clock. Don't keep me waiting. That's a good boy."

I wanted to ask her why he gets turned on by her monotone voice, by the detachment that makes clear everything she says is a lie? Does he like surrendering his power? Or is it the shame and humiliation of being reminded she's in control? But I wasn't about to draw attention to my stupidity. Instead, I decided to ignore the whole thing. Business, that's all it is.

"Thanks, Corinne, the trick was a cinch, just like you promised." I handed the madam one of my hundred-dollar bills. She made change. Her cut was eighty.

"I told you. I wouldn't steer you wrong, honey." She came over to where I had perched myself at the edge of her slippery chair and slapped me hard across the back. "Congratulations. You are initiated. You are officially a ho. Now we've got to drink a toast to your new professional standing."

After she had poured us both full snifters of Grand Marnier, Corinne took me by the arm and pulled me up, directing me to a spot in front of her large picture window. Below us, the East River ran, and to the north and south, the bridges outlined in bright lights seemed to celebrate the city itself, as if every day were a festival.

Once again, the propinquity of it all struck me as ironic, as wonderful and strange. I was separated from my childhood by time but not by space. A life so remote from any I could have imagined was, nevertheless, happening to me on the same ground where I had been raised. "What a small-town girl I am," I thought. Here I was, about to drink to my initiation into the priestesshood of the socially damned, looking out on the same view of the same sparkling river I had been staring at when, ten years ago, I had my first drink: champagne at the former senator Foley's townhouse on Sutton Place. My grandparents always brought their family along to the traditional New Year's Eve party. I was just thirteen, and I was wearing my first pair of stockings, a Christmas present from my mother. I had hitched them on with a big, lumpy garter belt, and the stockings bagged at the knees, but I felt beautiful and grown-up, as if I had crossed some invisible line into adulthood.

It was nearly midnight. The senator himself, then very old but still with the wicked twinkle in his faded blue eyes powerful men never seem to lose, had grabbed an extra glass off the passing tray and handed it to me as we stood together on his marble balcony, rejoicing in the bitter wind that charged up from the river. After I polished off the first drink in one gulp, which amused my corrupter,

I immediately went indoors and searched through the crowd for more. Outside on the balcony again, delicate glass in hand, I found myself alone. I hung backward over the low wall, my face turned up to the pale glimmer of stars, their neglected presence a dim reflection of the brightly lit bridge to my right. Then I downed that drink. The bubbles teased my palate, my nose. The sugary, sour taste of the champagne surpassed even the velvet sweetness of the white icing on the gingerbread cookies that Hilda, the Foleys' cook, baked every year. Alcohol made chocolate seem like an insult to the intelligence. I remember no longer feeling the cold. My spirits leapt higher than they had ever been.

"So this is what's been missing," I said out loud to the night.

Now the stately Corinne, in her loose caftan with its flowing hood, stood against the backdrop of the black sky above the river. When she raised her glass, her wide sleeve dangled from her white, dimpled elbow. Her face shone in the semidarkness.

"What's your full name—your handle? I want to make this official."

"Janet."

"Janet? That's it? Never mind...OK, here it is: To Janet the whore!"

The Traveling Medicine Show

After Corinne's, I cut over to the Traveling Medicine Show, a saloon on Second Avenue and my old hangout. I had been avoiding it for a year —that is, until a week ago.

In the late sixties, we had a real St. Vitus dance going there, a whirling dervish of sex, drugs and rock 'n' roll. Not only did I believe in magic then, I sought evidence, praying for signs, such as the supernatural handwriting that leisurely spelled God's message to me, carving words in the sawdust across the barroom floor. Miracles of this kind only happened when I was whacked on methamphetamine, which was also when the divine order of things revealed itself, when inanimate objects gathered together to portend, when colors became backlit with the unseen rays of the moon, and jukebox tunes reverberated against the otherwise undetected, hollow sound of nothing. Crystal meth charged the circuits of my brain, leaping over synapses, chasing L-dopa down sleepy channels as sluggish as damned rivers until the banks of my mind flooded with revelation.

I did not fear this state, the drug-induced madness rightfully called "amphetamine psychosis"; I pursued it, guided by my own benign, urbane Charlie Manson, Michael McClaren.

Michael believed in crystal methedrine. Speed is to cocaine what heroin is to morphine—a very strong, very hard drug. But we cherished the tattered government brochure always circulating somewhere in the bar classifying methamphetamine as a psychedelic. This confirmed for us that it was a sacrament. After a few sleepless nights, I would grow preternaturally calm, and the high began to seem indefinite the way love does when it's good. Michael administered lines of this powerful substance like a kind and watchful small-town doctor who runs a makeshift clinic full of locals come in for the cure. He believed and infected us with the belief that crystal methedrine could heal. We were all convinced. About this we were not cynics in the slightest degree.

Michael had invaded like a missionary from Greenwich Village in the spring of 1967, transforming a dreary Upper East Side singles parlor into what was for me a palace of the night. The corner saloon was lit by an eerie copper glow; the place oozed with drugs, and the small stage rang out with free music played by friends of Michael's who dropped by to try out new material. The barroom walls were festooned with photographs of these local and world-famous regulars. There were mostly black-and-white head shots of the men, musicians, along with bartenders and drug dealers, all caught in deep and inscrutable contemplation, while the women were displayed in garish color: go-go dancers spinning their tassels on tabletops, or young uptown girls, myself included, wearing tiny bikinis and sunglasses, sprawled over the hoods of shiny cars.

Nothing checked, no restraint, unless it was Michael's intriguing silences, especially intriguing because probably not a soul uptown or down consumed more speed than he did. And speed made most of us talk and talk in a shorthand of free association, broken sentences tumbling back and forth like flaming torches. But Michael stood out against the pack; he expressed himself in elaborate pantomime instead. He was always tacking something on the bulletin board with his staple gun, or spray-painting a lightbulb crimson red, or brushing his lips with the harmonica he never played, or tinkering with a mike onstage, or just running loose, a marvelous rhythm to his jerky step, the speed spinning him from wall to wall. All of us, his unabashed followers, loved to watch him. His long black hair streamed behind him. His skin was as white as candle wax, except for his flushed cheeks. His wide-set eyes were transparent ice blue, fixed with the vacant stare I once saw in a timber wolf's eyes. You could almost hear his mind, as high as a whistle pitched for wildlife, and his mind drew us there night after night, all the young girls you could imagine, and the boys, too: we were enchanted.

That was the sixties, before male charisma got discredited. Sometime during the past year, while I was avoiding the place and trying to be a practicing radical feminist, the Traveling Medicine Show had turned seedy. Its lights were too bright now; the jukebox played the same numbers over and over, and Jimmy, the bartender, looked wearily at his watch. The place was changing back into just another local gin mill, but when I returned, all I could see was that Michael was still at his post where I'd left him the summer before. I reluctantly noticed he had acquired a slight potbelly, in spite of the fact that I was sure he continued to snort mountains of crystal meth (it was the daily quarts of rum and Coke, I guess). And the mortal growth of hair that poured out of his open work shirt, obliterating his once smooth chest, was thicker and ruder than before. But what mattered was that Michael was still there. The sight of my old hero and the stench of beer—old, sticky stale beer— lured me past the door.

I didn't expect him to throw his arms around me after my year of pointed neglect, and sure enough, he went out of his way to shun me the first night back. He behaved as though I were a stranger all through the long evening, right up until last call. Even in decline, he had pride. *You think you can just waltz in here after a year and expect me to fall all over you, bitch?* But the truth is he had nothing better to do. The truth is he was happy to see me. I could tell from the way he immediately started stapling something to the bulletin board. Then he abruptly went and sat down at his long table, where he put his feet up on the neighboring chair and pulled open a copy of the *Village Voice* with a deliberate thrust of paper. He hid his face behind it, as if he had gone inside his house and slammed the door. All of this was for my benefit, I thought, but I wanted to make sure.

"I guess Michael isn't talking to me," I said to Jimmy. It was almost four by that time, and I was hanging on with both hands to the cool glass full of ice and booze and practically no soda.

"Of course he is. He's real happy to see you," Jimmy said, wiping the bar down with his wet, filthy towel.

"You could've fooled me," I said.

"Oh, Janet, c'mon now, you've been away too long. This is how he always acts when he's happy to see someone, you remember that much, don't you?" he said.

A little while later, I noted with gratitude that Michael had switched to *Penthouse*, which he was reading with a half-smile on his face. A good sign. I walked over, careful not to stand too close. He looked up and smiled outright, as if I had just come through the door.

"Have a seat," he said, getting up. "Want a drink?"

All of a sudden, after not having seen me for a year and then ignoring me all night, I was his guest.

He went over and got us both drinks, his a tumbler full of rum and Coke, and my umpteenth scotch and soda. When he came back, he sat down next to me and put his feet up again and stirred his drink with his long, graceful finger.

"You look like you could use a line," he said.

"Yeah, I'm dying for a line. It's been a year at least," I said.

"How'd you stay awake?"

"I didn't, really. I was walking around in a daze the whole time."

"Here, I'll put a little of this in your drink. It's not the quickest way to get off, but it'll do the trick."

He took a square of tinfoil out of the breast pocket of his red shirt, a dark red that made his eyes look extremely light blue. Then he tapped some of the tinfoil's contents, a thin trickling stream of white powder, into my glass.

"Try not to overdo it. I'm very clean, remember," I said.

"Yes, but when you drink it, it's gradual. Don't worry, I'll look after you."

As soon as the Traveling Medicine Show closed that first night of my prodigal return, Michael hurried me down the block to his apartment, as if there were urgent business to discuss. He lived right on Second Avenue, above a hardware store. His studio faced the back where an ailanthus tree had presumed to grow in the alley, forcing its way through the concrete and up past his window. Michael's house was the most hallowed cell, the most beautiful, whimsical shrine in the whole of the material world, as far as I was concerned.

For months, while I was out on the street picketing, or stuck inside the freezing offices of the radical feminist paper *Gutter*, sitting on a metal folding chair and hammering out policy with the other women, I dreamed of this forbidden little bunker with its dark red corduroy bedspreads, like something a college boy's mother might have sent, and the billowing white cotton curtains that hung down from the ceiling behind the two beds. The effect these closed curtains had was to make you feel, lying there, as if you were backstage. The beds were arranged in an L shape so that they might lend themselves to a variety of offbeat positions, but not to sleeping together all entwined and sweaty. Which was fine with me on a couple of counts. First of all, who slept? And then, even if you did crash there, who, crashing, wants to share a bed?

Crashing is a serious business. It is the other side. Speed whisks away revelation when at last it departs the body. The profoundest truth, the one you thought would change your life, evaporates as if it had all been just a shimmering, whimsical dream. You are a husk, and if you are wise, you do not stir for days. Your senses dulled to the point of uselessness, you might as well lie prostrate in your open grave-bed until life creeps back in, or, more likely, until you decide to do more speed. The apostates couldn't take it; they tended to get suicidally depressed. Speed never affected me that way, or Michael either. What happens, if you allow yourself to surrender to it, which is what you have to do, is that you go into a mild coma. This was no big deal as far as I was concerned.

But of course, when the time arrived, I would want to come down by myself. At that point, you are feeling so fragile, you had better surround yourself with the familiar. When you come to, it's as if you were sleeping in the womb and then had to bust out of the birth canal all over again. You look ugly as hell when you wake up, puffy, gray, dried spittle plastered over the entire side of your face.

The atmosphere in that small, hot room, with only one fan whirring in the window, bore down on us. It was charged with the unexpected, electric weight of intimacy. The drenched air, ringing with silence, wouldn't let us speak or even, for a minute, move.

At last, as if someone had started the reel spinning again, Michael stripped, always the first thing he did. He made us both a rum and Coke, and then he took a bubble bath. I sat by the tub and blurted out a lot of inane things. The drug was starting to hit, and I was caught off guard. I had forgotten how liberating it was.

"The speed's working," Michael said.

"I'll say it is," I said. "I feel like a fool."

"We're all fools," Michael said, lifting his leg out of the bubbles and soaping it the way starlets used to do in the movies. Finally, he got up and pulled a towel around his body, the front of which was covered with black hair. This made him seem human to me. I loved him even more for the humility his giant spirit had assumed stuck inside the lowly flesh of manhood.

Ah, speed, mother of hyperbole. The drug has left its mark, as if the machine of my mind lost a knob. Even now, I find it difficult to measure in degrees. When I am moved, the emotion wants to fly to its limit like an old horse making its way back to the barn. Back then, I was altogether blind to the subtleties of feeling and impatient with them.

I wanted to touch him. All those days and weeks and months I berated myself because I, a genuine feminist, I thought, could not stop wondering about the de facto harem I had left behind on the Upper East Side, of all places, and now here I was, overjoyed just to be watching Michael trail soap bubbles into the other room. He sat naked on his towel under the pin light, put his drink down on the table in front of him and then started to fiddle with the tuner on the radio. After a few minutes, he settled in and picked up *Penthouse* again, while I, recalling the order of our ritual, stayed behind and ran a bath for myself.

"Drink some of your rum, that'll take the edge off," Michael called out to me.

I lay back in the tub and drank the alcohol and felt myself float off, until I was hovering for an instant over the deserted street outside. Just a little out-of-body experience, nothing to get alarmed about, I told myself. Then I saw some writing form out of the cracks in the plaster on the bathroom wall. It said GET WELL over and over in big script, a very personal hand. This was not as odd a hallucination as it might sound. Remember, we were all preoccupied with healing ourselves. And we thought there was a better chance of achieving mental health if we became psychotic first than if we just stayed mired in our neuroses. Michael put it this way: "There is no cure for the common cold, but if you catch a cold and then go stand in the rain, you might get pneumonia, and that they know how to cure."

"What are you doing in there?" Michael yelled.

"Oh, I—I don't know," I said, pulling myself back into space-time.

"That's all right, you'll mellow out. Drink some more rum," Michael said.

He continued to look after me, taking responsibility for my state of mind, clocking it every so often to make sure I didn't go out and not come back.

I flashed on a memory of my handsome father, Rayfield, and I, driving in silence up to his riding stable in the countryside where he boarded his horse. I am about nine or ten. We are absolutely silent the whole time. He is shifting gears in his little Karmann Ghia and simply delighting in the drive. It never occurs to him that maybe his daughter next to him is feeling one long howling pain of rejection. Is feeling that he has so little interest in her that she, like a parcel, like a Sunday burden, is being driven up to the stable and put on a horse because she is an obligation he is now too sober to avoid. Unless—and here is where the fruitful imagination takes over for good—unless this is it. This is, in fact, love. Silence is the ultimate communion, the evidence of complete understanding. Yes, silence, sharing the solitude, that's what love is.

And now, freshly bathed and wide-awake, I sat silently with Michael on the other side of the pin light. If all women were looking for their father again, then I was set. They resembled each other: dark hair, strong black eyebrows and contrasting light eyes—a distinctly Byronic look. But the quality of Michael's I was most grateful for on my first night back was that he was such a stick-in-the-mud. Michael was still there, a castled king in his corner. Unlike other men who would probably go somewhere else or take up with someone else in your absence, unlike this father of mine who married again so fast, Michael never moved off his spot, never left the block. He was strangely reliable. True, I might have to share him with another woman from time to time, but it was vastly preferable to being outright excluded. Handsome, winsome Michael was still there where I had left him. That was compelling; it was the crux of his appeal.

I was thinking this as we sat together, naked. The soft, long hair on Michael's chest was glistening wet under the pin light. His body had matured beyond him, suggesting as it did a warm and nurturing kind of man. I felt like a little girl.

"Guess it was tough trying to make a living out there as a full-time activist. Orthodox feminists. Humph. Doesn't pay very well, does it?" Michael asked.

"Michael, don't make fun of me."

"I'm not, I'm really not. But I could've told you that wasn't for you. You have to find some other way."

"What do you mean 'not for me'? Because I like sex too much, is that what you mean?"

"Something like that. Listen, they're repressive. The way I see it, they want to turn things back, put more distance between the sexes."

"You aren't hearing what they're saying, that's obvious."

"Oh? So why did you leave?"

"Well, the truth is you're right about me. I couldn't handle it. It was too austere, that life. I'm just a sybarite, that's all I am. I give up, OK? I missed getting high. And, well, I missed you. OK? I really did. Now I'm here. So let's drop it."

Silence. He had to weigh those words, "I missed you." He had to let them echo for a few seconds above the sound of the whirring fan. And then he resumed his rightful place as the man who would run my life. From an amused distance. Nevertheless, he was willing to run it, which is more than I could say for any other man thus far.

"What are you doing for bread?"

"Nothing."

"Where are you staying?"

"At my mother's house right now."

"We gotta figure out what you're going to do. You can't live off your mother forever. Any ideas?" he asked.

"You know me, I always figured the world owed me a living," I said.

"Maybe it does, but don't be surprised if it doesn't pay up. Have to think of something...gotta have a gimmick, that's what you need, a gimmick," he said. He was sitting naked with his legs crossed, tapping his knee, smoking a Camel. He was getting that mischievous look, playing with me now.

"I know. You could start a circle jerk, advertise in *Screw*. You would be the supervisor. 'Supervised circle jerks...' No? OK, maybe not. Then let's see...how about 'Private Viewing of Blue Movies for an Elite Few'? You'd be amazed who'd pay to see sixteen-millimeter flicks, all those poor schmucks too uptight to go to Forty-Second Street. You could rake it in! What's wrong with that idea?"

"I don't even have an apartment, let alone enough chairs to accommodate a movie audience," I said, pretending to take his silly suggestions seriously. I lit up a Newport. I was pouting. I hated his cheery attitude. And I already knew where this was going.

"You know I got a good friend, Susannah, you remember Susannah?" he asked me.

"Of course."

Of course I did. The pretty, femme Susannah, with her honest-to-God dark corkscrew curls and her actual flouncy skirts, was the first woman I ever had. She was his southern belle contingent. Came up here just to see him maybe two or three times a year. It was preposterous. We all had to defer to her when she came, as if she were special, which was hardly the case, it was only that she was infrequent. Nevertheless, everybody had to make a big fuss over her. The last time I saw her, the three of us went back to Michael's house, and Susannah got to be the center of everything as usual, as if Michael and I were extending ourselves as host and hostess. I had not planned it, but I found myself going down on Susannah, after it was instigated by Michael, who lay underneath her. She was acting wild in a demure sort of way, sitting up with her back to him and rotating awkwardly on top like a helpless mewling little thing. While this was happening, Michael kept smiling at me around the back of her head as if we were in cahoots. Then he pulled out and pushed her toward me.

(In spite of the company I had been keeping, I had never seen a vagina that close up before, let alone tasted one. Not what I expected, it was, somehow, much neater. I had assumed it would be a flaccid, fleshy, amorphous hole, but Susannah's pulsed with muscle hidden inside. When I tentatively circled her clitoris with my tongue, it stood up, and I felt her whole vagina spasm ever so slightly. The clitoris embarrassed me; it seemed like such a vestigial little thing. Poor women, with our tiny imitations. Otherwise, from what I could see, with its swollen labia and its thick inner wall, the vagina was just like an inverted penis. 'But what a powerful sex organ,' I remember thinking, a little surprised and almost frightened by the gravitational pull of it.)

"Well, Susannah knows this madam," Michael went on. "I told you when she's in New York, she always turns a few tricks and makes enough to pay all her expenses. I could find out the name of the madam, if you'd be interested. Better yet, why not get in touch with Corinne? She'd fix you up. Corinne really likes you; yep, she'd do it in a New York minute.

"You and everybody else, me included, is already giving it away. But you're lucky. You can get paid for it. Who's going to object? Nobody around here. Do you care what the straight world thinks? Of course not. In fact, whenever it disapproves, I take it as a sign at least I'm doing something right. I don't see why you shouldn't get paid for it."

This was one of Michael's longer speeches. I understood he was encouraging me to be defiant. I got it. His motives were very nearly pure. But if I'd been capable then of being honest with myself, I would have had to admit that I was hurt. I wished that he would claim me, possess me, swear he'd never love another. I tried to comfort myself with the thought that Michael did want to possess me in his way by sharing my experience, because I already knew what he had in mind. I knew that Michael's own peculiar interpretation of pimping would never include taking money—he had such an aversion to money—but he'd insist on hearing all the details. 'Vicarious' was his favorite word.

"Do you think I could do it? I mean, I don't know whether I'd be any good at it," I said.

"You good at it? You got to be kidding. Anyway, from what Susannah and Corinne tell me, there's nothing to it. These johns are all straight businessmen, married guys, looking for a piece of strange. They're so excited by the idea, they come after a few strokes. Nothing to it," he said.

"I don't know. I'll have to think about it," I said, still pouting.

We were sitting naked together, I on one bed, he on the other, maybe two feet apart, not speaking. The only lights were the pin light and the glowing tips of our cigarettes. The radio was playing another tune, a preview from Europe the DJ said, something about a horse in a desert. Dumb lyrics I suddenly realized in an unwelcome moment of lucidity. Dumb.

Michael reached for his suede book bag full of vibrators. He pulled out a huge machine, which was flat across the top.

"Look at this, it's new on the market. Isn't it a beauty?" he said, a small boy displaying his latest gadget.

"What does it do?"

"The vibrations are so strong, they make the whole inside of your pussy contract. You come in about ten seconds," he said.

But then he put it away.

"That's for later," he said, a papa now, teaching his kid how to postpone gratification.

Also, the truth is he had only brandished the thing to get us on the subject of sex in the here and now. Neither one of us was in the mood for a vibrator. But Michael's problem was that he was shy. He was really soft-spoken and shy, and he could never get over the fact that women were so willing to sleep with him. Even after years of various girlfriends threatening to commit suicide on his account, he was still stupefied by the pitch of their desire. Not many men are ready to unleash a woman, watch her go, the way Michael was. So it's understandable he would feel like the sorcerer's apprentice sometimes.

He grabbed my nipple, which was standing straight up thanks to the tickling breeze from the fan, between his thumb and middle finger. I felt my clitoris jump like a little fish. He took hold of my other nipple. Then I think he actually kissed me. It was more like one mouth bruising another, the way children do it, but it was a kiss. He pulled me close, settling down right on top, skin to skin, heart to heart. The kissing changed. We opened to each other. It all came back to me, how it used to be when we first met, before the drugs took over completely. I remembered. We were back. No wonder I loved him. After a few generic thrusts, he recovered this stroke he had. The way his whole body moved on top of me—the sweetest rub, then the lushest friction, then throbbing velvet torture. God please let me come. I felt completely subordinated, pinned helpless and squirming under his big body. I held on tight. I could hear myself squeaking, grunting, moaning. I hated those noises, but I couldn't stop. He was watching me. I opened my eyes and there he was. My legs spread wide. After a while, he reached down with one hand and pushed them back closer together. Acute pleasure was forcing me to give myself up. Inside the fierce heat I was thinking, 'I love you.' Michael whispered in my ear. I heard him say, "You're here to stay. You're doomed." I wish I knew what it was he did. Not just in and out, he somehow slid up into me over and over until eventually even I would come. Not this time. I couldn't quite let go, and he couldn't hold it anymore. He stayed inside shuddering and twitching for a while afterward. I didn't want him to pull out; I wanted more. My tears on my face.

He let himself out of me slowly and reached for a cigarette. I felt a keen sense of loss. Maybe if I had really come, put my hand down there and really got off, I thought, I wouldn't feel so bereft now. But no, probably even that wouldn't have made much of a difference. I would have felt deprived anyway, at least wistful. The better it was, the tougher it was when it ended. I could never get enough when it was that good. I remembered now why I used to think he was indispensable. I sighed out loud. Everything was missing; I was manless once again.

But he kept close. I could be thankful for that at least. I knew there would be more; I could tell and felt relief. Michael would never leave a woman hanging. He was strangely devoid of ego in that area. If I weren't satisfied, he didn't make me feel like I was hard to please. Like me, Michael had come to believe it was absolutely crucial that everyone have an orgasm one way or the other. He had read all about Wilhelm Reich's Orgone Box, and he knew that sexual frustration caused most of the misery between people.

He was lying now to my right, on the outside of one of the single beds. He reached for my pack of Newports and handed me a cigarette, lighting both of ours with his Bic. We lay there in the faint glow of the pin light. Then, without warning, he switched his Camel to his left hand, turned over, and grabbed my face with his right hand. His left arm now dangled off the narrow bed. He lay half on his side with his face up against mine and proceeded to turn my head in both directions, back and forth, while he conned my face as if he were looking for clues.

"I can't get a handle on what you look like." He was staring into my eyes now. "What do you look like? I've never been able to figure it out. All year, while you were gone, I tried to picture your face, but it always came up different."

He continued to maneuver my head in the tiny glare of the pin light now as if my eyes didn't exist, as if my face were a many-sided crystal he was trying to make sparkle. Then he thrust my head away.

"Too many planes in that face or something," he said.

After which he collapsed on his stomach and lay there for a minute with his own face buried in his hands. Finally, when I was about to throw my arms around him, he jumped up, full of pep, a shining tribute to the regenerative power of speed, and made us both another drink.

Now I was back at the Traveling Medicine Show, waiting for the opportunity to boast to Michael about turning my first trick. I was armed with solid evidence of my intention to stay. Trading sex for money was the only way I could think of to get Michael to take me seriously.

I watched Tommy Shelter, an old friend of Michael's from their Village days, climb on the tiny stage at the back of the room for a second set. He started thumping chords on his acoustic guitar with so much urgency you thought the strings might break, and singing his signature brand of delta blues with a driving rock 'n' roll beat, preaching to the converted. The story went that Tommy had learned how to play guitar on the stage of the Black Box around the same time Bob Dylan was still passing the kitty around. This would explain why Tommy strummed and hammered with such poignant frustration. His voice, majestic and raspy at once, shot through with soulful passion, catapulted him to the top. The fact that Tommy was missing his upper front teeth didn't hurt either. The way he slid over his f's and dropped his t's made him sound like a very old, wise sharecropper. Really, he was only a year or two past thirty, with a Nubian cameo of a face. He was one of a dozen or so luminaries in the music business who still showed up periodically to try out new material.

The bar crowd was so blasé, so hard-boiled, so wired on speed and booze, it did not make a fuss over these musicians, who would otherwise get mobbed by groupies in the more fashionable clubs downtown. As a matter of fact, the regulars at the Traveling Medicine Show made a point of paying attention to the music but turned their backs on the performers themselves once they stepped off the stage. When two of the Beatles and their latest Uriah Heep manager showed up in the late sixties (at the height of their careers), Michael put them at a table in the corner, where they sat pointedly ignored by everyone until, perhaps deflated, they slunk back out into the night.

The real stars were the bartenders. These Irish Americans were big, handsome, and profligate with their drugs. They free-poured the booze and made generous love, drawing young women like me who, released by the Pill, would rather hang around getting smashed until last call in the hope that we might go home with one or the other of them than wait idly backstage at the ready for some stuck-up musician, or, God forbid, sit demurely by the phone, silently praying.

And here was Jimmy the bartender, still wiping the bar with the same dirty rag. A company man he was, devoted to Michael in this case, but Jimmy would have to have been devoted to someone. He was that kind of guy. Jimmy was a refugee from a big football school in Indiana. The army wouldn't take him for some reason; he'd tried to enlist. He was a large and, unfortunately for him, open-faced strawberry blond who blushed for no reason at all. Rather than play against type, Jimmy hung on to his midwestern guilelessness, oblivious to the mores of the scene in which he now found himself. Michael adored Jimmy—"4-H Jimmy," he called him—and took every personal kind of pain to drag him down into the muck with the rest of us. Right away, he had turned his hick buddy onto speed, derailing Jimmy off his career track. (Armed with a degree for it, Jimmy had once longed to go into the hotel business, but all hopes for that were gone now.)

Michael sat with his feet up on a second chair (he'd become more sedentary once he hit thirty) at his big, long table reserved for him to the left of the room against the wall. He had on a pair of giant earphones, which were not attached to anything; it simply meant he did not wish to be disturbed. He was polishing his cracked moccasins with a paper napkin as if they were Guccis, leaning forward to get a good look at them in the overhanging light. He kept pushing a lock of his long black hair off his face as he did so, until exasperated, he pulled his hair back in the fat rubber band he had been wearing around his fuzzy wrist. Michael seemed completely preoccupied with these self-appointed tasks, completely uninterested in his old friend Tommy, who was singing a mournful refrain about freedom on the tiny stage at the far end of the saloon.

And as always, Michael also seemed not to have noticed that I had just walked through the door. But 4-H Jimmy beamed and scooted over to where I was now standing at the bar.

"Janet, you sweet fox you—here again. I guess you really are back. And you do look fine tonight in that little black number...Dewar's," he said, pouring a glass with a few chips of ice in it full of scotch, spritzing the top with a little soda.

Then Bruno spotted me and broke out from a small crowd of regulars that hung wedged together in the corner. He sidled along the bar sideways like a crab, pushing his drink as he went, until he was standing next to me. He leaned over to Jimmy and whispered loudly in his ear, "She's a feminist now."

Bruno had cut one album about three years earlier that had produced one hit, the kind of upbeat pop tune lounge singers love to cover, and he'd been drinking in a steady, quiet way ever since, like an old railroad worker on a pension.

"A feminist? Nah. I never would have figured you for a feminist, Janet," Jimmy said.

"It's a fact. I saw an article she wrote for *Gutter* last year. That was you, am I right?" Bruno asked me, like a cop on the case.

Jimmy picked up the sticky bar rag and started pushing it around. "Is that true, or is he making it up?"

"It's true, it's true," I said.

"No, no," Bruno said, waving his hand and leaning over slightly as if to gather a thought from the sawdust on the barroom floor. Tommy Shelter was grinding away at his guitar. The rest of the customers were quiet.

"You don't know the half of it," Bruno said, pulling himself up. "She wrote about how men *objectify* women. How we use them like meat." He turned to me. "But I gotta say, you do look pretty objectified yourself tonight." He glanced at my breasts, still poking out of the low-cut black crepe dress, then at my crotch. "Pretty objectified."

"Yeah, well, I got horny," I said.

"Let's drink to that," Bruno said, waving his glass.

I turned away from Bruno to listen to Tommy's cri de coeur pouring out over the stoned dive after midnight. I had a new status: I was a whore. In other words, past human redemption now, I didn't have to be nice to anybody. Bruno sensed that he had been dismissed and retreated sideways again, guiding his drink along the length of the bar, back to his pals in the corner.

What I told Bruno about being horny was true as far as it went. In fact, I was chastened over the past year by the persistence of my desire. When I left the scene, I had been in a fury, a sweet, blind rage at men. I was tired of being pretty and playing a minor role. During the year that followed, I took to wearing hiking boots and a motorcycle jacket, I stopped shaving my legs and under my arms, and I joined up with a group of radical feminists who published

Gutter. I practically never went to bed with anybody during that time, since, after a few abysmal experiments and to my dismay, I was clearly an irrevocable heterosexual. Too bad, especially when so many of my colleagues were gleefully coming out. And then, not long ago, my libido started to rise like a gorge inside of me, ripping up into my brain, until all I could think about was getting a man, and I didn't care anymore whether I, the self, the person, was obliterated in the process. I needed rapture I decided, and fuck equality and fuck justice.

I had to come back. I missed Michael. Beyond that, I was a city kid who was used to hanging out. By the time I was thirteen, I was standing around with other delinquent teenagers on Madison Avenue street corners. There, as I posed coyly in front of Hamburger Heaven, I learned how to congregate. This is what I craved: the scene. Plans that normal people made, God, it was too much like work.

Having turned around to face the room, I leaned back with my elbows propped on the bar and, in my old black crepe dress, tried to convey the languorous attitude of a call girl. After a while, Michael removed his earphones. I was about to go over to his table when Melissa sailed in, dressed as usual in her halter top and cutoffs, her wild red hair shooting off in all directions, her scarecrow gait exaggerated-sloppy from quaaludes. She, too, had originally intended her destination to be Michael's table, but, her head leading the way, she overshot the mark. Windmilling by, Melissa lurched instead into the middle distance, somewhere perilously close to the stage.

"Just another falling sparrow," Michael said, sniffing the air, as she careened past him.

"The honeymoon's over," I said to myself. "Now I'm going to have to compete with this cunt. Well, fuck it. Maybe I won't. Let him have her. Yeah, let the motherfucker wet-nurse her back to life all by himself."

"Serves him right," I said out loud as I twisted my body around to face Jimmy. I had eaten no dinner; the two Dexamyls I swallowed hours ago, before I turned my first trick, were starting to wear off, and Jimmy had already refilled my glass with barely diluted scotch. I was pretty drunk.

Eventually, Tommy Shelter stopped playing, gently laid his guitar down on the stool, climbed off the tiny stage, and began moving through the crowd in my direction. Right away, Michael was up pumping quarters into the jukebox, which was crammed with sleeper hits he had recorded off his favorite albums at a friend's sixteen-track studio. A work of art, that jukebox. Michael panicked when there was no music. Keith Richards started singing, "You got the silver, you got the gold..." in his reedy voice. The smoke curling in the air seemed to be turning into incense, an ethereal blue. The whole room lurched into a downbeat rhythm. A kind of benign knowingness settled over the crowd, as if we had all been quietly blessed.

"You look fine, healthy. Your skin has a glow to it. The break from this scene did you good," Tommy said, taking my elbow in his palm. He was wearing a long, flowing dashiki. He could've been some visiting African dignitary.

"What'll you have?" Jimmy asked him.

"Oh, I don't know, just a ginger ale," Tommy said politely, modestly. "Would you like to come outside for a minute for a smoke?" he asked me, still cradling my elbow.

His bodyguard, Nighttrain, had moved up behind him, hugging the guitar now in its case, and was standing at his back.

"Sure," I said.

The three of us stepped outside. Michael had followed us as far as the doorway. He kept peering at us until we disappeared around the corner. We were worthy of stares from any quarter: two black men, one in an African dashiki, the other one in loose overalls, and me in my cocktail dress. It was late and dead quiet, except for the sound of crickets chirping in the potted trees. Tommy lit up a joint. We passed it around for a while, gazing at the shiny pavement, wet from a brief shower, which shone green, red, green, red, under the changing walk/don't walk light.

"Do you want to come home with me?" Tommy asked.

Nighttrain ignored us and stood watching the empty side street.

"The last time I went to your house, *he* was there the entire time, right in the room with us," I said, nodding in the direction of Nighttrain.

"Let's go to your place then."

"Yeah, well, I don't have a place right now. Crashing at my mother's house. As a matter of fact, I'm looking."

"That's no problem. Let me think, there's Jade, but no, she's too street for you. I know, Sigrid, just right! She's got a big pad on the West Side, right off the Park. I'm sure she'd put you up for a while if I asked her," he said. "Oh, Sigrid, she's a dream. You two will get along, I promise you."

"Is she straight?"

"How do you mean?"

"I mean, she likes boys, right?"

Tommy laughed. "Right," he said.

"That's good, 'cause my last roommate kicked me out for being straight," I said.

"Don't worry, those days are over," he said, sounding as if he knew.

Tommy took my number, or rather, my mother Maggie's number, and promised to call. He didn't ask me to go with him again. That impressed me.

After we finished smoking the reefer, which on top of the booze knocked me out, Tommy Shelter and Nighttrain took off, while I, sensing I was about to vomit and hoping to make it to the privacy of the toilet, marched myself back inside.

Escape

"Get up, get up!" my mother screamed, alarm in her voice, as she shook me. "It's Saturday afternoon already. You've been sleeping since you got home yesterday. I thought maybe you were dead. Hurry up, somebody's on the phone."

I turned over. "What'd you say?"

Maggie continued to shake me. "I said there's a call for you. Says his name is Tommy. Tell your street friends I don't want them calling here. I don't want them making their drug deals on my phone."

I jumped out of bed and started running to the phone in the big front hall. On the way I said, "Mother, that's Tommy Shelter, the singer, the one who was at Woodstock, you know?"

"Oh, no, I didn't know," she said. But she sounded chastened, even impressed. After spending her youth in the theater, she still worshipped fame, secretly of course.

"Hi, Tommy, sorry it took me so long, I was crashing."

"Your mother told me. She said you'd been asleep since yesterday."

"She told you that? What a pal, huh?"

"Don't worry about it. You can get out of there now."

"Really?"

His low voice was soothing. I hung on to the receiver and started to nod. I was dreaming.

"Janet, Janet, are you still there?"

"I'm sorry, what?"

"I said I just spoke to Sigrid. She wants to meet you. Call her. Here's her number. Got a pencil? She mentioned something about this afternoon."

"It already is this afternoon," I said.

"Her pad is right across the Park from you. Are you busy?"

"Busy? Let me think. Hold on a minute. Tommy? Hold on, I'll be right back. Tommy?"

"Yes, I'm here," Tommy said.

I ran in my room and went straight for my little black brocade purse. A dim memory was pushing its way to the surface. I was hoping I hadn't just imagined it. But no, there it was, a square of tinfoil, a care package of speed that Michael had slipped into my bag before I left, whenever that was. Wonderful Michael, in my life again. I sighed with contentment. Then I ran back to the phone.

"Tommy?"

"Are you OK?"

"Absolutely OK. I can go anywhere anytime. What's her number?"

The Sigrid solution came my way not a moment too soon. Maggie and I hadn't been hitting it off very well lately. It might even have been that she was preparing to kick me out. In the beginning, a couple of months before, when my roommate took in her new lover and asked me to leave, and I had to go home (no place else to go as usual), Maggie was undeniably delighted to have me back. I was her only child, and she and I had always been a smidgen too involved, according to every shrink I ever knew. In fact, I'd go so far as to say that when I first returned, Maggie was spilling over with an inappropriate amount of enthusiasm. She started laughing at her own jokes, buying tickets for us to Broadway matinees, ordering steamed lobsters from Rosedale Fish Market. She was full of hope. We joined Weight Watchers and cooked chicken livers stirred up with apples and onions in Pam and did the crossword puzzle together on Sunday. She honestly believed that I was turning over a new leaf.

Then I remembered to pull myself out of this jolly stupor.

My mother had been seducing me, as was her wont, and I'd been falling for it. My biggest nightmare was that, unless I fought it, she and I would float off into the sunset together like something out of Tennessee Williams, like Sebastian and his mother in *Suddenly, Last Summer*, only the single-sex version.

So my tactic was to turn churlish and mean. I never left the house. Maggie came home after doing the grocery shopping, and I was sprawled out on the sofa, my hiking boots—left over from the radical feminist stint—propped on the upholstered pillow. Maggie stood there in her low-heeled Florsheim "comfort pumps," shifting her weight from one foot to the other. Then she wrinkled her nose as if the air smelled and looked longingly at her sofa.

"I don't have a place to sit in my own house," she said.

"What's wrong with the club chair?"

"But you can't see the TV from there."

"You don't want to watch anyway. The movie's almost over," I said, wishing she would shut up.

"Yes, I do. I want to see the news," Maggie said, standing there in her miracle-fiber skirt-and-blouse ensemble, a big clumsy pocketbook hanging off one shoulder, still carrying two shopping bags full of groceries, one in each hand.

"It's OK," I said, never taking my eyes off George Raft, "this movie will be over at six. You won't have to miss a minute of Vietnam, Ma."

My attitude wore her down. She looked so miserable by the end of the day—her soft, reddish-blond-dyed hair matted to her forehead, a faded housecoat thrown over her wilted body—a weaker child might have taken pity. Not me, though. I wasn't about to fall into her clutches. Just because I had to be there didn't mean I belonged to her, I told myself. As far as I was concerned—and several of my shrinks had backed me up on this—my mother was out to get me.

Before Tommy and I got a chance to hang up, Maggie came out into the hall where I had draped myself over the loveseat and started gesturing to me.

"That's enough now. Tell him you'll call him back later. I want to talk to you." Maggie spoke loud enough for Tommy to hear.

I waved her away.

"That's enough I said." The volume was pitched even louder now.

I put my hand over the mouthpiece. "Don't bother me when I'm talking on the phone. Go away," I hissed.

"How dare you speak to me like that. You are on my phone in my house." The volume was turned up full blast now, to shrieking level.

"Tommy? I have to go. Thank you." I slammed down the receiver. "You love humiliating me, don't you? It's how you get your jollies, isn't it, humiliating me. Always was, you sadist bitch. All my life."

"That's it! That's enough. You can just pack your bags and leave right now. I don't care where you go. I've had it!" Maggie screamed.

She looked ridiculous as usual, I thought, standing there little and pudgy in her shapeless, chocolate-colored miracle-fiber pants and a lavender T-shirt, which had, coincidentally, a chocolate-colored stain on the front of it. Were the pants and shirt supposed to go together? Never exactly chic, Maggie had been extremely glamorous when she was young. Daddy's little girl, the gay divorcée about town, sexy and colorful; she was a lush, sweet orchid that bloomed at night. This was so right up until lately. Then I don't know what happened. Once she passed fifty, she simply let the whole thing drop as if it were a stage role that had ceased to amuse her.

"It just so happens I was planning to leave today anyway," I said.

"And go where?" she asked. Her voice fell so fast, she sounded almost timid by comparison.

"Never mind where. It's none of your business."

"Oh yes, it is. How do I know you won't come creeping back here when this one doesn't work out. Is it that man you just talked to? Are you going to live with that man? Fine with me, as long as he's willing to pay for everything. Does he know how spoiled you are? How messy you are?

"And, Janet, put some clothes on. Maybe he won't mind, but I don't like you parading around my house naked."

"No, Mother, it isn't that man," I said, ignoring the last part but feeling, suddenly, naked. "It's a young woman, around my age. She lives off Central Park West and she's looking for a roommate."

"Who is she? Someone you know?"

"Not yet, but I understand she's very nice."

"You're going to move in with some stranger sight unseen?"

"I thought you wanted me out, no matter what."

"Yes, but I think you should leave here the right way. Get a job first, then find an apartment when you have some money saved. I know your father, if he were ever willing to take any interest at all, would agree with me. I'd call him right now, but he absolutely refuses to get involved. Might as well face it, whenever there's a crisis, I've got to handle it alone. He's useless, your father."

I was tempted to tell her that my handsome Yankee cavalier of a father, with his history of wives—four of them, present one included—had just been passing through. He was an empty well, I wanted to say to her, an empty well. Instead I said, "But you're doing fine all by your lonesome. Didn't you just kick me out?"

"Maybe I did. And probably that's what I should do, but you know I'd worry. OK, I'm sorry. I lost my temper. You can stay."

"Tough shit. I'm going."

"Please stay, Janet. I think you'd better stay, Janet. You're asking for trouble. This isn't right. You're not going about this the right way."

"Too bad. I'm already gone," I said.

"What are you going to do for money? That girl isn't going to put you up for free."

"I said none of your damned business." This over my shoulder. I was eager as hell to just split. Suddenly, the desire to break free was acute. Must get out quick, before she destroys me. Must get away from the cloying pink-and-cherry-red bedroom of my childhood, the ever-widening mesh of private jokes, shared Weight Watchers recipes, and heated after-theater discussions. This was a warm and easy life but not the one I chose. Help. A few more tricks and I'd have the rent. God, hooking was great, the money changing hands in a flash. Hooking was my ticket to ride—ride or otherwise fall into the great gaping maw that was Maggie.

It could only have been a bullet hole smack in the middle of the plate glass oval in the front door of Sigrid's apartment house. This was right before gentrification, when the West Eighties still looked like the working-class neighborhood it once was, only worse, dilapidated. No buzzer system, so, as we had arranged over the phone, I banged on the ground-floor window, which was where Sigrid lived. The face of a princess, of a blond Rose White, peered at me through the venetian blinds.

"It's plenty big enough for two," she said once we were inside.

The apartment was one room, with a homemade plywood partition about five feet high that ran down the middle. Sigrid had decorated her home with beds. Beds were everywhere. One queen-sized number was made up with sheets, the others, three or four single beds, were draped with tie-dyed cotton coverlets in various hues of green and purple, big pillows in psychedelic primary colors thrown around on top of them. Besides the extensive bed collection, there was a card table with some metal chairs over by the kitchenette.

"This looks great," I said.

"Supremely functional. Beds are all-around practical, the only kind of furniture worth having. You can do anything on them: sit, eat, read, sleep, fuck, anything. What else do you need?" Sigrid said. "Want some tea?"

I was quietly speeding. My pupils were crowding out my irises, otherwise you couldn't tell. But, as always, the drug made me romanticize. What was really getting to me was the china-blue, angel-blond, porcelain look of my hostess as she elegantly poured the boiling water into a potful of bancha leaves. Even though she was wearing jeans and a faded-blue man's shirt with a hole in the shoulder and padding around in bare feet, there was a quality she had that I was sure inspired men to throw their coats over mud puddles in her path, send her flowers. She was a lady, a very white, delicate lady.

"The thing is, I'd like to move in immediately if I could, except I don't have a lot of cash right now," I said.

"Oh, that's easy, no problem. I know how to get money any time," she said.

Sigrid made it sound like getting money was a hobby, something to do when you had nothing better to do.

"Tell me," I said.

"OK, but I don't know what you'd be up for. Maybe it would bother you," she said.

"I doubt it."

"Good. Then I'll let you in on it," she said, pouring the tea into two mugs and sitting down across from me, where she proceeded to tuck one foot over her opposite thigh, then the other one, lotus style. She took a dainty joint out of her pocket, lit it, and passed it to me. It was very good dope.

"I've got these friends, Vincent and Candy," she said, sucking the smoke into her lungs and holding it. "You never met anyone like them, a trip, really. They run this, well, how should I put it, 'emporium,' I guess you'd call it, off Times Square. There's a big theater in the back, where Vincent stages these live sex shows, only they're actually morality plays that he wrote himself, allegories, you know? They're really beautiful, except I don't go in for that, that's not my bag.

"But in the front, he's got this mini–massage parlor going. It's just a roomful of massage tables with screens to simulate privacy, you know? Here's the best part: each customer gets a timer. Fifteen minutes. Hand jobs, that's all. It's a piece of cake. Twenty-five dollars for a hand job. We keep fifteen of it. Do ten of those and you got the rent plus mad money. And you can do it for as long as you want. The guys are lined up in the hallway. It's so easy, it's like having a trust fund. Any time I'm feeling broke, I just call Vincent. We could pop down there on Monday if you like."

I shivered. Hand jobs—that is cold. I didn't mind going to bed with someone for money. That had turned out to be a cinch, but mainly because it mimicked ordinary life and normal relations between a man and a woman. I could fantasize anything during the act; I could pretend, if it helped things along, that the john was my lover. But hand jobs? They were mechanical acts that exposed the whole enterprise for what it was: orgasm for money. Everybody likes to come, but men could and would pay for it. Even the poor ones would pay to come. The only sentimental note is that they preferred a delicate female hand to their own for a change. Meanwhile, I would be stuck with the reality of what I was doing. Hand jobs. But I looked at the fair Sigrid, the lovely lady who would inspire gallantry in the worst of heels, and I had to admit my attitude was silly and impractical.

"I'll definitely think about it," I said.

I went home and packed the few clothes I hadn't lost or ruined somehow and generally got ready to move in with my new friend, Rose White. Before I left, I kissed and hugged Maggie good-bye, as if I were a kid on my way to Europe for the first time. She kissed and hugged me back, always willing to jump into the charade of a loving, uncomplicated parent-child relationship. We were the same size, so whenever we embraced, our bosoms collided. We were standing there in the hallway, pap to pap. It made me nervous. I had told her that my roommate did a term at Swarthmore, which was true, and that now she was studying to be an actress, which was also true.

Maggie seemed relieved. She would go to bed that night telling herself I was just a child of the sixties after all, rebelling in a harmless and probably short-lived way, and all was right with the world. It made me sad. I didn't enjoy in the least deceiving her and disappointing her over and over again. This was because despite years of the best adolescent therapists money could buy, despite one eerily removed professional after another telling me to get away from that destructive bitch who actually unconsciously loathed me (one guy did say exactly that), in spite of all this, a part of me had to admit, as I stood there in the middle of the warm hug, that I wanted desperately to please my mother. Even though I knew I wasn't supposed to love her, because in enlightened psychiatric circles you had to hate your mother first before you could finally love her, I was never able to bring myself to go through the required healthy hating part. OK, so she neglected me when I was a kid. OK, so what. We also had a lot of laughs then. Right after I started third grade, my governess, Josephine, quit because, she said, she only took care of young children, and, at the age of eight, I was no longer one. From that time on, my mother hired a series of live-in maids who did their best to keep their distance. After Josephine left, there had never been anyone else. It was Maggie then or nothing.

No Frills

The taxi sailed downtown along the East River, on its way to deliver me to my first whorehouse. Corinne had referred me to her colleague Evelyn for a week's work. She said it was part of my initiation into the Life. The late-morning, late-August sun poured its benign light over the dirty water, and the oily rivulets seemed to dance as if fish were chasing each other just below the surface. A compact little tug scooted under the Fifty-ninth Street Bridge, reminding me of lives lived in the open. Mick Jagger's taunting alto blasted over the car radio. I was preening again in the large hand mirror I had brought with me and singing along, occasionally catching the young, long-haired driver's eyes in the car mirror staring at my shiny black hot pants that twitched to the rock 'n' roll beat.

In an hour's time I would be sequestering myself with the first of an endless trail of strangers, all of whom would be sticking their strange penises into me, from eleven A.M. to seven P.M. for the next five days straight. And the truth is, rather than gritting my teeth, I was jumping with excitement, behaving more like a bobby-soxer on the way to her first hop than a prostitute booked for a week's work. Appealing visions of iniquity danced in my head: satin sheets the color of wine, heavy drapes blotting out the street, and foreign men who looked vaguely like Marcello Mastroianni drawing on long cigarettes and appraising my delicate limbs through hanging corridors of smoke.

Imagine my disappointment when confronted with the most ordinary of garden apartments, a floor-through on an equally unremarkable side street somewhere in the no-man's-land of the teens. In fact, the single detail that might suggest "bordello" was the beaded curtain dividing the bedroom from the rest of the lackluster apartment.

The madam, however, stood out against the backdrop of her beige-carpeted, brown-laminated living room.

"You're chicken pussy," she said, "am I right?"

"Excuse me, I'm what?"

"You know, fresh. Take off your clothes. I want to be sure, have to check you for needle marks, sores, that stuff. My clients don't want junkies, and they don't get junkies. Capiche?"

Evelyn had a nose and a chin that looked like they were going to get closer as the years went by, but those eyes were like shots from the soul, and her body was out of this world, slim and curvy like something out of a jerk-off magazine. She was wearing a tiny, fringed vest that just covered her breasts and silk hip huggers. Her straight brown hair hung down below her shoulders suspiciously like a hippie's, I thought.

As I stripped before the madam, who scrutinized the inside of my arms and the cheeks of my behind, I continued to look around. Finally, I couldn't hold back anymore.

"But I don't get it."

"Get what?"

"I don't know. I expected somehow something more, you know, sexy. This is strictly dentist-office decor."

"Rented. Everything in the joint. Rented. By the month," Evelyn said.

"Well, how's a guy even supposed to get it up in an atmosphere like this?"

"Put your clothes back on and sit down. We've got a client coming any minute," she said.

I did as I was told. "Sorry, it's none of my business."

"No, no. I'm not offended. OK, let's put it this way. Janet—that is your name, right?"

"Yes, Janet."

"OK," she said, sitting down next to me and poking her face into mine. "OK, Janet. Here's the point: you got a lot to learn about men, girl, a lot. That's obvious." She leaned back, crossed her legs and stretched both arms out along the back of the rough brown plaid sofa.

"Why do you say that?"

"Because," she said, pulling her arms down and putting her hands on her knees after uncrossing her legs until they hung wide open, "a stiff prick don't need atmosphere. That's the last thing a hard-on wants is atmosphere."

After she spoke, Evelyn paused for what seemed like a long time and trained her eyes on me as if she were looking for signs of life on the moon.

"This is a whorehouse, honey. A whorehouse is no different than a men's room, and we whores are the toilets. Capiche?"

"I see. Toilets. Uh-huh."

"OK, I'm crude. But you might as well know what it is you're getting into. Illusions don't make life any easier. We're douche bags, baby, that's all. Still, it's a quick buck, can't take that away."

"I guess I never thought of it quite like that," I said.

"Nah, not too many girls in the Life do. The truth is tough to take." She patted my knee, stood up, and stretched. "Ten to one you didn't get into this on account of your high self-esteem."

"The hell with self-esteem. OK, maybe I don't have any, but I don't want any either. I don't estimate myself at all. Maybe I'm great; maybe I'm shit. What measure would I use? It always comes down to what other people think, other people's opinions. I'm not interested," I said, glad to vent one of my pet theories.

"Good, that's a good trait for a ho to have," Evelyn said, glancing at the electric clock on the wall. "OK, sixty-forty split. Blow job is fifty, straight is seventy-five, half 'n' half, a hundred. Up front. That covers it. Nothing fancy—my clients don't go in for it. They're meat 'n' potatoes, salt-of-the-earth, happily married, two kids, two cars, Long Island, New Jersey kind of guys. You'll sail through this week. All my girls love it here."

Evelyn's little no-frills whorehouse was an ideal introduction to the Life. If I'd had to compete with other comely young things, as I later would, or if I'd been expected to cater to those kinky, hard-to-please types (those idle, jaded whoremongers, usually remission men, who haunt the fancier cathouses around town where they spend hours sizing you up before they finally pounce on you), then I'm sure I would have bolted. But as it was, I could ease into it. In fact, hooking at Evelyn's with her benign, singularly unimaginative clientele was less of a challenge than my own private love life had been for a long time.

The first john of the day's name was Frank. A mild, curly-haired Jewish fellow from the Five Towns, he sold appliances wholesale, lived happily, just as Evelyn had said, with his *goyisha* wife, Marion, and three kids somewhere out there on the flat moraine.

He shared this information proudly (as so often was the case with these men, he was exceedingly proud of his domestic life) within the first fifteen minutes in the living room, where we three sat while he drank his highball, after politely requesting a coaster from the hostess. I don't know why he thought I needed to know all this about him, but meanwhile, I was afraid he might be stalling because he wasn't attracted to me. Finally, when he sensed he must get to it—time is money after all—he smiled shyly at me and stood up, offering his hand. It was the first intimation I had that he liked me. Probably too eagerly, I took it and waltzed off with him through the beaded curtains into the simulated motel-chain bedroom.

I indiscriminately loved hard-ons. This made whoring a lot easier. I told myself freedom is loving the opposite sex—or, if you're gay, your own sex, same difference—freedom is loving the whole thing because you love desire itself. Why is it women still aren't free to love desire itself? I believed that I had dodged societal repression, that I was breaking out into a wild zone beyond male jurisdiction. In fact, my lust did act to save me. Only the palpable feel of a man, his very foreignness, could literally and otherwise penetrate my bad-dream state. Drugs and booze fixed it, too, but sex most of all.

This was perhaps why my first inclination was to make love to the stranger, allowing him to undress me, as I never would later on. He got more than his money's worth that lunch hour, tousling my funny hair, which was growing out in all directions, and playing with my clitoris until I came. I was still just a lover then, a sweetheart of a girl, no more sophisticated than the local high school slut when it came to sex. I wanted to be loved; some part of me wanted Frank and every other man to take me home to meet his mother.

Evelyn was quick to set me straight. "You spent too long in there. I heard you moaning, too. What the hell is that all about?"

I blushed with shame.

"Janet, Janet, honey," she said, pushing her face up against mine again, "you don't make love to these clowns. That's why they call it a 'trick.' Capiche?

"Listen, now, to what I'm going to say. It's the best piece of information you're ever going to get. Lay the chump down and squat on him. Push your tits up, hold 'em there all squished tight, show him your cleavage, and make him come. The sooner the better. Save your juice for the pimp or whoever. But come on, kid. Get with it. You're a whore now. You're a pro. Act like it. OK?"

To illustrate her point, Evelyn had grabbed her own large breasts and shoved them together while she talked. They were staring at me accusingly.

"Yeah, OK," I said, still weak with shame, remembering how Frank had actually hugged me there in the pitch-dark, and I had hugged him back.

One thing I did get for my trouble was that he took my number. Frank was my first whorehouse trick and the first entry into what would become my own sizable book of clients, a valuable commodity that retiring whores sell to other whores, sometimes for thousands of dollars, just as a doctor sells his list of patients. Stealing a madam's john is sure grounds for immediate dismissal, if you get caught. Corinne had warned me of this, and it was the first thing Evelyn had said to me over the phone. But every whore I ever knew gave out her number whenever she got the chance. And madams will look the other way, as long as they like you and as long as you don't get greedy. Anyway, not every john will ask for your number. It helps if you happen to be his type. You wait to be sure you've hooked him, or otherwise he might even snitch.

But Frank went for me. When he finally came to see me at Sigrid's, he behaved like an ardent suitor, showering our humble digs with presents: an electric grill, a steam iron, a water pick, and a state-of-the-art clock radio. For this reason, Sigrid tolerated him, although she was pretty uncomfortable with the whole idea. According to her code, it was OK to jerk off anonymous strangers, but turning tricks with men who knew your name was another matter.

One more aspect of Evelyn's business that worked in my favor was the unhurried nature of it. Often, I grew restless, and eventually, I came to resent the empty hours I spent waiting for the next call or the next appointment. But it gave me a chance to ease into the job.

Evelyn liked to smoke reefer; I preferred to duck into the bathroom and snort lines off my big hand mirror. Finally, toward the end of my first week, I told her about it. She did a line with me but regretted it immediately. Speed made her too hyper, she said.

"I don't see how you can do that stuff and then just sit here, without even booze to take the edge off," she said.

Liquor during working hours was forbidden by Evelyn, as it was at most of the smaller houses; not so the big ones, where drinking at the bar with clients went with the job. But usually if a house featured only one whore, that one had to be self-contained, almost demure. The long afternoons did not in any way resemble a party there in the garden apartment; rather, each john's visit was meant to be a restful interlude, and I was offered up as the equivalent of a soothing tonic.

The time I spent at Evelyn's was tranquil and easy once I got the hang of turning fast, efficient tricks in the darkened bedroom. A shaft of southern light trained itself against the vacant living room wall, and I would sit there for long stretches watching motes of dust and threads of smoke swim slowly inside its circumference, dreaming my drug-induced dreams of Michael McClaren and me living blissfully in a thatched-roof hut in the Irish countryside. Sometimes I wandered outside into the erstwhile garden, now reduced to two dirt plots divided by a path of stepping-stones. The remnants of bushes and other living things, the thin, bare cords formerly of ivy that climbed the brick wall, made me long for I could not then have said what.

Evelyn taught me how to play backgammon, but we didn't gamble. Money was too serious to her. Nevertheless, we played ferociously, both of us hating to lose. My madam began to warm to me. She dropped her bravado as if it were a clunky burden to be discarded all of a piece. We talked about ourselves, or at least Evelyn did. She was more forthcoming than I was, because I was ashamed of my background. I don't know why I was so reticent about having been brought up on Park Avenue. Perhaps I sensed that the details of my childhood were too much of an anomaly, too far-fetched. I alluded to my past, of course. I had to acknowledge it in a general way, or else Evelyn would have known I was lying or trying to hide something. She would have known because even though I continually censored myself, eliminating ten-cent words before they could spring from my mouth, my private-school diction gave me away.

Evelyn owned a big two-story house in a cul-de-sac by the water near the tip of City Island. There were two kids it turned out: a girl sixteen and a boy seventeen, almost eighteen, both born out of wedlock by different fathers. The first time Evelyn got pregnant, she was a junior in high school living with a taciturn mother who prayed most of the time, some brothers and sisters, and an Italian drunk of a father who beat up everyone occasionally. It did not occur to Evelyn to get an abortion. For one thing, she loved passionately the father of the baby, a petty hood, an honest-to-God Sicilian.

The girl's father was Irish, and easier to forget, she told me. I didn't argue with Evelyn about their comparative merits, because I had never been with a Sicilian, and I had never experienced the unassailable fidelity she described. Even after all these years, it was obvious he had been the love of her life. He had been true. The other one, the Irishman, was cuter maybe but disloyal. He screwed around. She made him sound trivial by comparison.

Sadly, Eddie's father did disappear, first to Rikers Island, then to Sing Sing, and finally to the city of Albany, where he now ran the numbers or worked at some other low-profile job. She wasn't sure. But as proof of the grandness of this first love, it had produced Eddie, her gray-eyed Sicilian, Eddie Carnivale, because she gave him his father's surname, the hell with the birth certificate.

"Oh, but he's trouble, big trouble," Evelyn said, her fierce brown eyes lighting up whenever she mentioned her son. Her daughter, Ava, had just started to rebel. Up until sometime this year, she'd been tractable, an adult in miniature, shopping for food and sometimes even, unbidden, sweeping the kitchen floor. Eddie, on the other hand..."Oh, never mind," she said. "He's a JD, that kid, a little wise guy, a con man, just like his father, no good at all. But a charm boy, I swear, and not because I'm his mother, the boy could sweet-talk an old lady out of her Social Security check before she even makes it to the bank. He doesn't have to steal; all he has to do is ask for it. I never knew anyone, even his father, like it." She sat up straight while she spoke, bristling with pride.

"You'll see for yourself," she said at one point late in the week. "I want you to come out some Sunday and have dinner with us. You take the number one train, the local, to the last stop and then the bus to the last stop. It's a drag, but I'll get Eddie to drive you home. Nothing fancy, capiche? Oh, but a gorgeous sunset over the city, bright red on account of the smog. And it's pretty where I live. So you'll come. I want you to meet Eddie, and Ava, of course. Maybe a week from Sunday. OK?"

"Yes, sure, I'd love to," I lied. I hated traveling anywhere except by cab, but I couldn't think of a reason to say no.

By the time Friday rolled around, Evelyn had booked me again for the following week, the last week in August. Even though most of her clients went for the novelty of different whores, at least rotating whores, business at that time of year was as slow as it got; besides, I was new talent, so Evelyn figured I could carry two weeks. And she trusted me not to run off with her clients if any of them happened to get attached. Well, it wasn't trust exactly. Instead, she didn't entirely believe that I was in the Life, that I was committed to building a book of my own. But I was, and I gave out my number a half a dozen times at least while I was there.

I became good, too, at hustling the men in and out fast. The bedroom decor helped, it was so impersonal, so brown and laminated like the living room. Impossible to forget where you were in that atmosphere. But I loved it, free as it was of personality, the demands of domestic life, the awful reminders of a happier past, the worn-out, broken-down, sad and familiar things we surround ourselves with and then grow to hate, until the prospect of going home looms like the horror of last night's ugly dream suddenly recalled. Evelyn's whorehouse bedroom, by contrast, reminded me of life on the American road, of toilet seats wrapped in paper to prove how sanitary they are, of little individual bars of soap, enough so you could open a new one every time. This bedroom freed me from the burden of self, from the petty responsibilities of daily living. With the solemn reverence ritual inspires, tricks dropped their used condoms in the special metal wastepaper basket reserved for that purpose. I washed the men off again just as reverently before they put on their suits and knotted their ties in front of the cheap mirror attached to the low dresser.

And on it went, except for the hours when no one called and no one came, hours spent waiting on the sofa with Evelyn, waiting and waiting for the insurance salesmen, the Seventh Avenue wholesalers, the cheerfully settled family men with small retail stores in the neighborhood. I waited for the prosaic, but to me foreign, worlds they brought in with them, for the money, and, not least of all, for the chance to practice my profession, to seduce them.

I learned how to spike the simple acts we performed together with low-key drama, with a sultry voice and an artful stroke. I learned how effective it was to lower myself on him slowly, to strike a pose in the dim light. Sometimes I brushed my hand lightly across a hard penis, making it seem almost accidental. I knew then the trick would be sucking in his breath and holding it, afraid I might disown the action if he asked for more. I might say, 'enough of that,' or some other preemptory thing. It felt so good, all the more because it was out of his control and because I was not aroused. Perverse as it was, the trick often liked being the only one who enjoyed it. Maybe he felt relieved not having to please the woman, not having to worry about her orgasm for once. Underneath that, there was something both humiliating and at the same time exciting about it, succumbing to the all-powerful, remote mother of his infant dreams.

Even as I began to enjoy the power I had over these tricks in the bedroom, I did not like at all the feeling of helplessness I experienced waiting for them in the living room. Evelyn seemed to take it in stride; not me. More than anything, I had always hated waiting for men. But in the hooking profession in those days, only streetwalkers could escape it. Meanwhile, this is what had drawn me to the saloons, where I could come and go, where I could hunt men instead of the other way around. Now, even though I had chosen to outright reject the society I was born into, I found myself once more obliged to wait for the attention of men. I could barely stand the frustration. If it weren't for the fact that I was also waiting for pretty good money, I might have hit the street.

Waiting

When I was almost seven, my father, Rayfield, called. This was the first time I'd heard his voice in two years. He had come home from Korea with the Bronze Star. He wanted to see me. I couldn't believe it. My father wanted to see me. It was like the president, or a famous actor, suddenly calling up and saying that he wanted to see me, so outsized had my fantasy of him become. In the two years that he had been away, I had received one unsigned valentine. My mother had to tell me it was from him. The fact that he hadn't bothered to sign it even, this drawing of a cavalier monkey in his funny, tilted cap, with only the printed words "Be My Funny Valentine" inside, broke my heart. Maggie patiently, emphatically explained that it was a Valentine's Day custom, that my father was pretending to be a secret admirer.

"Couldn't he have at least put 'Love, Dad' on it?" I kept asking. "Just 'Love, Dad'?"

Anything would have been better than nothing. I was convinced that he was in a hurry, popped the card in the mailbox, and that was it. I figured he had forgotten about me, and I pined for him. I became seriously depressed. How I did that, I remember, at the fickle age of five, was by vowing to be unhappy all the time. Not just some of the time when I felt like it. That was not serious enough. Grown-ups think you're simply in a bad mood if you look sad, then ten minutes later start to laugh at something someone says. No, the trick was to stick with it, make them see you're not just being a kid. It had to be full-time. I was going to be unhappy every waking minute if I could help it.

When I entered the first grade at an enchanted, strange little European school, where they cosseted neglected uptown kids like me, the depression gradually started to lift. I didn't want it to, because I was afraid that I would forget my father, just as he had forgotten me, and then it would be as if we as a duo had never existed. To prevent this from happening, I turned my absent father into a love object and began to revel in the attenuated refinements of unrequited affection. I was determined that I would not forget. Singlehandedly, I would keep this thing we had alive. Before he left, he said to me, "Remember, darling, true love is like this rubber-band. You can stretch it, but it never breaks."

So there. So it was true.

But then, after the initial call in September, we didn't hear from him. I went into second grade. Thanksgiving passed with no word. Finally, he phoned again. He was settled now, with a job at the copy desk of the *Tribune* and a room somewhere I never had heard of, White Plains I think it was.

It was on a Saturday in early December at my grandparents' penthouse on Fifth Avenue, and my father was coming. I see myself sitting on the window seat, my knees tucked up to my chin, the blue velvet skirt pulled taut over them, staring out the living room picture window at Central Park, twenty-two stories below. I liked to search out an empty space in the rambling apartment where I could pretend that I was living alone. The best way to do this was to enter a room after Bridget had finished cleaning it, preferably when Josephine had slipped off to an afternoon Mass (poor people were Catholics; rich people like my grandparents were nothing at all). Today Grandpa had gone out to his club, but he often took his nap then. My grandmother might try to get me to take a walk in the Park, but the old woman shuffled along on the sidewalk, going nowhere, until she hit a bench. I needed a destination, and I hated the pavement. Instead, I ran for the fields, the big rocks, the densest part of the woods, where you couldn't even see the buildings.

Sometimes my grandfather took me there, the Ramble it's called, deep inside the Park. That morning, the two of us—my round, bald grandfather and I—had skipped down the hill as far as the miniature boat pond. Grandpa bought a small plastic bag of salty peanuts, which he said were for the squirrels. Then, according to ritual, I ate them. At this point, the old man shook his head like his granddaughter was beyond hope and called me a "squirglar," a thief who stole from the squirrels. I giggled. He had made that word up himself. Grandpa liked me wicked. Good children, he said, were hiding something. And they were dull.

Now that I was seven, he undertook to lecture me on a variety of subjects from literature to politics. On this particular morning, he had decided it was time to warn me about two phony writers from my father's neck of the woods called Emerson and Thoreau. These men were muddled thinkers. It was self-evident in their prose, which was filled with parentheses inside of parentheses. Obviously confused. "Never use a ten-cent word when a two-cent word will do," he told me.

I was thinking about Emerson and Thoreau and that word I couldn't pronounce, "transcendentalism"—"a lot of hooey" was how my grandfather explained it to me. The two guys lived on a pond, or one of them did. Well, why not? But if I knew anything, it was that Grandfather was right. His warning tone implied the world was full of fools.

I was looking out the window at the far side of the big boat pond in the middle of the Park, where the woods grew thick, imagining those two men perched at the edge there rubbing sticks together to make a fire. I pretended I could see them under the trees. I also granted a short audience to Horatio (a clown of a sidekick I had been trying to banish, since everybody except Horatio himself knew and accepted that he did not exist).

Josephine came out from the back of the apartment, through the dining room, stopping at the staircase adjacent to the front door in the hallway. She looked at me across the wide-open space of connecting rooms and then looked at the door. Then my nurse sighed and started up the stairs. From where I sat, I could see her nylon uniform pull at the seams across her wide, rolling back. She stopped on the landing to breathe, a great demonstration of heaving in and out.

"C'mon, Janet, I'll brush your hair again," she called out to me.

I got up slowly and walked to the stairs. Josephine had already brushed and brushed my straight ash-blond hair that morning, and still it fell in strings around my head. I wished I had curly black hair like the second grade class leader, Betty. My ears poked out. My white nylon socks were slipping into my black patent leather shoes. I began climbing the stairs, grabbing the polished banister directly above me and pulling myself up one step at a time.

"Stop that," Josephine said from the landing. "You're not an old lady."

We went into the big guest room, where we sometimes spent the night. It was furnished, draped, and carpeted in tones of beige. A few of my stuffed animals sat bright and incongruous on a pillow. Usually chatterboxes, always arguing among themselves, even they got quiet here.

"I see Bridget cleaned the room this morning. Isn't that nice?" Josephine said.

"Bridget always cleans the room, every day," I said.

The nurse sat down on a taut coverlet. "Not everyone has someone to clean up after them," she said.

"Mother says when she was growing up everybody had a maid," I said.

"If everybody had a maid, who were the maids then, I'd like to know?" Josephine asked, taking the hairbrush in one hand and my arm in the other. She pulled me between her legs and started to brush, first the left, then working her way around.

Outside the penthouse window, one tall fir tree, standing in its own tub, fought back the sun. Along the glass fence, holly bushes and mistletoe had been planted that week. The earth was still moist and turned. The winter light splashed the roofs of the other apartment buildings, which stretched as far as the East River in this direction, each one of them studded with evergreens growing out of miniature walled gardens, high up in private communion with the sky.

A little later, Josephine and I sat on the light blue linen sofa in the living room, sinking deeper into its wide cushions, watching *The Big Top*, a live circus show for kids. I was glaring at the set. The front door slammed and Grandpa swooped in, still wearing his hat and coat, trailing cold air. His delicate hooked nose was red, and behind his bifocals, his blue eyes watered.

"Hello, girls," he said, meaning Josephine and me. "Where's your pa? I was going to steal Ray away from his daughter for a chess game."

"Good afternoon, Mr. Abram," Josephine said. "Mr. Chace hasn't arrived. He hasn't called either. I can't imagine."

"Well, I'm going to my study. Let me know when he shows up," he said.

I tried not to look at him when he kissed me before he went away.

Grandma was still at Elizabeth Arden, getting made over. My mother had gone out for a long lunch with some writer friends. The phone had not rung since after breakfast, so when it did, Josephine patted my arm and said, "That'll be him, to say he's on his way."

A second or two later, Bridget appeared in the doorway and nodded. Josephine went to the phone in the hall, followed by me.

"Yes, yes, I understand. Circumstances," she was saying into the phone. "We were expecting you at one for lunch, but that's all right. Just hop into a cab. Janet is so anxious to see you."

I tugged Josephine's elbow. "Does he want to talk to me?"

"No, no. He just called to tell us he's on his way."

"Where is he, in New York?"

"He's in New York, right outside Grand Central. He was detained, but now he's coming," Josephine said as she hung up.

"Didn't he want to say hello to me?"

"He's on his way," she said. "You'll see him in person in a few minutes."

"How many minutes?"

She hesitated. "Fifteen."

I pulled my nurse's wrist down and read her watch. "It's exactly two twenty-one." I began counting with my fingers. "Two twenty-one plus ten plus five, two thirty-six. He'll be here by two thirty-six."

"If not before," Josephine said, and we went back to take our places on the sofa.

At three o'clock I got up and changed the channel. A still shot of the city at night flashed on the screen. The theme from *Gone with the*

Wind played behind the familiar voice of the announcer introducing this afternoon's "Million Dollar Movie," *Mr. Peabody and the Mermaid*. I had seen the last half of it three times that week after school. I loved the part, without knowing exactly why, where the mermaid lay close to Mr. Peabody, drinking out of a glass, a helpless creature, locked in a fish's tail, rolling around on his patio. I didn't know whether it was funny or sad. The mermaid wore bright red lipstick; even when she popped out of the sea she was wearing lipstick.

After the movie ended, with Mr. Peabody looking out his New York window at the falling snow, Josephine put her arm around me, patting my shoulder. "There, there," she said. That made it worse. I shook off my nurse and went to the picture window. Directly across from me, the deep orange sun began to slip behind the left tower of the Majestic. Suddenly, in between bare trees, the streetlights in the Park came on. An occasional car wound along the drive inside the Park. It was that time of day on a weekend in winter when people find themselves alone and caught off guard by the early darkness.

The doorbell rang. Josephine leapt to her feet like a fat girl jumping rope and went to the door. Maggie rushed in, the cold air surrounding her like a strong perfume. She threw her dark, sheared beaver coat over the banister. She looked like her father, short and compact, the same periwinkle-blue eyes set in a heart-shaped face. She was wearing a fitted gray flannel suit with a deep red fox collar. A little gray suede hat perched itself at an angle on her head from which flew a gray veil, covering her forehead like a gossamer flag. Her fine hair shot out in loose waves from underneath her hat, suggesting angles in her plump cheeks. She was grinning, as if someone had just told her a joke and she was still laughing. Clutching her purse, she walked deliberately on her high heels, as if she were following chalk marks on a stage floor, and stood at the wide entrance to the living room. Then she was no longer smiling.

"Where's your daddy?"

I turned back to the window.

"He called, missus," Josephine said. "He's running behind."

Maggie looked at her slim gold watch. She tossed her head. "Well, that figures," she said.

She went over to me, reached out to touch my face. I pulled away as if I had been stung and moved closer to the window.

"I'm sorry, honey," my mother said. "You know he means well. He just can't help it."

The doorbell rang. Everyone turned to face the sound as if they were expecting the enemy. The bell rang again, three rapid sets of *ding-dongs*. The two women and I sank back. It was Grandma then. Bridget ran out from the kitchen, taking mincing steps as if she were hobbled, and pulled open the door. She half curtsied in an eager dumb show of fear. A tiny woman wearing long blond hair swept up in combs shuffled through the door. She was bowed under the weight of a silver fur. Bridget stood with her arms outstretched at the old woman's back, ready to receive the coat.

"Good evening," Grandmother said.

"Good evening," Bridget said, as she scooped up Maggie's abandoned sheared beaver from where it had fallen on the stairs and threw it on top of the undulating mink.

My grandmother's eyes were the color of ice on a lake. She turned and peered into the living room. "Don't you people believe in electricity?"

The room was dark. Josephine hurried around it, first turning on the running lights along the bookshelves and then a three-way standing lamp in one corner. The old woman smiled without showing her teeth.

"Good, I'm glad everyone is here. We won't be late for dinner. Mr. Abram is in his study, I take it?"

"Yes, madame," Josephine said.

"Well, I'm sorry that I missed Rayfield. Such an attractive man. You will tell him how sorry I am, won't you, Maggie, the next time you speak to him?"

"He hasn't been here, Mother," Maggie said.

"Oh?" the old lady asked without surprise. "I had understood that he was visiting Janet today."

"Well, he stood her up," Maggie said. She went to put her arm around me and I pulled away.

"Perhaps he will turn up yet. Bridget, kindly tell Anna that there will be one more for dinner and set another place."

"No, Bridget," Maggie said, walking over to the maid and retrieving her coat, which she hung in the closet behind them. "That won't be necessary. I don't want him here drunk."

"Maggie, must you continually contradict me and confuse the servants? Set another place, Bridget. That will be all. I don't want to be disturbed until dinner." The old woman disappeared into her room. They heard her door slam.

Bridget pulled a large, polished oak hanger from out of the hall closet and very gingerly folded the big coat around it. "Will you need anything, Mrs. Margaret?" she asked my mother.

"Yes, Bridget, some ice. I need a drink."

Bridget nodded and left for the kitchen.

Maggie turned back to the living room, where she went over to the television and switched it off. "Josephine, what did you do all afternoon, just hang around waiting for the bastard?"

"Hush, hush, missus. Don't talk like that in front of the child, even if it is the God's truth."

Maggie pulled off the little hat with one hand as she rubbed her hair around impatiently with the other. "It was better when he was in Korea. Janet shouldn't be subjected to this," she said, sitting down abruptly on a white loveseat against the wall, which ordinarily was never used, and patting an empty space next her.

"Come here, Janet, come sit," she said.

I shook my head. I couldn't bear to let anyone see me like this. Everybody's parents in my second grade class were divorced—well, practically everybody—but the other kids' fathers made a big fuss about their visitation rights. Sometimes, someone might not even be able to attend a birthday party because that was the father's day. I knew how it was supposed to go.

Bridget appeared again, framed in the large entrance to the living room. She was carrying an ice bucket in both hands. "They've announced Mr. Rayfield on the house phone. They want to know if he's expected."

Maggie looked at her watch again. "It's after five. He's got a hell of a nerve."

"What should I say?" Bridget asked.

Josephine took the ice bucket and set it on a shelf with interior running lights, next to the empty fireplace. "Tell him to send him up. Better late than never."

"But, Josie," Maggie said, sounding very young to me then, "do you think it's wise?"

"Janet has been waiting all day. Better she see it than blame you," Josephine spoke matter-of-factly.

"But I don't care!" I said. "I don't really." Tears flew out of my eyes like flecks of spit from an angry mouth. "Tell him to go to hell."

"Shame on you. He'll hear you all the way in the elevator," my nurse said.

The bell rang. Josephine was there before Bridget could arrive.

"At last," she said as she pulled it open, "at last. Come in."

But the tall young man, still in his thirties, stood outside, his wrinkled raincoat hanging off him as if he had not been able to make up his mind whether or not to wear it.

"Are you sure, Josie?" His mouth dropped in that self-deprecating smile. "I thought I might be too late to be welcome."

"You're always welcome, Mr. Ray," Josephine said. "Now in, in." She shooed him past her as if she were corralling a truant rooster back into the yard.

"Hello, Daddy," I said, and went over to meet him.

He scooped me up and began to stagger. Together we fell onto the carpeted stairs, adjacent to the door, where he continued to hold me, burying his head in my hair. "Oh, baby, baby, you OK?"

I ran my hand across his chin.

He pulled his face. "Seems like it's growing," he said. His skin was pale and fine underneath the stubble. His green eyes were dull and misted over as if his mind were traveling great distances without him, hovering over the refracted lights of the city outside the living room window. He had a high forehead framed by a mass of dark hair, which he combed straight back, but which now fell forward in looping waves over his heavy eyebrows. He began to run his hand through it, but then abandoned the gesture, as if he had been distracted, this time by the front door that Josephine had just closed behind him. Something or someone on the other side of it grabbed his attention. The white turtleneck (the kind he always wore; he had an aversion to ties), which was still tucked into his pleated pants, may have been clean earlier that day. Now it advertised his afternoon. Vague brown spots, possibly spilled coffee, covered the front of it. I watched my mother screw her face up in disgust.

She got up from the white sofa and marched over on her high heels to where my father sat on the stairs. "Why did you have to do this today? Why? Just one day you could've laid off it. For Janet's sake. You know the problems I've been having with her. She's totally withdrawn. The teachers say she won't respond. She mopes around the apartment. Is it always going to be like this with you, Rayfield? Is this what I have to look forward to? What gives you the right to turn your back on her when she *needs* you?"

I broke in, yelling, "Stop it, stop it!"

I stood up in front of him, facing my mother, to protect him.

Then he reached up and took my hand and turned me around. Our eyes, the same slanted green ones, met. "Maybe I should leave, princess. I'm a mess. I'm sorry." He put his elbows on his knees and covered his face.

I continued to look at him, memorizing his hairline, the grooves on the sides of his square mouth, the way his eyebrows arched, the Adam's apple. He was the handsomest man that I had ever seen and I did not know when I would see him again.

"OK, go," I said, without moving, the hot penthouse air ringing in my ears.

"That's not very kind," Josephine said. The big nurse took my father by his other hand, pulling him to his feet. "Have some black coffee first."

Maggie pushed past her ex-husband. "Well, I can't stand it. I'm going upstairs. Josie, don't leave Janet alone with him."

"Not to worry, missus," Josephine said. "We'll have a little black coffee. Janet, kiss your father. Tell him how much you love him, how much you missed him. Go on, now."

I shook my head. Pride, the price we sometimes pay for survival, had suddenly taken over. 'It's not my turn anymore, it's his,' was all I could think about. 'I held my end up for a long time, but now it's his turn.' He moved a few steps until he could just reach out and touch my small shoulders covered in velvet. Cautiously at first, he began to massage them with his palms. I could smell his stale whiskey breath as he leaned over and kissed me gently on the cheek.

"Janet, darling Janet. You're all grown up. Did you miss me?"

What I wanted to know was: Did he miss me? He had to say so first. I kept my mouth shut. My father dropped his arms and shrugged. "Josie, I'm sorry. I tried, but the kid's too smart for her old dad. She's through with me, too, fed up. And she's right, she's right. I'm going."

He pulled me to him, clutching me like a small belonging that someone else had tried to steal away. Frightened by the abruptness of it, I let out a little scream. Grandpa Abram came to the door of his study at the far end of the apartment wearing a silk smoking jacket, his black eyeshade pushed over his forehead.

"What's going on here?" he asked, his watery blue eyes raw and blinking without his glasses.

"Hello, Sam. It's Rayfield here. Sorry to have missed you, just leaving." My father pulled his dirty raincoat around him. "Janet," he said, his hand on the brass doorknob, "I know I'm a no-good bum of an old man, but I'll always love you. No matter what. Remember, darling, love is just like a rubber band. You can stretch it, but it never breaks."

Then he was gone, the thick metal door thudding shut behind him. I ran, pulling it open with both hands. "Daddy, I'll wait. I'll wait."

He looked at me as if I were a stranger, or as if he had forgotten why he was there.

"That's my pet, that's my Janet," he finally said, just as the elevator arrived. He slipped past me behind Jake, the operator, turning inside where he continued to wave and smile that doleful smile until Jake heaved the car door shut.

The Visit

Michael and I stood not particularly close together behind the wall-sized picture window of the Traveling Medicine Show. Michael was gazing out on the early birds spruced up in their ties and jackets and high heels and makeup as they headed south.

It was an early Friday morning, still hours before what would be the last day of my second week at Evelyn's. We were speeding to the point where everything is hushed and time quits, gives up, stops shoving you. The hard white crystals melting in the brain had catapulted us headlong into a Faustian dream where we hovered beyond mortality. We had escaped hunger, thirst, exhaustion, anxiety, frustration, sadness of all kinds. I felt cool and shameless, as numb as ancient sand blowing in the desert wind. Freed from the struggle. The contrast between us inside and them outside further heightened our already exalted state. We were dimensions away from the solemn taxpaying lot on the other side of the dirty windowpane.

"I never get tired of watching them go to their offices." Michael shook his head in mock disbelief. He shivered with incomprehension, hugging himself and rubbing his muscles underneath the sleeves of his black T-shirt as if he were cold. In fact, the air-conditioning was on the blink, and the day already promised to be good and hot.

We continued to look on for a while in silence, too grateful to speak. I was feeling particularly blessed because lately I had Michael all to myself. Safe inside the dark bar, dressed in blue-jean cutoffs and a child's T-shirt stretched taut over my flattened bosom, I imagined myself to be protected forever from ordinary life, from panty hose and hairdos. My contempt was perfect; I even found it in my heart to pray for them, that alien breed trudging along in quiet desperation, their numbers increasing with the rising sun. Why had I been spared? Just lucky, I guess.

"They look like the British raja, don't they? Everybody buttoned up, covered from head to toe, the sweat already dripping. See how everybody ignores each other and keeps their eyes glued straight ahead. Why? And they're always in such a big hurry, no matter what time it is. I can't figure it out," I finally said.

"All I want to know is how come I have everything I need, and I don't have to do what they're doing? God, good God..." Michael shivered again. A broad, smug smile shone on his face. "Wonder what the poor people are doing today?" he said, as if watching the nine-to-fivers were the sport of kings. Then, a moment later: "Maybe I could check out Evelyn's sometime."

"How do you expect to do that?"

"You know, I could pretend to be a john. I'd pay, of course, what the hell, we all gotta pay sometime. I'd just like to see what it's like, the inside of a madam's house. And Evelyn sounds interesting."

"Really, Michael, you're playing with me."

"Nope. No, I am not."

"But you don't look like any john I ever saw. You'd never pass. Then she'd think we had some kind of conspiracy going, like we were casing the joint, planning to rip her off or something."

"All righty, let's see...I know, I could pose as your friend. How about that? Come over at the end of your shift. You'd introduce us. How about that, pretty clever, huh?"

"But honestly, you gotta believe me, there's nothing to see down there. It's the dreariest little setup."

He turned his back to the window and walked over to his long table, where he sat down, put his feet up on the neighboring chair, pulled open the *Village Voice*, gave it a snap and disappeared behind it.

"OK, OK," I said, following him.

I pushed the paper down below his face. He looked up then. There was a shady little smile playing on his lips.

"OK, I'd be delighted to introduce you to Evelyn. But, of course, she's gonna assume you're my pimp. Even if I tell her otherwise.

And madams vie for ascendancy over pimps—did you know that? Well, they're sort of competitors, aren't they?"

"Since when do pimps wear moccasins with holes in 'em? I'm a mighty lousy pimp then," he said.

At seven P.M. sharp the doorbell at Evelyn's rang. I was shocked, overwhelmed. In cities, lives stretch out linearly. We show bits and pieces of ourselves, like shards of different-colored glitter on a string. Our friends very often have no use for one another. Work and home rarely intersect. Our past is discarded, detached like empty boxcars. We live in discrete worlds that we imagine are mutually exclusive. When two of these seemingly incompatible worlds combine, it feels as though two broken parts of the self were coming together.

I went to the door. Michael's black hair was clean and pulled back in a ponytail. His blue jeans were the newest pair he owned, and he was wearing my favorite scarlet corduroy shirt, the one that threw his pale blue eyes in relief.

"Michael, meet Evelyn," I said, leading him straight into the living room.

Evelyn kept her seat on the sofa. She was wearing skintight toreador pants, a half-unbuttoned black cotton shirt, and red high heels. The cleavage poured out; her long brown hair hung against her smooth white skin.

Michael approached and she put out her hand. I thought for a minute he was going to kiss it, but he shook it. Then he sat down in the armchair where the johns ordinarily sat.

"Janet likes it here," he said.

"She's a very good worker. Too bad business has been so slow," Evelyn said.

Even though it was true, the reason she made a point of saying business was slow was because she wanted to back me up. If Michael were my pimp, it would figure I told him business was really slow so I could keep some extra for myself. She was assuming like a good whore I had lied, and this assumption was based on the original wrong one that he was my pimp. In other words, Evelyn was acting in some other scene entirely.

Meanwhile, Michael had assumed I never told Evelyn I was new at this, because that's the way he would have handled my situation. He thought an admission of inexperience was the kind of tenderfoot confession that would automatically be exploited. When he told Evelyn I liked it here, he put the emphasis on "here," as if there were other whorehouses to compare it with.

They were both wary and streetwise, and they were trying to look out for me, each in his or her way.

Sitting back in the armchair, Michael said he was comfortable. I realized I had never seen him sit with his feet on the floor before—come to think of it, I had never seen him in anything as bourgeois as an upholstered chair either. It was like letting in the outdoor cat for the first time and watching it make a beeline for the fire, where it curls up familiarly on the softest cushion.

Michael looked around at the brown-laminated living room. He nodded. "To the point."

Evelyn offered him a drink.

"I drink rum," he said apologetically.

"Not a problem," Evelyn said, all of a sudden eager to please (no different from the rest of us poor fools as far as I could tell). She took coy little steps in her red high heels over to the small bookshelf-turned-bar, and it occurred to me that I was getting a first-time look at a whole other side of her. Evelyn the lady: no slang, no curses, no acid wisdom. As she mixed our drinks, she spoke deliberately and with an arch politeness. Not even the johns got this treatment.

After she had delivered the alcohol—a rum and Coke, a Dewar's, and a Finlandia on the rocks—Evelyn rejoined me on the sofa, where we sat facing Michael. Following her lead, I crossed my ankles in an attempt to appear demure, but I doubt I pulled it off. I was dressed in one of my working outfits: black satin hot pants, granny boots, a tiny, puff-sleeved pink angora child's sweater stretched across my bosom. Michael leered at me politely.

We let a moment of silence pass while we savored our drinks. Twilight slipped into darkness; longtime foes of the sun, the three of us heaved sighs of relief. No one thought to turn on a light for quite a while. Finally, Evelyn reached to her left, where an early example of Lucite supported the three-tiered plastic lamp. She lit the top bulb and turned it away. Still no one spoke. Michael and I would have sat drinking without saying a word until the stars came out, until the liquor had hit, as we often did when left alone, but Evelyn was better socialized. Eventually she more or less announced to the shadows against the wall in front of her that soon she would hop into her old Mustang and take off for City Island, where her daughter would be finishing up dinner, washing the dishes.

I pictured a raw domestic scene too brightly lit and needlessly busy. It was depressing, repugnant even: the tart smell of tomato sauce hanging in the air, the daughter squabbling with her brother and a mutt yapping at somebody's heels, the TV playing a sitcom rerun, its canned laughter numbing the senses like a tab of Thorazine, drowning out the sweet chorus of late-summer crickets. But obviously, Evelyn looked forward to it.

"Eddie might be home. It's too early for him to go out yet. Sometimes he just hangs out at Rocky's on the corner. Sometimes he goes who the hell knows where. Never mind, I don't worry about him anymore; it's the street I'm worried about with him on it, if you want to know the truth."

A few sips of vodka and she was beginning to sound more like her usual self.

"You should tell your daughter and Eddie, too, to come into the city and stop by my saloon." Michael was fondling his glass, making the ice tinkle. Now he seemed restless and eager, talking about the bar, the home he so rarely left. "There's free music most weeknights. We have a lot of good musicians who showcase their material there, like Tommy Shelter and Lionel Pike and, let's see, Max Ghostly... Freddie Bombay played there last night...Omega's going to be around this week. Remember her?"

"Lots of famous people." Evelyn nodded politely.

"They like to try out new stuff. It's on Seventy-Sixth and Second. The Traveling Medicine Show. Come by with Janet. Have a few cocktails on me," Michael said.

"Eddie would like it. He's into music, plays the guitar. I don't hang out much anymore. Got other things to do at home. I never told you this, Janet, but I live with someone. A good man. He does hate to leave the island, though. Can't drag him into Manhattan. But he keeps busy. Any kind of work out there he can get. He can do everything: carpentry, painting, even a little plumbing."

"What's his name?"

"Danny. Mr. Fix It. Local fellow." Evelyn swallowed more vodka and started smiling over the rim of her glass. She was musing. "He's simple in some ways, at least that's what people think, but really he's very wise. He's taught me everything I know about plants, their names and when they grow and where, too. I never figured there were so many varieties of wildflowers right on City Island. Well, you'll meet him, Janet, when you visit this Sunday.

"Michael, why don't you come along? Plenty to eat. Nice view of the bay and the city. We get these really intense red sunsets out there on account of the pollution."

For one instant, an entire dream blazed in my mind. Michael and me going somewhere together as a couple. Then, sure enough, he started to squirm a little and crossed an ankle over his knee. He hung on to his crossed leg as if he were trying to pull himself away.

"Sorry, gotta work."

Michael never had to work, mainly because Michael didn't do anything.

"Michael's like those rare Beaujolais that don't travel well," I said.

"You mean we're not going to be able to import him to City Island?"

We all laughed. Michael tilted his head and smiled at Evelyn as if he were seeing her just then for the first time. He uncrossed his leg, letting his foot drop to the floor. Usually he was not only shy, not just wary, but, truthfully, a touch paranoid as well, because he was always slightly psychotic from the methedrine. But he seemed to relax now.

When I came across someone I thought was worthy of Michael, I would make a case for that person, and I had devoted a good deal of time over the last few weeks to descriptions of Evelyn. Michael and I were both fiercely sentimental about our friends. For instance, there was 4-H Jimmy, the bartender from Indiana. Michael had regaled me one almost garrulous night with descriptions of Jimmy's first studio apartment in the city: matching flour and sugar canisters in the kitchen, felt flags from Indiana State's football team pinned to his wall. Jimmy used to wear madras Bermuda shorts on his day off back then. He was in such earnest then, breezing into the Traveling Medicine Show for a few cocktails before he went to work as a maître d' at his clip joint on Third Avenue. Four-H Jimmy was so guileless it broke Michael's heart. He made me appreciate his protégé. "Don't be a snob," he said.

The truth is I had very much wanted my madam and my Svengali to meet, and when Michael's curiosity finally got the better of his fear, if I demurred at first it was because I felt I had a lot at stake. I wanted Michael and Evelyn to approve of each other. Now, I sat gloating between the two of them like an indulged only child.

He casually asked if he could check out the bedroom. "I'm curious," he said.

"Hate to disappoint you, fella, but there's nothing to see. Of course, you're welcome to look. That much is on the house," Evelyn said.

He went out into the hall and turned to his left. Facing the bedroom, he pushed open the beaded curtain with both hands and stuck his head inside. We got up and followed him as far as the edge of the living room.

"You can walk right in. No one's gonna grab you and ravage you," Evelyn called out to him.

"More's the pity," he said, but he didn't go inside.

I shrugged my shoulders. "He told me he wanted to check it out, where I work. I told him there was nothing to see. I think mostly he just wanted to meet you." I spoke softly so he wouldn't hear.

"Handsome, that one," Evelyn said.

City Island

I thought it was about the ugliest, most forlorn-looking house I had ever seen. Chunks of brown paint were flaking off the wood shingles. A crumbling porch had been partially screened in on the left side of it, but the screen was full of holes big enough to stick your head through. The poor thing looked as if it had been abandoned, left to rot. So much for Mr. Fix It. And none of this would have been so bad if the one tree shading the house, a spindly oak about twenty feet high, hadn't been drooping as if it wished it were dead. An old-fashioned wheelbarrow sat by itself in the dirt yard; behind it I could see rusted engine parts splayed out on the ground, an incidental arrangement of inner tubes, coils of rope, a snarl of rubber hose, and, to the left at one edge of the property, an empty doghouse with half its roof caved in. Long, bold weeds shot up through all this debris in unlikely places. And I could see the rear end of the old Mustang, its tailpipe dragging, sticking out of a small shed next to the house. A hedge about five feet high ran along the left side of the property, and a tall, unpainted wood fence bordered on the right, which created the impression Evelyn's neighbors had done their best to block this scene out.

The single charming detail was the healthy-looking Saint Bernard that had begun to bark at me from just inside the front door, which swung open presently to reveal a man in a red T-shirt and blue-jean overalls. The man bounded toward me, down the sandy path leading from the house. His black hair, underneath a dirty white sailor cap, was greasy and combed close to his scalp. As he got closer, his soft blue eyes shone with pleasure and he smiled, revealing an open space and the clean outline of pink gum where at least four of his upper front teeth should have been. But the smile was so confident and sweet, like a baby's grin, that I found myself thinking about the superfluity of front teeth. He extended his hand and shook mine warmly.

"Dan's the name."

"Hi, I'm Janet."

"Yes, I know that much."

The Saint Bernard was jumping up on me by this time, trailing a fibrous length of drool that threatened to glob off and drop itself perhaps on my face, now that its own was next to mine. Dan pulled the dog by the scruff of its thick neck so that it danced a minute backward on its hind legs. Then it fell to all fours and lunged again, tongue out ready to lick, the gooey saliva dangling dangerously above my outstretched hand. I was hoping the animal would settle for a pat, but it ignored the gesture, throwing its front legs around my neck like an old friend who'd been dying to see me.

"All right, Bear, that's enough," Dan said, too calmly, I thought, as I stood there trying to keep my balance. I watched the spit swing over my sandaled foot.

"C'mon now, you silly brute," Dan said, this time giving it a man-sized push.

The animal galloped to the left; in three swift strides it reached its destination, a hole in the high hedge. I followed, curious to see what was on the other side. Above the hedge, another house stood, the mirror image of Evelyn's, only this one was trim and tidy, its wide clapboards painted a crisp white. Little beds of pink and blue hydrangeas posed at the corners of the emerald-green lawn. The smugness of it inspired one of my acute attacks of longing for the orderly assumptions of middle-class life. For a few seconds, I suffered a driving impulse to go visiting over there instead. Meanwhile, the dog had planted its feet squarely before a mysteriously empty-looking break in the neatly clipped hedge. It was barking viciously at something.

"She seen a squirrel, or maybe it was a groundhog. But it was them squirrels ate up my strawberries out back. She could kill one or two. I wouldn't mind," Dan said, joining the dog and me.

"You grow things behind the house?" I asked.

"We got near half an acre stretching all the way to the edge of the cliff above the water. I started a patch of berries and put in an orchard of apple trees, oh, this was ten years ago, before I was living here myself. Evelyn had her heart set on an apple orchard back there for some reason. The apples don't seem ever to ripen proper. They fall out the tree green. Doesn't matter really. It's a pretty kind of tree."

Dan spoke in an unexpected, loping cadence—unexpected because City Island lies right off the Bronx, after all. But this thin strip of land has always been a forgotten stepchild of the city, nothing more than a sandbar boasting a row of cheap fish restaurants that feature local lobsters, along with a large marina just beyond us at the far end of the island.

"You from around here?" I asked.

"Never left. I mean, I been to the city, but I never traveled yet. Maybe one of these days," he said, sounding as if he meant it. "Let's go in the house and I'll fix you a drink."

The inside was a Mary Poppins surprise: gleaming blond wood; a ceiling with exposed beams; yards of sofa covered in a cerulean blue, which looked pretty clean, not counting the animal hairs (a fat little calico cat was there to start rubbing up against me as soon as I crossed the threshold); state-of-the-art hi-fi center; accommodating-looking brown leather swivel chairs with ottomans to match; and a long glass coffee table with nothing but a couple of brimming-over ashtrays on it. The living room and the stairway were carpeted in wall-to-wall shag. The entire house smelled like roasting meat.

Dan caught the look of shock on my face as he rejoined me with my requisite scotch and soda. (Sometimes I could be persuaded to have a beer in the morning, but any time after midday was scotch time.)

"Everybody does the same when they first get a look at the place. Taxes, you see, the IRS. Can't flaunt nothin'. She keeps most of what she makes in a box at the bank. Not even too much jewelry or anything else fancy. Doesn't believe in attracting attention. Smart one, she is," Dan said.

Just then, a set of legs could be seen at the top of the staircase followed by the rest, one lithe teenage girl with long hair like her mother's, coming down the steps. She stopped midway, greeted me with a dull hello, turned and disappeared upstairs again.

"That's Ava. She likes to stay in her room most of the time."

Dan had poured himself a large drink of something. Couldn't tell what it was because the glass was tinted. We were about to go and sit on the couch when we heard the kitchen door slam. Evelyn, dressed in jeans and a halter top, came bursting into the living room, her arms outstretched like a school crossing guard blocking traffic.

"Hold it, hold it. Don't sit down. There's an emergency."

"What's the matter, anyone hurt?" Dan asked, looking genuinely anguished.

"Nope, but somebody's gonna be if we don't find that damned snake."

"Where's the snake?" Dan asked.

"That's what I'm saying. The snake booked, vamoosed, took a powder. I just went out to the shed to get a few bottles of wine—he's gone! No telling how long it's been. We got to find it before Eddie hears about it, or we're all dog meat, capiche?"

"But that's impossible. He's in a cage," Dan said.

"Yeah, well, somebody left the cage door open. The snake's gone, I'm telling you."

"Eddie's most prize possession, a boa. Keeps it in the shed," Dan said to me.

"I'm organizing a posse right now," Evelyn said. She went to the foot of the stairs and yelled, "Ava! Come out of there now!"

The girl appeared immediately.

"Go over to the hedge. Look up and down it until you see Eddie's snake. You didn't open that cage door, did you?"

"No, Mother," she said, stressing the word 'mother' in a fairly cheeky way.

"Doesn't matter. You're part of the expedition. Go on to the hedge." She turned and faced Dan and me. "Dan, you look up and down the fence—on both sides, I don't care what the McCormacks or the Kravitzes have to say about it. Capiche?" she said, addressing herself to everyone. "OK, go. Look carefully. Dan, wear your glasses. C'mon now"—she waved Ava down the stairs and out the door—"I'm taking the road. Oh, Janet, you go out back. Check the orchard.

"We'll catch him. How far could a snake travel in a day?"

No one knew the answer to that.

I didn't particularly want to be the one to find it, but I went through the kitchen and out the back door, where I intended to sit under a tree until I thought an appropriate amount of time had passed. If the snake were on the ground somewhere, I would just as soon miss it.

The orchard was a maze of apple trees, a few green apples already fallen and rotting in the tall weeds. I was wandering in it, lost in some romantic dream about Michael, when I heard a voice.

"What's up?" it said.

I looked around, didn't see anyone.

"Hi, what's doin'?"

I followed the voice into a tree. There, naked to the waist, with his blue-jeaned legs stretched out on a branch, sat a faun. He had a nimbus of long, soft ringlets framing his boy-face. His shoulders were broad and knobby. His skin was so pale it was translucent, touched with the faintest patina of green, but it didn't look unhealthy. It looked more like the wings of a gypsy moth, or the tint of something that had turned recently from a leaf-thing into an animal shape. He might have just conjured himself up minutes before I got there. His gray eyes were murky, like smoke. He was smiling in a beatific way. Instead of pipes, he held a cigarette to his mouth and pulled on it.

I jumped a little. He laughed.

"Who are you?" I asked.

"I live here. My name's Eddie, Eddie Carnivale, but they call me Eddie Apollo. I'm tripping on a thousand mics right now."

"You seem very calm," I said.

"Acid always calms me down," he said.

"Didn't mean to disturb you. I was looking for a snake," I said.

"Look no further," Eddie said, smiling.

There were other hunting parties arranged by Eddie in the following weeks, and Evelyn told me later that everybody walked outside more or less with their heads down for a long time after that, but they never did find the poor snake.

Finally, conceding temporary defeat, we assembled in the dining room. Evelyn disappeared into the kitchen. I had offered to help, but she wouldn't hear of it, preferring to steer Ava ahead of her through the swinging doors. That left me to entertain the two men, Danny and Eddie. Danny was tucking into another highball. Eddie was still tripping his brains out and for the moment seemed the least concerned of anyone that his pet was missing.

"He's a brave boy, gone out to see the world," Eddie said, sounding philosophical and maybe a little proud that his boa got away. If it were my snake, I would've been worried about it, but then I didn't have the perspective a thousand mics of acid was likely to provide.

Eddie poured himself a tall glass of what looked like rum. I was on my second scotch and soda by this time. I was almost hungry because I'd had no methedrine since early in the day, before I left on my long trip on the Seventh Avenue 1 train to the last stop, followed by an interminable bus ride to the end of City Island. I was getting sleepy, too. So I excused myself and went upstairs to the bathroom, where I promptly did a line, a fat line. I came down buzzing and no longer in the mood for dinner.

Eventually Evelyn and Ava emerged through the kitchen door carrying a big platter of pot roast adorned with carrots and potatoes and another platter piled high with surplus vegetables. They went back and came out again with a gravy boat, a bowl of penne, and a large tomato-and-iceberg-lettuce salad already dressed and tossed, this time accompanied by the Saint Bernard, almost within slurping distance. Danny took the dog by the collar and pulled it outside. He came back in and poured the decanted wine to the rim of each person's big goblet. I was grateful for that. Then he raised his goblet as if to toast but thought better of it and just drank. Evelyn, still standing, piled our plates with food and passed them along. The entire elaborate meal seemed out of place. Everybody but Danny sat staring at their plates for what struck me as an ungracious amount of time.

"C'mon, kids, eat up. I worked my ass off and this is good food. You gotta eat! Janet, I know that's not your bag, but you probably need the calories. Eddie, you, too. You're going to disappear if you don't eat. And, Ava, I'm sick and tired of your anorexia or whatever the hell it is. Eat, eat. Capiche?"

We tried to oblige, pushing the meat in its heavy gravy around and around on the plate. I was shoving food into my mouth one carrot at a time, which I would then chew and chew in the hope I could break it down enough to swallow it.

"You kids are crazy. You don't know what you're missing. Great dinner, Evelyn! We got to do this more often," Danny said, taking a big long drink of wine.

"Seems sacrilegious to be eating when my boa is out there somewhere starving to death," Eddie piped up. He was using the snake as an excuse not to eat. Can't hustle a hustler.

"Yes, I know, Eddie, but you won't bring him back by starving yourself," Evelyn said. She probably knew he was playing her but liked being his foil all the same.

"What about you, Ava, are you mourning the snake, too?" Evelyn asked.

Ava barely looked up. "No, of course not. I'm glad it's gone. I'm just not hungry, that's all."

"You're never hungry. What, you think that's sexy, the skeleton look?"

"Honestly, Mother, you are such a drag. Did anyone ever tell you that?"

"Hey, Ava, cool it, man." This from Eddie.

"I don't understand you two girls—why can't you get along?" Danny said, helping himself to another round of food.

"May I be excused?" Ava asked, her tone as hostile as she could make it.

"No, that's rude to Janet, our guest. Besides, I want to see you eat something."

"OK, Evelyn, Mom, let the little bitch go. We don't need her around anyway, bringing me down for sure," Eddie said.

"Maybe Eddie's right. You're bringing us all down," Evelyn said.

Ava left the table immediately and went upstairs, where she disappeared inside her room and slammed the door.

I had moved on to my second carrot, which I was chewing endlessly like it was a tiny bone. The gravy was starting to congeal on top of my largely untouched meat and pasta. Lucky for me the family was dysfunctional. I was blending in.

Finally, Evelyn, with Danny as helpmate, took all the platters and our food-laden plates back into the kitchen.

Evelyn came out and said cheerfully, "Judging from your plates, I see that no one wants dessert."

"What's for dessert?" Eddie wanted to know.

"Ice cream and cookies," Evelyn said.

"I'll have some of that," he said.

"Oh, that's nice, you can't eat all that food I prepared, but you're suddenly hungry for dessert," Evelyn said, but she went back into the kitchen, where Danny was loading the dishwasher, and came out again with bowls, ice cream, and a box of Entenmann's chocolate chip cookies. I could tell that nobody expected me to have any. I was off the hook.

"You don't want to go home in an old crate like that," Eddie said.

We were standing behind Evelyn's old Mustang. The moon hung over us, low and full.

"Why not?"

"Nah, this ain't the right kind of short for a girl like you. I can do better. C'mon."

He fished a metal wire about a foot long out of a pile of junk at the back of the shed. Then I followed him onto the road, where we turned right, passed the fancy neighbors, and came to a parking lot. A lit-up sign said MEMBERS PARKING ONLY. It belonged to the yacht club. Eddie darted ahead of me and trotted up and down the mostly empty rows. Now and then he circled the occasional car and peered in its window. He stopped, put his hands on his hips. His curly locks, his skin, the white T-shirt and blue jeans, turned a monochromatic gray in the moonlight. I came up and stood beside him. He pointed to the far corner.

"That one."

As little as I knew about cars, it was unmistakably a Corvette, a cream-colored Corvette. Eddie went to the edge of the lot and motioned for me to get behind him. I stood in the weeds just beyond the asphalt. The crickets around my feet stopped singing. I could hear the tiny scratch of wire in the lock. Once the door opened, Eddie stuck his head in and leaned over the front seat. He connected something up underneath the dashboard. Then the engine began to hum. He went around and opened the other door for me.

"You should always ride in style," he said.

We were both drunk, and Eddie must have still been tripping, too, but the road was empty. He gunned the gas pedal right away and did not slow down to a fast cruise until we reached the main part of the little town. We swerved all over the Throgs Neck Bridge. On the highway, the cool air assaulted me steadily from the wide-open window. I felt giddy. I couldn't keep from grinning.

"Smokin', ain't it?" was all Eddie said.

I turned to look at him. The wind was blowing his hair back away from his determined face, and for the first time, I could really see it. He was much less ethereal than I had supposed. In fact, his face was bottom-heavy, dominated by a strong chin. His lips were sultry, his nose straight and a bit wide. Thick lashes framed his gray-blue eyes, which were splintered with tiny specks of white like a hundred blind spots. The bone above his eyebrows was strangely prominent, and his forehead was smooth and low, with a clearly marked widow's peak. While I stared at Eddie's profile, he ignored me, keeping his eyes on the road, both of his white-knuckled hands gripping the wheel. He knew he was stoned and drunk.

The air turned acrid and warm and stung our eyes and our noses even before we entered the midtown tunnel.

"Where to?"

"Seventy-Sixth and Second. And thanks."

When we got to the Traveling Medicine Show, Eddie pulled up with a squeal of the tires, then burned rubber again after I slammed the door. I watched him tearing off down Second Avenue, just making the graduated green lights. I remember thinking he was hip for a kid.

Mystery Plays

Evelyn held me over for yet another week. She liked having me around, and, in all modesty, I was good for business. Meanwhile, Frank, the enamored john, was coming to see me once in a while in the evening. He was my first regular client. By the time I got through at Evelyn's, without trying, I had saved almost $2,000, which I kept under my mattress. After finishing my third straight week of steady employment, I took out the bills and counted them for the first time. *Damn*. I didn't know what to do with all of it. I had been buying clothes here and there: jeans, lace-up boots, a cashmere sweater that caught my eye on Second Avenue, and one of the first midis to appear that season, a long, subtly flared black skirt that made me look like a wisp. Even so, I was still rich.

I decided it was time to stop depending on Michael. It was time, in other words, to buy an ounce of speed on my own. I left the whole transaction up to him, and he was glad to do it. He approved. He got me a special price—what he paid, which was practically wholesale—seventy-five dollars an ounce of what was barely stepped-on liquid meth. Considering a matchstick end's worth would keep a three-hundred-pound man awake all night, an ounce would go a long way—or should have.

"A lot of girls don't know how to be on their own out here," Michael said.

When he handed me the tinfoil, he told me the stuff was so clean I had better keep it cool. Otherwise, it was liable to melt. And the dealer had etherized it, which made it seem milder than it really was. He warned me not to overdo it.

"You know how you are. Be careful," he said.

"Yeah, well, try not to patronize me, will you?" I said.

I could smell the sweet ether in my nostrils. The speed was so pure, it was an aromatic paste that stuck in the short straw and stuck in my nose. I put a dollop on my tongue; it disappeared. Where did it say in the New Testament "and if they drink any deadly poison, it will not hurt them"?

I careened on foot uptown and down. I found a black-magic bookstore in the East Village and read Aleister Crowley sitting as if frozen there on my bed at Sigrid's. She began to avoid me, I thought. Or maybe I was imagining it. Anyway, I couldn't take her where I was, and she was too bound to those feeble three dimensions for me to want to be where she was. I even stopped going around to the Traveling Medicine Show. It didn't matter, because Michael and I were connected telepathically by that time, I was sure. I began to talk to him out on the street. Then I began to talk to God and His Consort/Mother. They laughed at me a lot and cheered me on.

Later, I started zigzagging up and down the island of Manhattan in taxicabs at all hours, ready to explore other scenes. I can remember, for instance, one early morning some old drunks in the West Village depositing me into one of these taxis and waving after me as if I were leaving their country to go on a long trip. I sailed up Eighth Avenue just before dawn, past the sunburst of marquees and billboards around Forty-Second Street that advertised girls with great, ponderous breasts, girls masturbating, girls leaning over with their backs to the street and spreading the cheeks of their behinds, all in living color, and I felt like Lilith on a rampage after she was kicked out of the Garden of Eden.

Back at the apartment, Sigrid began to eye me suspiciously. Now I knew she was avoiding me. She kept to her side of the plywood partition. When she brought someone home, she no longer bothered to introduce me. I could hear them whispering.

Jesus, it felt great to be thin. After what I thought of as the girlish flesh on my face had fallen away, high cheekbones emerged. Nothing could be more captivating than that spectral look, I thought. I could feel the knobs of my hips, the outline of each rib. I was in control of my body at last. Every curve now obeyed me. I became amazingly limber: I could do backbends all the way to the floor; I could sit in lotus position for hours.

Somewhere in there I asked Sigrid to take me to the Times Square emporium because I wanted to do the live sex show she had told me about. I was suddenly in the mood. She raised an eyebrow when I announced this and shrugged.

"What the hell, you're so wacky these days, Janet. Flaky is what you are. But if it weren't this, I guess it would be something else, so, OK, you're a big girl. But why, Janet?"

"What difference does it make? Something to do. A little adventure," I said.

What I didn't say, because I knew it wouldn't go over too well, was that God and His Mother, my now constant companions, had suggested I might look into it. Acting in Vincent's morality plays would be good for my moral education, they said. It is true these two had a serenely cosmic sense of irony. They were not bound by conventional mores, that's for sure. And, as if usurping the devil's job, they goaded me on. Playfully, gleefully, the two of them teased me, exhorting me to go after experience. "Be wholehearted," they said. Even Michael couldn't have whisked me down and through this netherworld as fast as God and His Mother seemed to want to go.

Sigrid led me up the narrow staircase to Vincent and Candy's emporium, where Vincent sat behind a front desk taking money off an assortment of men, from the look of it, poor men. This was the massage parlor part of the operation. Before we went inside, we could hear one of his employees around the corner hawking tickets to the "mystery plays," the two one-act dramas shown back-to-back. "Live sex, live sex," he kept barking over and over into the street. Behind Vincent, Candy stood in stiletto-heeled boots, all of at least five-foot-ten solid brick of her, dressed in a merry widow with a black leather jacket draped over her shoulders. Her hair was ice blond, not a particularly common shade at that point in time. She was lavishly made up, with thick black eyeliner, another anomaly in 1971. The eyeliner extended, Cleopatra style, into sweeping wings. She had a smirk on her face, a twisted, sardonic grin. It gave me the impression she was performing. I guessed that she was the shill.

When Sigrid had finally called the two of them to tell them she was bringing her roommate along, Vincent's only question was "Is she white?" Now he stood up and grinned at me. He was obviously pleased that I was indeed white, and young, and certainly not too fat. I felt like a winged insect crawling out of its husk, supple, thin: I weighed now under a hundred pounds. It was the first week of autumn, still warm by day, but cooling off at night, and I was wearing a long-sleeved, full-length bodysuit (no bra, of course) and a leftover micromini. Sigrid stuck to her jeans-and-old-shirt outfit. Unlike the rest of us, she didn't believe in dressing for the occasion.

Vincent walked over to me and extended his hand. Here was another charismatic leader, in this case the guiding light, the impresario, of Times Square. His handshake was firm, like a salesman's. He was wearing a T-shirt and black jeans, and his arms were covered with luxurious tattoos, spirals of jewel-colored serpents and dragons. I took the opportunity to examine his nose, which Sigrid had told me he had fixed. It was a trifle on the small side. He smiled again, a smile that you'd expect to see in an eight-by-ten glossy. His front teeth were all perfectly uniform caps, except for one incisor, which was pure gold. He had pomaded his straight, dyed blue-black hair into a DA, one lock hanging over his forehead, fifties style.

"I hear you want to be in my play. That's great. I'm always hoping for someone who might be able to understand the material. Let me introduce you to your fellow cast member. Then I'll explain the plot to both of you and rehearse you a few minutes before the first show. There isn't much time. National Broadcasting's studio is headquartered just down the street, so we get a big lunch shot, all them horny execs. Sigrid, you know what to do," he said, leading me away.

"I'll be fine," Sigrid said as she and Candy stood close together, whispering.

The men who had just paid for their hand jobs seemed content to hang around. Inside the sunny, large room next door, with the massage tables and the screens, there were only black girls and Puerto Ricans working, girls like the men themselves. They preferred to wait, staring at the two blondes.

My costar sat in the last row of the balcony of the huge theater, an abandoned movie palace. He had his feet up and he was smoking a doobie the size of Manhattan. It was the first time I'd seen a Rastafarian joint, or dreadlocks either for that matter. It shook me up. Vincent introduced him as Elijah. He was a Jamaican who was quick to tell me that he managed a reggae band back home. I had never heard of reggae. Vincent told me it was religious rock 'n' roll. Rastafarians believed they were the descendants of Sheba and, therefore, one of the lost Hebrew tribes.

"Which is why Elijah is such a good person to interpret my play. He has a sense of its mystical dimensions," Vincent said.

Elijah nodded. He looked solemn. "I don't go with white women," he said.

"What do you mean, you don't go with white women? Why didn't you tell me that sooner? Anyway, Janet isn't white, she's Jewish—same as you—c'mon, we haven't got time for this," Vincent said, starting to panic.

Elijah stood up. He towered over me. He looked at my body, then he cupped my face in his hand, tilting my chin until we were within kissing distance. There was a glint in his eye. Was it humor? Anyway, he had a lovely build, so lean, broad shouldered. I could overlook a lot, even the snakes coming out of his head. 'I'm really a good sport,' I thought.

"All right," Elijah said, pulling on his sweet cigar, like he was doing us both the biggest favor.

Vincent went limp with relief. "Thanks, Elijah, thanks, brother," he said, patting the man on the back.

Vincent was showing signs of being a truly great director. At least he knew how to placate his actors. He sat us one behind the other in aisle seats. Then he ran down to the small stage bathed in pink lights. A fake Christmas tree with a real apple hanging off it stood drooping to the side in one corner, the only prop. He ran back up again.

Vincent raced through an explanation of his mystery play in two acts. "This is how you make your entrance, from back here. Most of the customers will be in the front, but they always get a little thrill when the actors come down from the balcony, especially since the actors are naked. You won't run, of course. Adam will be leading Eve by the hand.

"See, the first act is the Adam and Eve story. In the beginning, you have to look lost, lost and innocent. It's the Garden of Eden. You wander around the stage, oblivious. Then I yell from up here—I play God—you can eat every fruit but the apple. That's OK with you. Adam lies down to take a nap. Eve just wanders around some more by herself. Joe, he's the ticket taker, comes on stage right and talks to Eve from behind the tree. He's the Serpent, convinces Eve to take a bite. Well, you know the story. Have to rush through this part, because the second act takes more explaining. She turns Adam onto the apple. How she does this is with a sexy dance. You know, seduce him. He goes for it finally. But, Elijah, man, you gotta pretend to be reluctant at first.

"They are suddenly aware of each other, of each other's bodies. They stare, they begin to touch, and so on. Then they make love. You can simulate that part, of course. Finally, after they're finished and are lying in each other's arms, I yell down again, curse them, and drive them out of Eden. Adam cries out in agony, 'Woman, what have you done?' Then you exit, your heads bowed in shame, up the aisle.

"OK, here's act two. It's called 'Salem Witch Trial.' Elijah, you play Cotton Mather, who, in case you don't know who that is, was an uptight prude. Janet is being condemned as a witch. You lead her down to the stage, her hands bound in a big chain. When you get there, you condemn her to burn at the stake. She pleads for her life. She says that if only you would let her dance for you, the dance would prove, by its beauty, that she is no witch. She pleads and begs, writhing in your grip. Finally, you say OK and unravel her chain. She begins this dance. It is really lewd. She seduces Cotton Mather. You make love (simulated, of course). He is undone; all his power is stripped. He becomes putty in her hands. At the end, he is lying exhausted on the stage. Janet, you wrap his hands in chains and then, triumphantly, you put your foot on his head.

"'You fool,' you say, 'I *am* a witch. I was a witch all along. You fool,' and so forth. Then the stage goes dark. The end. Got it?"

"Yes, we've got it," Elijah said.

"Can I run to the loo first?" I asked.

Vincent looked over the seats. A few customers were starting to file in, one at a time, most of them dressed in suits and ties.

"Make it snappy," he said.

As soon as I shut the bathroom door, I whipped out a small mirror, a short straw, and the tinfoil of crystal meth from my bag. Even though the adrenaline was racing, I didn't want to take any chances, run out of energy and suddenly lose heart. I knew if I hesitated now, if I started to think, I would lose more than heart, I would lose the power of momentum that was promising to carry me and my psyche further out than anyone had ever been. I was by now deliberately going crazy, under the aegis of God and His Mother, or so I told myself. Then better to sail drug-ridden through this event, zoom through it mindlessly stoned if possible.

When I got back to our 'dressing room' high up in the dark balcony, Elijah was already naked. I pulled off my clothes, and we both just stood there, shivering slightly in the big, cool auditorium, waiting for our cue. Finally the orchestra section was about full. The lights went dark, just like real theater, I thought. I got a rush of stage fright and looked over at Elijah. He was stroking his beard in an agitated way. Vincent nudged us.

"Go on," he said.

Elijah took me by the hand and led me down the center aisle and up a small flight of stairs at the edge of the stage. His hand was cold and moist, but his grip was gentle and firm. It inspired confidence. The audience was so quiet it was hard to remember they were out there. The two of us wandered around, trying to look lost and innocent. Then Elijah did an inspired thing. He sat at the edge of the stage and let his legs dangle, as if he were splashing his feet in a stream. I hovered near the tree. God yelled down to us, as promised.

"Eve," he said, "stay away from the apple. You, too, Adam."

Adam jumped up and pulled me to him. We both quaked. I couldn't get over what a fine improvisational partner Elijah had turned out to be. Except that he already had a huge hard-on, long and lean like he was. So much for prenubile innocence.

He went and lay down to take his nap. As soon as he did, the Serpent stepped out from behind the curtain at the back of the stage and started calling, "Eve, Eve." Adam was lying there with his penis sticking straight up, and I had to wake him and convince him to eat the apple. He did shake his head appropriately and turn away, but before we knew it, we were clasped in each other's arms. A combination of circumstances precipitated our sudden embrace: our fear; the hot pink lights; the exciting contrast between the dark brown and white of our skins; both of us being stoned literally out of our minds on our respective drugs—and the fact that we were Adam and Eve at the time didn't hurt either. Adam scooped me up in his arms and carried me to the center of the stage. He lay me down slowly on the wooden floor and gingerly spread my legs out. We made love, noiselessly, as if by keeping quiet, we could shut out the forty or fifty pairs of eyes that were fixed on the action. In other words, we no longer cared where we were.

No fool, Vincent in his role as God waited for Adam onstage to come. As soon as he did, God started thundering from the balcony. He banished us from Eden. Elijah lifted me in his arms again and carried me offstage and up the aisle.

An eerie silence hung over the huge theater. The men in the audience weren't even shuffling in their seats, let alone applauding. Vincent seemed unperturbed.

"Fine, fine," our director said when we reached the balcony, "but listen, Elijah, man, you're not supposed to get a hard-on before you eat the apple."

"I don't see why not. Anyway, it couldn't be helped," Elijah said.

"Another thing. If you keep fucking like that, you'll never last through four shows," Vincent said.

"It's all right, mon, it was worth it," Elijah said, smiling at me.

Vincent wrapped my hands in a big chain, and Cotton Mather pulled me down to the stage. As excellent an Adam as Elijah had been, this next role was a real stretch. Elijah as Cotton Mather stood there condemning me to the stake.

"You got to die, woman. You're a witch. No, no, you got to burn," he said in a deep voice.

I found myself dancing tentatively, more the suggestion of a dance than the real thing, my hips swinging back and forth slightly. As halting as my movements were, I could sense the audience responding to them, and Elijah gave me plenty of time to seduce him with my supposedly irresistibly lewd performance. Together, we managed to drag out the second act, building suspense, if there could be any suspense left. Finally, I stood in a pose of witch's triumph with my foot on Cotton Mather's head, and the stage went dark. When the lights in the theater came up, one or two men in the audience started to clap, but most of them filed out in a hurry.

Word of mouth must have spread through the corridors of National Broadcasting, because the orchestra for the next show was just as full as it had been for the last. It was unusual, Vincent said, to draw that big a crowd in midafternoon. Elijah and I dallied in foreplay now that we had overcome the worst of our stage fright. Basking in the pink light of Eden, we began to caress. I finally got up the nerve to touch his dreadlocks, which were as soft as knitting yarn. Later, freed from my chains, and according to the spirit of Vincent's morality play, I took the lead, straddling the defeated prude Cotton Mather and riding high.

While I was wiping the sweat off my body with a Warwick Hotel towel that Candy had given me, Vincent gestured to Elijah, taking him off to the side where he said something to him. They shook hands, and Vincent handed him some money. Elijah came back and started putting on his clothes, bell-bottoms and a tie-dyed T-shirt. He tucked his mad hair into a big woolen cap. Then he sat down and began lacing up his sneakers. I went over to him.

"Why are you leaving? I thought we were doing great," I said.

"Ask Vincent. He's got his regular player back. Besides, you wasted me, darlin', I'm all used up. But it has been grand, just grand, girl," he said in his Island-English accent.

He stood up, pulled me to him, and kissed me on the forehead. Then he was gone.

Vincent came over to me with another man. This one was white and beefy looking. His name was Lester. He had to be the original

Midnight Cowboy, but there was something threatening about him. A gray shadow hung over his snub nose and popping eyes.

"Lester's my buddy from the gym. He's a regular now, been doing this all week," Vincent said.

"I thought Elijah and I were good together. We were packing them in."

"Yeah, sure, honey, but you're a killer. You wore him out. He was spent, finished."

"Oh, I'm sorry. I didn't mean to. I liked Elijah."

"Don't worry about it, Lester's a pro. Anyway, look at those muscles. Ever see muscles like that?" Vincent asked me, poking Lester, who was stripping now. I took Vincent by the hand and pulled him away from Lester, out of earshot.

"No, no thanks. I got to pass. He's too creepy, sorry."

Vincent looked over at the naked, exceedingly white hulk of a man and nodded.

"He does seem a little sinister at that, now that you mention it. But hey, thanks, Janet, man, you are very hot. Maybe you'd be willing to do this again sometime if I can find the right partner," he said.

I was touched and gratified by his words. Thanks to my psychotic state, I was beginning to find myself ostracized almost anywhere I tried to go. When I was particularly high, I wandered and chatted to the invisible, I laughed and sometimes cried out loud in the street, and even when I wasn't behaving like that, I was now giving myself away just by my dilated pupils; my long, electrified straight hair that shot out from my temples; my increasingly odd outfits; and my unnaturally skinny body. But there were always certain people, certain nonjudgmental people who were either as crazy as I was or close to it, or simply very kind, who accepted me as a whole human being. Vincent seemed to be one of these sympathetic allies.

I went to check on Sigrid, to make sure she was still on the premises. I poked my head around a screen in the massage parlor room, and there she was, chatting casually in Spanish with a customer while she stroked him absentmindedly.

"Just wanted to see how you were doing," I said.

"Racking it up," Sigrid said. "How about you?"

"Lost in the footlights," I said.

"Any time you feel like leaving, let me know," she said.

The customer must have been turned on by the sound of us talking. He groaned and started to dribble semen into Sigrid's hand. She grabbed a tissue and wiped him off with the calm and aloof air of a nurse bending over her patient.

I stood around in the front room, trying to summon the courage to go behind one of those screens with a patient. Just wasn't up to it. Anyway, I'd had enough for one day. Candy was behind the desk, ordering the men to sit down and wait their turn as if they were schoolchildren. I went back out on the balcony, where Vincent was talking to Lester, who was putting his clothes back on.

"Don't worry, I got another pair to finish the set for today," Vincent said, as if I might be concerned about letting him down. "No really, it's going to be fine. Yeah, they're a couple of Okies, two young kids, just married and fresh—I mean fresh—off the boat. They're sitting down in front...say they're flat busted, could use the bucks...I don't know."

"Oh, let them try it," Lester said. He seemed perfectly content not to be appearing today.

"OK, but would you two mind waiting around just in case?" Vincent asked. He pulled out a wad of twenties and handed them to me.

"Hey, Vincent, this is a hundred bucks for two shows," I said, counting out the twenties.

"A bonus. You deserve it, kid. You're a star. When you shine, nobody shines brighter, Janet," he said, grinning his prefab grin.

Vincent called out to the couple, Jeff and Lee Ann. They came running up the aisle, hand in hand. He started to explain the plot and they nodded vigorously.

"Yes, sir," they said.

The seats began filling up.

"Take off your clothes," Vincent said.

The couple undressed quickly. They stood there, buck naked except for the shining gold crosses they both wore around their necks. Lee Ann took a minute to fold their clothes neatly in a pile. She stared up at her husband, all trust.

Lester had disappeared by this time, but I stayed to watch. The two of them marched brazenly to the stage. Jeff jumped onto it and then lifted up his bride. It was immediately obvious that they hadn't paid attention to any of Vincent's directions. No point in God sounding his warning, it was already too late. They started to soul kiss, and then Jeff went down on Lee Ann, just like they always did. She yelped and moaned. He pushed her onto the floor.

"Oh, great. What a pair of rubes," Vincent said. He threw his hands up. "Fuck it."

Jeff started humping with a regular, married-style rhythm.

"Oh God, oh God," Lee Ann started screaming, "I'm gonna come, I'm gonna come. Oh God!"

All of a sudden, the place was thick with cops. It reminded me of the time termites in nuptial flight hit my grandparents' home in Palm Beach. One minute, the house was still inside, the next minute it was moving, swarming with twitching insects. Cops were everywhere: cops on the stage, pulling the couple apart like they were two dogs; cops on the balcony surrounding Vincent and me.

"You go by the name of Vincent Damone?" one of the cops said. He slapped cuffs on Vincent's wrists before he could get an answer. He read him his rights.

"Who are you?" another cop asked me, pulling me through the door into the massage parlor waiting room. As he did, I watched the audience full of suits stampede for the exit.

They were holding on to Candy. She was screaming, "That Lester son of a bitch. He set us up, that motherfucking rat bastard!"

Three cops were holding her now. She kept crying out and thrashing her head from side to side like some kind of modern-day Sabine woman. The cops meanwhile fell right into their roles, behaving like perfect Roman-style straight men, gripping her by the arms and the back of the head and standing fast with grim expressions on their faces.

"All right, Candy, cool it," Vincent said as they dragged him through the room.

My cop threw me down into a chair, and I found myself sitting next to a very composed Sigrid.

"You don't understand, officer, if you'd been here earlier, you would have seen for yourself. This play is a work of art. It has redeeming social value," Vincent was saying as they hauled him and a kicking Candy out the door.

"OK, girls, what's your story? Your blond friend here says you was just visiting," my cop said.

The massage parlor workers from the next room had been lined up in a row. A short little cop was pushing the last one along, as if they were all attached. They filed out in an orderly manner, looking bored.

"So, girlie, your friend tells me you two are roommates," my cop said. He was plainclothes, dressed in slacks, a corduroy jacket, and a tie. "You should be ashamed of yourself. Well, what were you doing here?"

"Visiting, officer, visiting our friends Vincent and Candy," Sigrid said.

"I'm not talking to you. I asked your little friend."

"That's right, officer. I've never been here before. I thought it was kind of an adventure, you know?" I said.

"Adventure. That's pitiful. A nice girl like you, like both of you." He was shaking his head.

There were only a few other cops left in the place, along with Sigrid and me. The bust happened so fast. I worried for a moment about Vincent, then thought better of it. He could take care of himself. But Jeff and Lee Ann, the poor kids.

"Here's how it is. I'll let you two go this time. But if I ever catch either one of you in my precinct, I'm going to make it real tough. Get it? Names, please."

While we gave him the information, another plainclothes cop took it down. He kept looking up at us and shaking his head.

Two cops in uniform put Sigrid and me into the back of a squad car. As we headed up Broadway, they seemed to be making a point of ignoring us, perhaps to show what honorable, upright officers they were. This made us giggle. Here we were getting chauffeured home by the law.

When we reached Sigrid's apartment, one of the cops got out of the front seat and actually came around and opened the door for her. She took the policeman's outstretched hand and alighted from the car. I followed. The cop stood in the street, his eyes trained on Sigrid's behind. Maybe it was only in that instant it hit him: this elegant white girl was a whore after all; she could be had.

"See you around, hot stuff," he called to her. "You little slut," he said under his breath.

When Sigrid heard that, she turned around and winked.

Outcast

Maybe as long as a month had passed. Toward the end of it, my extreme speed run had thrust me into kairotic time. Instead of roaming around town talking to God and His Mother, I began to travel deep inside my own mind, where I explored other dimensions and the origin of the universe. Instead of chatting with the two of them, I actually turned into God's Mother, who, I realized, came first. Before there was anything else except me, I was so lonely that I kept falling into unconsciousness, only to come to into nothingness once again. Finally, I woke to find another being there. It was obviously a he, who smiled smugly as if he thought he was alone and glad of it. He seemed to be enjoying his solitude immensely. "I Am," he said. The great "I Am!" I was so thrilled to see him, I never bothered to seriously question whether he might be just a figment of my own tortured imagination. I was so glad of company that I was happy to let him think I was the latecomer.

Aha! The secrets of existence laid bare by a mind fueled on crystal meth! The true story of creation hidden for all time until now: what a discovery! And it just might explain why we women are still so quick to acquiesce. Sure, let them think they started it all. Anything's better than that nothingness and no one.

I had news for the world! I was planting a flag on the furthest reaches of the human psyche. Meanwhile, not only was I losing track of what day of the week it was, I was beginning not to know what millennium. I was out there.

OK, enough. I knew I had to confront the great "I Am," a.k.a. Michael, to bring us once again into the three-dimensional world, our humble stage after all for as long as we lived. It was seemly to communicate with our voices and not just telepathically, as we had been doing.

At midnight I strolled into the Traveling Medicine Show in a spanking-new brown suede fringe jacket, the cashmere sweater, and a pair of jeans that were no longer as tight as they used to be. I felt I looked, well, divine would not be putting it too strongly. How could I not, sylph that I was?

Michael eyed me in a critical way. I didn't expect him to jump up and throw his arms around me, but considering how connected I thought we now were, I had hoped he would beam radiantly at least when I returned. Maybe he was angry that I had stayed away so long. While continuing to stare at me, he actually stood up and slammed his *Voice* down on the table. He was pissed.

The only other time I had ever seen Michael so angry was not that long ago, at the end of August, when one night his mother, frantic to reach him, called the saloon. He had an extension rigged to the wall next to his table, but he never answered the phone himself. He let Jimmy do that, even when the bar was three deep and Jimmy was scrambling up and down behind it. As it happens, the place was busy that night. The jukebox was playing Neil Young's "The Loner." Jimmy moved from behind the bar and cut a path through the regulars. He signaled to Michael, pointing to the phone. Then he came over to the table, where Michael sat reading the latest *Playboy*, and where I just sat.

"I don't know whether you want to take this call," Jimmy said, looking more red-faced than usual.

"Who is it?" Michael asked.

"Your mother. She sounds upset about something," Jimmy said.

In a continuous, sweeping motion, Michael got up, toppling his chair as he did so, walked over to the extension on the wall next to him, picked up the receiver and, with one swift jerk, broke it clean away from the rest of the phone. It was such a pure gesture of righteous indignation, like Jesus taking a bullwhip into the temple. How dare *his mother* call him at one in the morning here, in the sanctuary, where he was speeding so calmly. Those customers sitting close enough stopped talking and stared, covered with awe. Michael handed the receiver, its severed cord dangling, to Jimmy.

"Tell her I'm not at home," he said sweetly.

Now his pale face wore that same stunned expression, as if I had done him a great injury. He looked elegant, his lustrous, nearly black hair spilling onto his cream-colored cowboy shirt. And he looked formidable in his wrath, like someone I wished I had never crossed. But what had I done? Was this meant to be a test?

"Dammit. I knew this was going to happen," he said.

"What do you mean?" It was my turn to appear stunned.

"You're crazy, Janet."

Something really was wrong. Ordinarily, he never called me by my name. It sounded too intimate.

"Well, if I'm crazy, so are you," I said.

"That may be, but at least I'm not disappearing."

"What are you talking about?"

"Go home now. Get something to eat."

"Go home?"

"You can't hang out here, not in your condition."

"What condition is that?"

"All right, let's take a walk."

He pulled me out of the saloon and next door to his building. He pushed me up the stairs. Oh, what a relief. He was only joking, or maybe he didn't want the bar to see how much in love we were. Once inside his hermetically serene apartment, with its angel-white curtains and its lusty red bedspreads, once more in the cool and the dark of it, I felt safe.

"Stay. Don't move until I get back," Michael said in a loud voice, as if he were talking to a dog with hearing trouble.

Overjoyed, I sat very still. Then it was true. He loved me, he loved me. I had a vision of us living in the forest in Shaker simplicity. I was wearing an apron and sweeping the wide planks of a hardwood floor with a handmade broom, a bunch of straw tied with a string and attached to a stick. He was outside the house, turning the earth with a spade on the slope of a hill. The entire scene, inside and out, glowed with a singular harmony. We were two halves of a whole.

Then I switched to a heightened version of my current reality: I imagined us sitting at his reserved table night after night, presiding over what remained of the regulars at the Traveling Medicine Show. Not a particularly exalted dream.

Michael returned carrying a paper bag. He put it down in the kitchen and poured me a glass of pure rum with a dash of Coke.

"Here, drink this."

I sipped it. The hot liquor just booted the speed along in my veins. I almost swooned.

He returned to the kitchen and came back with two take-out plates full of food, which he set on the big wood coffee table. One plate had a liverwurst sandwich on it, the other, congealing fried eggs with home fries. He threw down the side of toast wrapped in white paper.

"Eat something," he said.

"I can't."

"OK, how about a piece of toast?" He held up a piece of white toast dripping with butter.

"OK." I forced it down.

"Now, how about an egg?"

"No thanks."

"You better eat something or you're going to die."

"Aren't you being a little bit melodramatic?"

"I don't think so."

I bit off a piece of egg and chewed and chewed. It didn't seem like it would ever go down.

"Maybe liverwurst is easier to take," he said.

Liverwurst.

"Have you got any downs?" he asked.

"No. I hate downs."

"Never mind. We've got to get you down. I'll go find some at the store. Don't follow me. I'll be back. Here, listen to the radio while I'm gone. Try to rest."

The radio was playing "Till the Morning Comes" by the Grateful Dead. The refrain was "Make yourself easy, you're my woman now." What clearer message could have been sent? I did make myself easy. In passing, I wondered why Michael had seemed so alarmed. It was the look of love I supposed that must have thrown him. I was pure in countenance. I was grace incarnate. It was most likely hard to take.

A lot of time passed. Michael returned with two big red Seconals. He handed my glass of rum to me along with the pills.

"Swallow these. Don't fight 'em. Go to sleep when they hit."

He disappeared again. I waited, but the pills did not make me sleepy, they only made me hallucinate more. Michael and me rolling in grassy fields behind the stadium. Michael was a girl and I was a boy. He was a brown-eyed, long-limbed girl with soft lips, and I was a sloe-eyed, downy-faced boy. I was taking her up in my arms...It was the beginning of a Van Morrison medley on the radio. I realized I had been watching his lyrics come alive in front of me: "behind the stadium with you..."

Before long, the shadowy, romantic movies degenerated into a series of garish, jeering cartoons. I decided to focus my attention on the physical world instead. As my eyes adjusted to the darkness, objects began to leap out at me from nowhere. A small carving of a bird I never remembered seeing before suddenly appeared where I could have sworn there was nothing a second ago. Things—like the ashtray, an idle vibrator, a pile of books lying flat on the shelf behind the bed—began to unfold before me in a stately procession, as if they had been brought into being by the power of observation. Speed can have this effect, can make inanimate objects seem to happen into existence like events in time. It was getting too busy; I decided I wanted to go. Nevertheless, I debated with myself for a while first, knowing I was taking a risk. Something told me that once on the other side, I might not get back in again so fast, but I was too loose now from the combination of speed, booze, and downs to stay put. When I let myself out, the door automatically locked behind me. Immediately, I regretted my decision. All of a sudden, the night turned ugly. I felt displaced and estranged, as if I belonged nowhere at all on this earth.

"That does it. Get out of here" was all Michael said when I appeared again at the Traveling Medicine Show.

I didn't budge. He came over abruptly to where I stood and for a second I thought he was going to hit me, but he merely took hold of me and shoved me out into the street. I would have been mortified if I weren't so overcome with grief. The pain was precisely the same kind of hurt as ordinary heartbreak, only magnified and intensified by the drugs and the madness to a gargantuan, God-mocking degree. The torment was primordially great; it literally took my breath away. I gasped and reeled with it. I staggered over to a lamppost and put my forehead up against the cool metal. I could not take it in. 'He must be testing me,' I thought. For one instant, I entertained the possibility that I was crazy, but quickly dismissed it. No, the love was real. I must hang on to that. And God was real. I wrapped myself in a zealot's faith, in the faith of one who has apprehended God; like the true believers patrolling Times Square, I began to rant. I couldn't believe Michael's cruelty. One image remained fixed in my mind: how my true love had stared at me, the whites of his eyes showing, when he pushed me roughly out the door. He was in a silent frenzy.

"Your chosen one is weak," I said to God and His Mother, referring to Michael and his inability to love me.

"Don't worry. Be patient," they said.

"How long do I have to wait?" I was pleading with them.

They never answered me with specifics. I went into a fury of frustration.

"How damned long? A week, a month, years?"

The opaque sky blinked.

"What, years? No, I couldn't stand that. Tell me a year. I could bear a year."

The night blinked again.

"At the most?"

The black sky revealed nothing. God and His Mother were gone.

The bullet hole in the middle of the glass oval in the front door of Sigrid's apartment house began to swing and toll like a bell, until I realized it was the methodical beep of the garbage truck pulling up to the curb. Once inside, I don't know how long I sat on the bed without moving on my side of the partition behind the closed venetian blinds. But I remember it seemed like too much of an effort to acknowledge Sigrid when she arrived home the following afternoon.

She came over, sat down next to me. Her large, generous blue eyes stared into mine. "You're very ill, Janet."

"It's even worse than that," I said. I was referring to the pain in my heart.

"Yes, I know. Listen, I'm going to call your mother."

I started. "Oh no, please don't."

"But I have to, Janet. I don't know what else to do."

"Haven't I paid the rent? On time? Well then, you've got no right..."

"It has nothing to do with that. Please try and understand. You're *gravely* ill, Janet, please understand. I have to do something. I can't just stand by and watch you destroy yourself this way."

"Why not? What business is it of yours? I have every right to destroy myself, if that's what you think I'm doing. What's so great about life anyway? Chummy, cozy animal life. Either you're eating or shitting or sleeping. And I've got news for you, you're always dying. What's so goddamn virtuous about longevity? Is it some kind of moral objection you have?"

"No, it's got nothing to do with morality—"

"Then let me go, friend."

Sigrid shrugged her shoulders and made as though she were going to pick up the phone.

"All right, all right, never mind. I'll go, I mean I'll go home to Maggie's. I promise, OK? Just don't call her. I don't want her coming by here and making a scene. I'll pack up right now, OK?"

Sigrid came over and grabbed me by the shoulders. "You do promise? To go right home, I mean? You will call me then to let me know you're OK?"

I shook her off. "Listen, pal, don't act so concerned when we both know you couldn't give less of a shit. You're adding insult to injury now. All you want is to get me out of your hair and I don't blame you. Just cut the caring act, OK? It gives me the creeps."

"Janet, since when did you become so cynical? Don't you believe that anyone could care about you?"

"Hey, stop laying that hippie love shit on me, will you please? Sure, lots of people could care about me. The streets are full of 'em. Now get out of my way while I pack."

In spite of my recent spree, I still didn't own much of a wardrobe. I threw what clothes I had in my suitcase along with the few books I had acquired, my sacred speed-inspired labyrinthine drawings, and my precious, cryptic poetry and dragged the thing out onto the street, slamming the door behind me. The fifty- and hundred-dollar bills from underneath the mattress and what was left of the speed in its tinfoil I had shoved recklessly into my jeans pocket. I was caught in a drizzle on a bleak October day that prophesied winter. For the first time in a long time, I felt tired, bone-tired. I was afraid I might collapse. Sigrid watched me from between the slats of the venetian blind while I stood very still in the rain until a cab finally turned down the street. She did not stop watching me until I climbed inside it.

"Seventy-Sixth and Second, please, the northwest corner."

I didn't go there willingly; I knew it was hopeless. But it was as if some vicious dybbuk had moved into my soul and was now dictating every humiliating move. I guessed this phase was part of my trial, something I must endure for a greater good.

"Where do you want me to put this bag, miss?" the handsome, young Vietnam vet driver, still wearing camouflage army fatigues, politely asked me as he hauled my suitcase out of the trunk.

"Just leave it on the curb, thank you."

I tried to act as if I had a will of my own, as if this were not on orders from some hostile spirit that had invaded my being, but I could not march through the door confidently, head high. I could take only a few feeble steps until I was just across the threshold.

"There, that's as far as I go," I said to my dybbuk.

At four o'clock in the afternoon, the place was nearly empty except for one or two customers at the bar, the bartender, and Michael, who sat with his feet up on a second chair, his face hidden behind the *Village Voice*. His hair still damp from his wake-up shower, he was sipping the first rum and Coke of the day, slowly stirring the liquid and the ice together with one long, patrician finger while he held the folded paper against his face with his other hand. He pretended not to see me.

The imperious soul-invader forced me to approach the table where he sat.

"I love you, Michael."

He lowered the paper and looked at me, and for one instant I thought I saw compassion pouring from the inflated black pupils that were his eyes. Then he snapped the paper open again.

"That's not my problem," he said.

I turned and left, my sole intention having been to plant those words on him like a curse before I surrendered to Maggie.

She looked stricken when she saw me shivering wet, and she ushered me through the door as if there were not a minute to spare. Perhaps there wasn't. Through persistence, Maggie managed to find a doctor willing to come to the house. My old pediatrician, semiretired now, finally agreed to do it. He shook his head when he saw me as if I were one of his uncooperative patients at risk of being denied a lollipop. In spite of his parietal manner, he was a wise old doctor; the first thing he did was to make me get on the balance scale in my mother's bathroom. I weighed ninety pounds. "Big deal," I thought, "gymnasts weigh less than that." But the doctor shook his head again, more vigorously this time. Then, although he had no experience with amphetamine psychosis, he knew enough to take my temperature, which was 105. He gave me a shot of penicillin and a big dose of chloral hydrate, and made me get under the covers in my pink-and-cherry-red bedroom.

'Not this place again,' I thought.

I heard the doctor and my mother conferring in the hallway, and I knew it was just a matter of time before she put me away. I could see that one coming, even in my state, even as heavenly zephyrs swooped around my body and a host of much gentler spirits softly sang lullabies. God and His Mother were allowing me to rest.

But sleep, which I wasn't much courting anyhow, still eluded me. I waited until I could hear Maggie snoring, and then I threw on some clothes and snuck out. I had to pass Oscar, the wall-eyed, arthritic doorman who worked the shift from two until ten A.M., and I was afraid that like a prison guard, he might try to hold me back, but he just said, "Isn't it a bit late, Miss Janet? Let me hail you a cab."

When I reached the Traveling Medicine Show, I went and hid under an awning across Seventy-Sixth Street. Whatever I had expected to see, somehow the last thing was Michael emerging before closing time with the Comanche hanging on to his arm. Everyone called her the Comanche because in the sixties she always wore a headband around her long, dark hair.

No, not the Comanche.

She was a cunning woman about my age, with a gorgeous little body and great brown pools for eyes, who always managed to be there when Michael was trying to shake someone loose.

I ran up to them and pulled her away from Michael's arm. I thought it was a coy move anyhow; it never would have occurred to me to take his arm in such a familiar way, and this in spite of the fact he belonged to me now.

"Jesus, Janet, you scared me, coming out of nowhere like that. What do you want?" the Comanche said.

"Get away from him," I said, inwardly wincing at my own histrionics.

"What's the matter with you, honey?" the Comanche said. She sounded genuinely bewildered.

"I said get away."

"All right, that's enough. Better leave us alone now," Michael said.

"Wow, Janet, you flipped or something? I think you flipped," the Comanche said, and the two of them hurried into his building.

I followed them up the stairs. They shut the door in my face. I reluctantly started to bang against it, not wanting to, but once again in the thrall of that evil force. I banged and banged my fists against the door. Madness procures strength from its own untapped resources, hidden valleys of energy in the brain. I called on those resources now, throwing the weight of my entire body against the door, slapping up against it hard in a relentless rhythm. There was no response. Eventually I sank to the floor and started to wail, scratching at the painted metal with my fingernails. Throughout all of this, I felt as though I were only going through the motions, as though I were a slave to an inferior script, coerced by the bluntest and the crudest of devils into imitating another bad actress in another foolish scene I had witnessed a long time ago.

Finally Michael opened the door. Defensively crossing his arms and hugging himself, he stood against it and looked down at me crumpled up on the ground. I could see the unlikely combination of honest shame and twisted pride dance in his glittering eyes.

"You better get out of here 'cause I just called the cops."

He slammed the door in my face.

'No, he wouldn't,' I thought, but then I heard their sirens in the street. As I came out, I saw the flashing lights from the tops of two cars that had pulled up in front of Michael's building. One was parked on the deserted avenue at a right angle to the sidewalk, movieland style. I tried to look dignified, but the cop riding shotgun nailed me. He pulled his big lumbering body out of the car and yelled for me to stop.

"You causing a disturbance around here?" he asked.

"I'm sorry, officer, I was overcome by heartbreak. My boyfriend's up there with another woman."

He chuckled. "I don't think he wants to have anything to do with you. Better let it go," he said.

"No guy's worth that," his partner said. "Why don't you just go home now."

At least when I got to Maggie's, she was still safely snoring. I don't know if I could have withstood any more confrontations just then. As soon as I lay down in my pink-and-cherry-red bedroom, I fell into a peaceful coma-like sleep.

Highcrest

Around the turn of the century, Highcrest was built as an homage to the great English estate, with its wild gardens, faux woods, gazebos, and vast, rolling lawn. In the sixties, a few enterprising psychiatrists, sensing a buck in the drug-plagued generation, had transformed Highcrest into a profit-making institution, designed almost exclusively for the recalcitrant sons and daughters of the well-to-do. It was not what is now known as a "rehab," where the staff educates the patients about addiction. There were no meetings, not even group therapy. Instead, Highcrest was a last bastion of the traditional brand of psychiatry that subscribed to the theory if the patient's problems were confronted and dealt with, the excessive behavior would simply disappear. In other words, analysis alone could cure anything, except psychosis. They held out small hope for me.

But then, few of my fellow inmates were as messed up as I was when I arrived, as evidenced by the fact that I was confined to the "seclusion room" on the attic floor along with a Jamaican nurse's aide. Lucy, my own private warden, hugged the same bright green acrylic cardigan around her sagging, white nylon bosom every day and read strange tabloids with photographs on their covers like the one of the two-headed baby or the man who hiccupped to death. I don't know where she found these weeklies; I had never seen them in those days on any newsstands in Manhattan.

The doctors had decided at my intake that I was "too euphoric." They prescribed elephantine doses of Thorazine and Stelazine to bring me down, but in the meantime, I wasn't allowed to mix with the other patients. From my attic window, I watched those patients, my contemporaries, as they were ushered out onto the great lawn for their morning recess. They tramped slowly back and forth in groups of twos and threes, bundled up in their Saks Fifth Avenue duffle coats. Keeping their heads down, they shuffled the leaves along underfoot and flapped their arms in the cold, the first frost making their breath smoke. I didn't particularly envy them their relative freedom. Except it was hard to get comfortable where I was being held, under fluorescent lights in a low-ceilinged room that had been furnished like a kindergarten lunchroom, with long tables built close to the ground and miniature plastic chairs. There were no toddlers at Highcrest. My guess was the doctors got a deal at the local nursery-school tag sale.

In the beginning of my stay in the attic, I saw handwriting form in the scratched red linoleum. It began by printing GET WELL in jaunty, raised block letters, which was all fine and good, but then it turned into looping script and became prolific, as tomes full of hysterical directives and exhortations began to appear. I had to ask the incorporeal author, or authors, to please stop; it was not appropriate in a nuthouse. Before the Thorazine and the Stelazine could shoot me down entirely, I had one final vision—the most panoramic of them all.

The vision had been triggered by something I read in Plato on one of my sojourns into a secondhand bookshop downtown. From what I understood, the philosopher contended that we started out whole but were torn into halves, and then spent the rest of eternity looking for each other. No wonder it was so excruciating for me, I thought. I was the torn and ragged half, the open wound that knew itself. By contrast, Michael was in denial; nevertheless it was true, he was my other half. Inside the hospital I discovered just how right I was when one night, in the dark safety of my private bedroom, I witnessed Michael and me cast in a variety of roles across the arc of centuries. I was watching a succession of tiny movies inside my head, except the images were more vivid than celluloid; they were three-dimensional and shimmered like holographs. Pictures came to the surface lit up with the detail and texture of living memory.

Over two thousand years ago, our home was in the desert. Michael was an Old Testament patriarch, loyal to the tribe but most of all to his father. He studied holy books six days a week and often late into the night, and he neglected me, his obedient, illiterate wife. Why was his first duty to God instead of to me, who loved him so? Such a Goody Two-shoes Michael had been in this incarnation, such a self-righteous, inflexible man. He ignored me, and it hurt.

Then I saw myself as a young woman, oiled with patchouli and draped in silk, living in purdah. My lord visited me. I worshipped him, but he treated me with silences. He made love to me from a great emotional distance; I was so far beneath him, it was as if he were depositing his seed into the earth.

In a more recent incarnation, eighteenth-century Europe, we saw each other only once, one night at a ball. I was dressed in a ravishing white gown. Our eyes met across the grand salon; we danced; he disappeared. The pain of trying to love—of being heterosexual in a world that, until lately, had been determined by such inequity—was beginning to wear on us, I could see that. It was getting hard to do more than meet for an hour or two during the course of a lifetime. But at last, on the eve of 1972, the conditions were right (well, close enough).

Afraid that the Thorazine would make me forget, I repeated my vow through the night like a catechism: I would win Michael back. I would make him understand. Nothing they planned to do to me, no amount of tricky brainwashing, could make me be false to my obsession.

And that is what Highcrest taught me, the secret of the recidivist, the glory of duplicity. I walked stiffly through my days like a hardened criminal, avoiding any body language that would betray me with the inverted integrity of one who will not be coerced. I discovered a gritty, spiny bedrock of resistance deep inside that I could touch at will, and yet, during all the hours spent under scrutiny, I was the model patient cooperating fully with authority. I secretly harbored what I thought of as my true self, keeping sight of that self even in my dreams at night. I never surrendered, even as I was assaulted with the routine crucifixion of mind-crushing drugs and the desolate monotony of imprisonment. Despite how it looked on the outside, I never flagged in my resolve to get back to the street.

This was not the case for many of the other inmates. A lot of those kids quickly saw the errors of their ways, and it wasn't just an act they put on for the doctors either, because during those few furtive moments when we were left to ourselves they had no reason to pretend. Same as taking candy from a baby, I thought, as I watched them fold up like so many dashed kites in the wind. They were only fooling when they were out there, these day-tripping hippies, just along for the ride. Once trapped, they navigated through the corridors of the locked hospital together like a cartload of Flying Dutchmen; their former lives robbed of meaning, they searched bewildered—I could see it in their frightened eyes—for a new world safe from punishment. The whole debased mansion seethed with jailhouse tension.

Exactly what was happening there came home to me on the morning when the entire male staff, a brawny crew disguised as nurses in their benign-looking white suits, dragged two frisky teenage boys who had run away at recess back onto the great lawn. First they trussed up the boys in straitjackets. Then they stuck needles in them and threw each one into isolation. And what had been those fugitives' original crimes that landed them in Highcrest? I understood the youngest one, a sophomore in high school, had been caught smoking hash in the family rec room, and the other slightly older boy had taken a bad acid trip.

I watched the male patients undergo the solemn ritual of haircuts once a month on barbershop day; I watched the females become passive and demure. It wasn't going to happen to me. I would not fall for my captors. The way I saw it, Highcrest got results by instilling fear, same as any correctional institution, except the hospital, operating for profit, offered less in the way of rehabilitation if possible.

One method I had for keeping aloof was to expose my cute, short, chubby shrink for the supremacist he was. As a young hired hand, he lacked the sophistication of the higher-ups. He was easy. So I asked him what he thought of a world in which women were expected to take care of the kids and men go out and do everything else.

"Did it ever occur to you that men 'go out and do everything else' because they can't stay at home and have children?" he asked me in a Korean accent so thick his words were nearly indecipherable. But I got the gist. His eyes, full of his good nature, were twinkling with the romance of what he just said. This sexist was not going to be my undoing, that much I readily promised myself. As part of my cover, however, I would faithfully report my dreams to him, like an obedient analysand. I excelled at that—he was only the latest in a long line of shrinks, after all.

Then there were my father Rayfield's frequent visits. Maggie had tried with no success to get him to take responsibility, play the heavy. But precisely because, unlike most people over thirty, he was so laid-back, I could trust him, and I looked forward to seeing him. Before I went completely loco, I had occasionally gone up to see Rayfield, who was now long sober and living quietly with his fourth wife, Betsy, in Cobb's Wharf, a commuter town on the Hudson. He and I would take drives in his Porsche, during which it became clear he was complicit, comparing my insanity to his own fond memories of the late 1920s, when he was a young byline reporter calling in his stories from a speakeasy.

Add to this our ancestors, a long line of rebels. The first American in our family had run off from English boarding school with two classmates and stowed away in the hull of a ship—one of the few Pilgrims to sail into the harbor at Plymouth Rock who was decidedly not a Puritan.

My mother was enamored of this New England background. Her German Jewish antecedents had come over before the Civil War, and by the middle of the twentieth century, her family's identification with WASPs was nearly complete. The marriage, while lit up by passing mutual attraction, mostly represented the hallowed tradition of a money-for-pedigree trade. (Except that much later, after my grandmother died, Maggie would learn there would be no inheritance after all. Maggie and I were "nouveau poor"—the other side of the American rags-to- riches story.)

While I was incarcerated at Highcrest, Rayfield and I began to get to know each other better. His stable was near the hospital, so, smelling of leather polish and horse, he made a point of stopping by after his ride. (He was the night news editor on a New York daily, which allowed him to avoid most people most of the time and ride his horse in the afternoon.) Rayfield had done considerable time in sanatoriums himself and obviously felt right at home. We became coconspirators scheming for my release.

"Don't worry, all you have to do is learn how to play along and you'll get out of here soon," he said, patting my hand. One day he said, "You know, some of this is my fault. I'm sorry I neglected you, but I felt so damned guilty, I was paralyzed. Do you think you could ever forgive the old man?"

I didn't respond right then, but no doubt about it, he knew how to sweet-talk me. Anyway, even if it wasn't much of an excuse, at least it sounded true.

Naive offender that I was, I continued to be openly defiant, but Rayfield was persistent. He kept telling me I had to act "as if." "That's all they're looking for. Listen to me and you'll get out of here a lot sooner."

My shrink decided to take the same candid approach. He smiled one of his twinkly smiles and waved a batch of keys in front of my face. "If you want to be free, you better behave." Unless I *appeared* to be making progress, I would never even get out of seclusion, let alone win any privileges, such as the much-coveted two hours of prime-time TV after dinner. I laughed out loud. Of course, how simple. Act the part and you're as sane as anybody. Once I figured that out, I applied myself. I made friends with some of the other inmates and took up canasta.

The biggest threat to my criminal resolve proved to be the narcoleptics, the Thorazine and Stelazine. Some bunch of pharmaceutical wizards finally managed to encapsulate hell. When administered in large enough doses, these drugs do nothing to soothe the soul; they merely break the circuits of the mind. My imagination shut down and it became impossible to sustain a thought. Each minute was suspended by itself like a sixty-second island without a bridge. The natural flux of emotion was lost to me, and my libido sank into an abyss. I felt marooned inside a now larger body I could barely stand to lug around. There was no escape from the passing of time. Like everyone else, I watched the clock sixteen hours a day.

"Why won't you let your mother come to see you?" my shrink asked.

"Because the bitch put me in here."

"She did it to save you, you know that."

"All she had to do was park me on a beach somewhere. I just needed sun and rest. And it would have been a lot cheaper. No, she didn't do it to save me. She did it to punish me. So fuck her."

My will survived. *Never, never again.* Huddled freezing against the wall on the great lawn so I could smoke, standing in line for my cups of medication, in bed after lights out, or even while I was shoving homemade brownies into my mouth (in a desperate attempt to simulate pleasure), I continued to silently curse everybody.

After months of this, and finally in the spirit of playing along, I consented to a visit from Maggie. She arrived dressed as a demure, beyond-reproach mother in a modest wool shirtwaist. I refused a hug, so she sat primly on the sofa and sniffed. "Don't stare at me like that, Janet. I had no choice. The beach was out of the question. You were much too ill. You would've died, Janet. I hope you stop blaming me, because nobody's going to let you out of here until you do. But they tell me you're getting much better. Thank God. This has been the worst ordeal of my life. You have no idea what you put me through. And then you won't speak to me? As if any of this was my fault. Please get well, Janet. Then you can come home."

Home? Oh boy, back to Maggie's again, that famous bastion of sanity. But it was the only way out. Anyway, it was rigged from the start. Maggie was the one holding the keys. Sure enough, after about ten months of incarceration (which some, but not me, might call a short bit), they let me go on condition I stay with her for a while. I damn well wasn't so-called cured, but I'd learned my lesson. From now on, I would snort speed more intelligently. Crystal meth was like the ocean: you can swim in it; just don't turn your back on it for long. I understood that much. Each night before I went to sleep both at Highcrest and then right after my release in my pink-and-cherry-red bedroom, I clenched my bloated fists and swore in the unseen face of the now distant God Almighty they would never take me again.

PART II

Highrise

The picture window spanned the better part of the east wall. On the other side of the window, the electric outline of the Fifty-ninth Street Bridge hovered at eye level like a giant Peeping Tom. In my new silk slip, slimmer than I had been in a while, I stood with my arms spread, the upper half of my body pressed against the cool, tinted glass. I imagined I was an ebony-hard thing, invincible, leaning into the brink at the prow of a ship. The sounds of the street could not reach me, only the hum of the air-conditioning that whispered through its vent and fanned out unobstructed through the bare L-shaped studio.

The week before, I had put down two months' rent and one month's security, and as soon as the check cleared I moved in. Once again my mentor, Corinne, had come to the rescue. She knew of a few vacancies in another Sutton Place building a little farther south. Even though it had all the trappings of an exclusive apartment house, the Coventry was actually full of transients far less reputable than met the eye. Although I managed to get a reference from our pompous family lawyer, it turned out to be unnecessary. The Coventry was an emporium of whores and other fringe types, all of whom had palmed the rental agent and the doorman and then slipped in as happily as eels sliding off rocks.

Through the dense bourgeois patina of the Upper East Side there has always run a stunning brass thread, an underweave of polished chicanery—like Berlin between the wars—that the ponderous, academic Upper West Side, for instance, could never hope to match. A few blocks away, ritzy hookers, drug pushers, smugglers, and mafiosi milled unselfconsciously through Bloomingdale's on weekday afternoons, past worldly, insular Upper East Side matrons who had mastered the rarest of urban skills: deliberate oblivion.

This was the milieu I now prepared myself to enter. Here a woman was free to be greedy and wicked. Here the hierarchy collapsed, inverted even. On the East Side madams hoarded sin in their exclusive fiefdoms. They tucked away their blue money with childlike glee, hiding their jewels in safes, their lives behind compliant doormen. As long as the whores were discreet, their remarkably disinterested neighbors looked the other way. The whores' materialism grounded me; their sensuality reassured me. High above the street now, I was beyond reproach, beyond the grasp of those doctors waiting to sweep loose women onto locked wards. As long as I had money, they couldn't touch me. As long as I paid the rent, I was as good as sane.

While I was stewing in Highcrest, I had evolved a working definition of sanity: street-smart. That's what I aspired to: the habits, the values, the what I thought of as common sense of madams and call girls. They understood the importance of sumptuous textures, sexual novelty, the imperious pleasure of beholding Manhattan at night from a penthouse window—that must be the secret to surviving out on the street, I decided while at Highcrest: live in the senses.

And I made it. Here I was sailing high into the purple dusk. Below me, tugs and yachts bobbing in the channel teased the majestic skyline like jestering dwarves. I was nursing a Dewar's, swilling the liquid around my mouth to savor the aroma, the bittersweet taste, its acrid tang incense to the palate, promising deliverance. My blood was humming with a lowly diet pill, a Dexamyl. I was playing it safe. The pill provided the energy I needed while sparing the visions the white powder induced. If you had told me then that I was living for booze and drugs, I would have laughed. It would be like telling me I was living for the sound of music. So what?

But I had never ceased to be political in my own skewed way. I did need to believe I was living for something. My life had to stand for something. Well, hooking stood for something. The profession had always been a form of de facto underground resistance to male control. Otherwise, once you let them prohibit experience, once you let them proscribe certain kinds of pleasure, then you might as well give up hope for self-realization. Once they control your desire, they hold your head in a vise. You don't dare look too far off in any direction. And, because the breadth of experience is forbidden, you will have to rely on their word—on received knowledge.

Men had divided us, I realized. Like house niggers and field niggers, good women and bad women were kept apart. We were the victims of myth, of half-truths. No dialogue, no hope for understanding. I would build an arch across this ancient fissure. I would free myself from all the hobbling generalizations, past and present, which thrive on ignorance. We are not the rapacious bottomless pits of lust, the unreasoning animal half of humankind that the Middle Ages and parts of the Third World paint us to be. Nor are we the frail eunuchs of the late nineteenth century, and most certainly not the clitorally fixated pets of my time, the *Penthouse* era, waiting to be diddled to climax in a quaint echo of male virility. On any given day, I could feel like any one of these monstrous stereotypes or a combination of them—but no, none of what I heard about my sex was true, and I longed to discover what really was the difference. I had to explore; I craved experience. I thought that maybe if I just got around enough, took a broad enough consensus, I would understand the truth about men and women.

For a long time after Highcrest finally released me into her custody, my mother stuck close. She hovered solicitously, making no demands. She would gingerly broach the subject of meals, what to watch on TV, forcing her gaiety, only seeming to gladly embrace the shopping and cooking rituals of Weight Watchers if it would please me, anxious above all to please me. When I tried to talk about leaving, she would pat my shoulder and say there was time to think about all that. I later discovered the doctors had told her after I arrived at Highcrest that I was nuts: schizophrenic, or maybe it was manic-depressive, or both. It must be hell to love a cracked thing, a thing so fragile you're afraid to touch it. Maggie humored me, waiting for signs of either recovery or another outbreak, she knew not which.

Meanwhile, I concentrated on dropping, week after abstemious week, the sluggish narcoleptic fat that felt like a pod sealing my limbs, robbing me of grace. And I plotted my next break. Eventually in March, after about six months of lying low and losing weight, I recovered enough confidence to call my two contacts, Evelyn and Corinne, who were more than willing to take my situation in hand.

The madam Evelyn sent me to was the eminent Annabelle, originally from New Orleans. Still living at home with Maggie at first, I slyly worked the afternoon shift. Annabelle owned a penthouse on lower Fifth Avenue overlooking Washington Square. She was a crone, with torrents of gray hair that she sometimes piled up and sometimes let fall any which way. But her girls had to be neat, pristine even. Annabelle would make us sit, shivering from the air-conditioning in her vast, sunken living room with our legs crossed. She made us wear skirts that at least covered our knees; nothing shorter would be tolerated. No false eyelashes, and not too much mascara either. When she wasn't lecturing her charges, you could find the old lady pruning and watering on her wraparound terrace. The regular customers knew they would find her there. Annabelle had a green thumb. Trees and tall bushes grew in wild profusion outside the picture windows. At night it looked like a giant web, branches tangled and knocking against each other in the March wind.

And while she insisted on decorum from her girls, Annabelle herself was exempt. Nobody could accuse the old dame of being a priss. She loved to curse; she particularly loved the word 'fuck,' and she cackled a lot, especially when referring to the old days and what a great whore she had been. We were nothing; we were drips, but Annabelle had wowed 'em back then in the early twenties. She was proud of her adventures, the many times she had been squired to elite nightclubs and fancy-dress balls, the night she had flown up north on a private plane—and this was before Lindbergh crossed the ocean, she reminded us—with one of her more glamorous playboy customers. She called them all suitors, and they were as far as she was concerned.

"They loved to show me off in public," she said, cackling. "Oh, I was beautiful then, beautiful. I wore gowns covered in beads..."

She wiggled her fingertips lightly back and forth across her sagging breasts, after which she let them travel like the spinning legs of a centipede down her midriff and over her bulging stomach. Then she paused to look at the parquet floor beyond the shag carpet, as if she were peering into a distant mirror, where she caught sight of herself fifty years ago.

"Somebody gave me one of them cloches, the ones that hugged your head"—she patted her crown—"encrusted with real jewels...and I can't remember, I truly cannot remember, who that was..." Annabelle snapped back to the present. "I used to knock 'em on their ass..."

This last remark was accompanied by her doing the shimmy inside the big tent of a muumuu she always wore, at the same time running her gnarled fingers through the jumble of gray hair piled up with Spanish combs.

Sometimes, she would sit in the middle of one of her large sofas and draw all four of us girls around her as if she were about to let us in on a secret. Then she would start. "Listen to me, children, I knew how to fuck; I could do the lobster claw." She made her fist open and close rapidly to illustrate. "I could suck the come out of 'em with my tight little pussy whenever I felt like it. I called the shots. Yes indeedy, I was the best. They never left me..."

This much was true, because many of these same johns, a seemingly endless array of distinguished silver-haired gents in dark pin-striped suits, were still in evidence. Only now as often as not, they brought their teenage sons and grandsons to be initiated.

I was struck by the deference they showed to the vulgar old woman. It was not exaggerated either, as I would have expected; no, this was genuine respect. And as far as I could tell, the madam did nothing to elicit it. She never modified her behavior one bit, never bothered to rein in her foul language. Annabelle had marked out a wide-open territory, quite literally a no-man's-land, come to think of it, in which she was free to behave any way she liked. More than polite, these scions of business acted like cowed schoolboys around Annabelle. As I had from the first, I pondered this relationship between whores and men. I was taught that only respectable ladies had the right to command any show of respect, and such ladies were invariably those women who were the least excitable, the most quiet, the most repressed, is what I thought. To see these johns, these otherwise substantial citizens, sitting quietly at attention before the thoroughly louche Annabelle was a remarkable discovery.

They were the kind of Old World johns who believe that a man's first experience should be with a whore, representing the last wave of a grand tradition that may have since become obsolete. Where today would one even begin to look for a teenage virgin? The ritual had become a sham. As often as not, when I thought I was supposed to be the boy's first, he quickly made it clear he could teach me a thing or two and had tagged along just to get laid, out of curiosity, or because he didn't want to disillusion poor old Dad.

Meanwhile, I was afraid of Annabelle's tongue, which could slice a girl's vanity to shreds. If the old whore was in the mood, she could get reckless. "Oh, child, you do got a flat ass. Shame. Can't go far with that." Pat, pat on the girl's behind. "Why don't you stick that out some?" or "Brighten up, sourpuss. With a face like yours, you better learn to compensate. Personality, personality..." She stuck her face into the face in question, which belonged to a little streetwise tough from Sunnyside.

"Listen, Granny, you ain't exackly makin' 'em drop their drawers on sight these days yourself," the girl said.

They both laughed, a cackle and a derisive giggle. Then I realized that Annabelle's derision was meant to be all in good fun. I kept waiting for her to get to me, but during the months that I worked for her off and on, she never did. Probably I was exempted because it was obvious I was too tender and wouldn't know how to handle it. Besides, I think she appreciated that I hung on her every vulgar word, listened carefully to every bawdy instruction—when she told us, for instance, how to "bust a cherry."

"Be kind," she said, "otherwise they going to shrivel up on you. So go easy with 'em."

Dressed in my knee-length skirt, my brown hair pulled back, and wearing very little makeup, I saw myself as a *bayadère*, a maiden in an ancient temple—the temple of deflowering. I took the job very seriously.

Once, while going through my usual spiel, I got caught at my game. I was undressing slowly, pulling off the modest knee-length skirt (I never quite got the point of that—it was too dowdy for words). While I was stripping, I was telling the boy, "There's only one first time. This is a special event, a rite of passage."

"I don't know about you, but it sure as hell isn't my first time," the boy said.

He was snarling. He looked, suddenly, adorable.

We connected. No longer john and whore, we were just two kids. The way we desired each other in that tricked-out boudoir made it feel strangely illicit and innocent at once, as if he were a lover stealing me from the harem. I remember gentle kisses.

Suddenly the *bam, bam* of the old madam's knuckles rapping on the door. Too much time had passed, and then come noises from the wrong party. We emerged flushed pink with love, defiant.

But you know, I don't think Annabelle entirely disapproved. She liked my enthusiasm. The popular idea that prostitutes obey strict rules about when to give themselves and when not is a total misreading of the average whore's psyche, which is far from obedient to anything.

I discovered that spontaneous lovemaking, the unexpected victory of sexual chemistry over circumstance, did happen. It happened about as often as it does anywhere in life, which is to say rarely.

"Never forget one thing," Annabelle would tell us every day in her carefully preserved southern drawl, "never forget: the sun rises and sets on those peepees of theirs, rises and sets."

When I first got back to Maggie's and my pink-and-cherry-red bedroom, I pictured the star of my dreams still sitting at his rectangular table with his feet up at the Traveling Medicine Show just as I had left him. But then one day a few months after I was released from

Highcrest, out for a convalescent walk on Second Avenue, I ran into the big red-haired, pink-faced Jimmy, who threw his arms around me right there on the avenue, as if I were not the pariah I had convinced myself I was. I felt fat and awkward in my shapeless clothes and so shy in Jimmy's presence, who was only one removed from Michael himself, that I could barely whisper hello. I had thought my throat was going to close when I tried to speak.

"Where you been, darlin'? My God, you look so healthy, I hardly recognized you. You look as crisp as a new head of lettuce," he said.

"I've been in the nuthouse, Jimmy."

"Well, sure, I knew that. But for all this time? Shit, what were they doing to you in there, experimenting on you or something?"

"Or something."

Jimmy pulled me over to the curb, where he leaned up against a car. He grabbed hold of my hands and swung my arms back and forth while he looked me in the face. Then he started to play with my hands, examining my palms and my fingers as if he were a doctor conning them for symptoms. Finally he searched my eyes with an expression that told me he was afraid he was about to hurt me.

"Could it be you don't know?" he asked.

"I promise you whatever it is, I don't know. I've been out of it," I said.

"Michael's packed up his tent and moved downtown to Slim's Wide Missouri. He's really where it's at now. He's at the hub of everything. I was supposed to go with him, I kinda promised I would, but, hell, there's no *opportunities* down there, if you know what I mean. All my contacts are up here. Besides, I'm used to walking to work. Yeah, I'm still behind the stick at the old Medicine Show; it's like running a morgue these days.

"Oh, and, Janet, Michael's living with someone now. You remember Roseanna? Yeah, the Italian one, you remember her, beautiful, yes, but not my type...Anyway, she went ahead and had his kid, just a few weeks ago as a matter of fact. Maybe it'll be good for him, whaddya think...might settle him right down...don't you think? I guess it would be all right for you to go and see him, but, honey, try not to stir things up. Don't tempt him back into the old ways, all right? I mean, I have no idea what he does for fun lately, but I'd hate to see him blow his chance at happiness."

He kept playing with my hands, flip-flopping them around in his big ones as if they were too hot to touch, and staring down at them while he spoke, as if my limp hands were the go-betweens that were meant to relay his message to my now impassive face.

"Oh good, Jimmy, I'm glad to hear it. Sounds like he's doing great...Well, of course, I'll drop by to see you real soon, although I'm not drinking a whole lot myself these days."

"Doesn't matter, have a ginger ale...The bar's real quiet, Janet. There's no more music; most of the old crowd is gone. We get an early shot now, neighborhood guys. We got a big TV on the wall. Everything's changed but me and the sawdust on the floor," Jimmy said, slowly brightening with relief as it came to him that this was to be the full extent of my reaction to his news. "Jeez, it's good to see you, Janet. I was wondering this time if you'd ever be back...So, where you headed now?"

"Just out for a walk."

"I better pick up my laundry before the damn place closes. Come around soon, won't you? I missed your crazy little face, you fox you."

Jimmy hugged me again, gently enfolding me in his big arms and slowly rocking me from side to side as if he exactly understood. I stayed there against his king-sized chest long enough to detect the beating of his heart. Afraid my generally guarded misery might take advantage of this warm moment to leap out in sobs like a shameful deformity, like a hidden stump loosed and waving suddenly in the open air, I finally had to pull away.

This was a lot to take in: Michael playing house with a baby and, possibly even worse, not where I thought he was. I slunk back to Maggie's feeling shook up and betrayed.

Now that I knew Michael was downtown, after my shift ended at Annabelle's penthouse on lower Fifth Avenue, I would hail a cab and direct it to turn on Thirteenth Street and drive slowly past his new club. I would pretend I was looking for someone, which in a way I was, in that I always hoped and feared I might catch a glimpse of him. Sometimes I got out and let the cab go. In the quiet evening that belied the frenzy to come, I would stand there in front of the dark window and breathe the air outside the club as if it were pure oxygen. Once or twice the big man working the door questioned whether I planned to go in, but I hurried away without answering him when that happened.

I was terrified of rejection. What if, as 4-H Jimmy had suggested, now that Michael was a father, he really loved this Roseanna? I couldn't picture it, but even if he was the same old Michael, and even if he didn't know how to love Roseanna any better than he did anyone else, he still might not want to have anything to do with me.

I longed for his touch and just to watch him from across the room—his tender, sensitive mouth; his wistful, delicate expression—and, possibly, to receive one of his telepathic penetrating glances—that was what I missed most, how well I thought he knew me. His presence soothed me in a way nothing else ever had. But before I went to see him, I decided I would have to be so on top of things that whatever he said or did wouldn't have the power to destroy me. I needed more time.

On this particular evening in my new apartment, I stood at the window watching the sky darken, sipping my drink, my mind starting to drift out over the river and down, dreaming as ever in Michael's direction. Then the phone rang, jolting me back. It was Corinne.

"Hello, hon. Am I the first to ring you on your new phone?"

"Yes, as a matter of fact you are."

"Good. I wanted to be. We're pals. Don't you forget it. Listen, I've been thinking, I've got an idea. Your next step. Very exciting. Come over tomorrow night and I'll tell you about it."

Felix's

As I was strolling over to Corinne's house on a warm spring evening that had leapfrogged into summer, making it almost too warm for my blue-jean jacket, I passed close to Felix's, the other Upper East Side hang-out. Felix's had been billed in a magazine a while back as "the place where the underground meets the underworld," only I hadn't seen much of the underground lately. This gin mill was just down the street from the often talked about and written about watering hole Irene's, home to the intelligentsia. Irene's bartenders drank at Felix's. They made fun of their customers at Irene's, the famous authors who were famous down the street at Felix's more for their bumbling attempts to score cocaine than for any Pulitzer Prize–winning novels they may have written.

Sufficiently mangy and drug-ridden, Felix's was the only saloon left worth drinking at on the Upper East Side, but it had its drawbacks. The men were vicious; they hated women, and they weren't afraid to show it. Working-class, streetwise gamblers, they would just as soon bet on two drops of beer sliding down the back mirror as talk to the likes of me, with a couple of exceptions, one being Felix himself, a Damon Runyon throwback with a lopsided grin who lived for women, and the other his right-hand man, the bartender Charlie Mooney. Charlie was about six-foot-four and gaunt with high cheekbones and dark, almond-shaped eyes that made him look like a Hun. But Charlie was a dreamer, another Irish dreamer, and I had discovered a few years before that he loved to read. His height and his intriguing face made it difficult for him to effectively ignore women. I, for one, was extremely fond of Charlie. And there were others like me happily willing to wait for him until closing time, minus the one or two Felix managed to pick off first.

When I wandered in on this particular evening, Mean Bob, as he was called, sat alone at the bar having a quick pop before he went to work up the street at Irene's.

"How about a blow job?" he said over his shoulder by way of greeting.

"Not if you paid me."

"Then why are you here?"

This is what I didn't like about hanging out at Felix's.

Charlie stood back listening. He had just set up and we were his first customers. After we finished our exchange, Charlie waited awhile before he came over to me with a Dewar's and soda. There was always the possibility that Mean Bob would scare me off. Not tonight, though. I couldn't think of an alternative. Besides, I knew Mean Bob had to be at work at Irene's soon. Moments later, he polished off his drink and slammed the glass down.

"Time to go babysit," he said, addressing himself to Charlie exclusively.

Then he dropped a twenty-dollar bill on the bar and swaggered out the door. This was the custom; the guys who worked behind the stick around town pooled their money, meaning they drank at each other's saloons and left a tithing instead of a tip.

Once Charlie and I were alone, he leaned over the bar slightly. "Did you hear about 4-H Jimmy?"

"I was just in there to see him last week."

"He got busted."

"Busted? Jimmy doesn't deal anything."

"Passing counterfeit bills. It's a federal rap."

"Four-H Jimmy? He didn't know what he was doing. He's been duped."

"Don't worry. He won't go up. They got him a couple of hotshot lawyers."

"They? Who's they?"

Charlie leaned over the bar a little more. "You know: *they*."

"No, I don't know."

He looked impatient. "Wise guys, Janet."

"Four-H Jimmy and the Mob?"

Charlie threw up his hands. "Whaddya expect from a guy who voted for Nixon?"

"Jimmy voted for Nixon? I don't think I've ever known anyone who voted Republican."

"That's because the crooks you know are honest crooks."

"What have you got against Jimmy, Charlie?"

"Jimmy? I love the guy." He thumped his chest. "Love him. I'm just pissed off at his stupidity, that's all. Anyway, he's not working at the Show anymore. Gone"—he sliced the air—"out . . . Laying low for now."

"Charlie, is he going to be OK?"

"Yes, yes. He'll be OK—this time. God protects fools." He straightened himself up and shook himself off slightly as if he'd just come in from the rain. Then he took a bunch of quarters out of the till. "Here, Janet. Play the jukebox."

Charlie tucked in his chin and folded his arms across his chest in that parody he did of a complacent burgher, which is exactly what Charlie wasn't. He explained it to me once. After he graduated from college all set to go get a straight job, he went along to work one morning with his father, who had been employed by the same chemical company as a bookkeeper at that time for nineteen years. They boarded the subway in Queens. The car was filled to bursting. Charlie and his father had one stop to make it across the aisle to the exit on the far side so they could change trains. Charlie followed his not-so-big father as he frantically pushed and shoved his way across the car to the other door. Then it struck my friend that his father had been doing this five days a week for the past nineteen years.

"Not me," he said.

Now with his arms folded across his chest, Charlie marched solemnly to the far end of the bar, where he looked out the big front window for customers. I went over to the jukebox, which was one of those new machines, no more languid bubbles of incandescent color, only dull fluorescence behind the banners of commercial hits. The jukebox had been neglected here at Felix's. Music was too emotional for the regulars. I played "Bright Lights, Big City," by Jimmy Reed, and "The House of the Rising Sun," as covered by the Animals. After that, I had a few drinks, to clear my confusion about Jimmy.

When I got to Corinne's, she was already in bed with someone, but forever good-natured, she greeted me at the door in her negligee with her always professional, welcoming, dimpled smile and led me over to one of her slippery chairs, where she then sat me down and poured me a snifter full of Grand Marnier. I could hear the toilet flushing in the bathroom behind the closed bedroom door.

"All right, as I said on the phone, I have an idea. If you're going to do this, do it in style."

Corinne pulled me out of the chair as she said this and turned me in a full circle. Then, with her knees bent and her head at an angle, she peered at me from below, making a frame with her hands as if she were a photographer. She stood up, lifted my now long, limp brown hair away from my face and let it drop lifeless to my shoulders. I winced; comparing myself with Corinne—with her luxurious auburn hair floating down her back; the slinky, translucent negligee, her august ripeness underneath and the way her nipples poked through the lace; the smooth skin on her face so artfully made up, her lips glistening a soft watermelon color that contrasted with her hair in a provocative way—I was made to feel like the waif that I was.

"I think it's time you went to school. So tomorrow, come by at noon and we'll start. A makeover. We're going to turn you into a real call girl. That is, if you truly want to do this."

"Of course I do! A makeover! Just like in the magazines. I hope I look better afterward. Sometimes those women look worse, you know? Hey, just kidding. I really am excited. A makeover! Thank you, Corinne. I mean it. I can't get over it." I paused, and then asked, genuinely curious: "Why are you willing to do this for me?"

"Somebody did it for me once. Besides, I'm not going to lose anything by it. What goes around comes around."

"Corinne, you're really something, really terrific. I sincerely mean it. Listen, I'm sorry I showed up so late. But you know, I just heard 4-H Jimmy got busted, and it threw me, I guess."

Corinne was as incredulous as I had been and made me repeat everything Charlie Mooney had told me about 4-H Jimmy.

"OK, I'm going to leave right now. I don't want to keep you any longer," I said when Corinne was finally satisfied I had shared every detail I knew.

"Don't worry about him." She cocked her head in the direction of the bedroom. "He's a football player and it's off-season—we've got all night. You don't have to rush away."

"No, no, another time. I'll be here at noon," I said as I weaved my way across the room. The Dexamyl was wearing off and I was feeling tipsy—dizzy, actually. Corinne followed me to the door.

I had been dying all this time to ask her about Michael, because I was sure they were still in touch, but I didn't want to seem too curious. I wanted to be certain I could convey the right off-hand tone, and I was afraid an irrepressible note of anxiety, or eagerness, might give me away. The more I delayed, the harder it got. Finally at the door, I realized this was my last chance.

"Have you been to see Michael yet at Slim's?" I asked.

"Haven't you, Janet?"

"Not yet."

"What kind of friend are you? I mean, you've been back a long time. What's keeping you?"

Corinne was one more person who had not heard about how I went crazy and preyed on Michael. Whew. What a relief. That's the great thing about New York: if you wanted anybody to know your business, you practically had to take out an ad.

"I heard he had a baby...thought maybe he was being domestic or something," I said.

"What, who, Michael? You've got to be kidding." Corinne chuckled deep in her throat. "Michael being domestic, that's a good one... Listen, that poor girl, Roseanna, she has to look after the baby all by herself *and* pay the rent. The only time he babysits is when she has to go stand in line for food stamps. I know this because he told me so himself...I think her parents help out some, but they're in Milano, of course...Can you imagine having Michael's kid? I feel so sorry for her." Corinne shook her head. "You really should go by and see him, Janet. The music's great, too...well, you can imagine, the whole scene's great," Corinne said, encouraging me to go as if my not having done so were just an oversight.

"I'll do that," I said, trying my best to sound casual. The sudden color in my cheeks as soon as the subject of Michael came up must have tipped Corinne, I thought, but if she detected strong feelings on my part, she didn't let on.

"In the meantime, you're going to owe me one kid. I'm telling you, I'm going to make you a star," Corinne said, putting her arm around my shoulders and giving me a little hug before she gently closed the door.

Makeover

"You're late," Corinne said.

I was just a few minutes late, but late nevertheless, and bleary-eyed. The morning was so alien, I had become infatuated with the wash of light on the buildings, the cars, and the concrete sidewalk studded with shiny stones. My observations slowed my pace as I walked uptown to Corinne's. She answered the door already prepared for the day in one of her flowing caftans, shaking her head in open disapproval.

"There's a few things I want to make clear to you. Then, after you've thought it over, if you're sure this is the life for you, I'll book you."

"Oh, Corinne, I didn't realize this was an interview," I said.

Corinne ignored this and plunged on. "Number one, no decent man is ever going to marry you. Might as well kiss that good-bye. Number two, once you're in the Life, you're in. No way out. Blue money's too easy and it's too good. Understand?"

A decent man? I had no sense of what kind of man that was. A dull man, is that what Corinne meant by "decent"? No dull man would ever marry me. Oh well.

"But I know all this, Corinne. I've thought it over. Honestly I have," I said.

I started to look around her living room, which I had never seen in daylight. Corinne had pulled the curtains; a blast of piercing noonday sun assaulted the room, exposing every wrinkle and stain on the satin-covered furniture. The place looked like it had a hangover.

"So you think you got it all figured. Well, I'm gonna give it to you straight: if you really did, a girl like you wouldn't be here. I was a shanty-Irish lunk of a kid from the Jersey Shore. Grew up in a house crammed with people. I had to get out. Finally, one day, I walked onto the boardwalk and turned a trick. You, there's no point. With your background, you should be up at Columbia or somewhere hustling the intellectuals," she said.

"I'm sorry if you don't approve, but I can't stand intellectuals. Columbia gives me the creeps. I'll do whatever you want."

"All right, if you're that determined, come back tomorrow morning at ten sharp. I mean sharp. If you want to do this the right way, not like some flake, first of all, you have got to have discipline. That means regular hours," Corinne said as she pushed me out the door. The kid gloves were off.

"I won't be late again," I called out from the hallway.

And I wasn't. I went on a maintenance program, confining myself to a few Dexamyl in the daytime, a few drinks and a ten-milligram Valium at night.

Corinne visited the Coventry, and she approved. My L-shaped studio faced the East River on Sutton Place, and that was good. The dressing room, the indirect spotlights on the ceiling, and the mirrored wall, which looked out on the Fifty-ninth Street Bridge and the open sky above the river from the height of the seventeenth floor, all of that was good. But she suggested it might be time to furnish the place, especially if I planned to run a business out of there.

My apartment still stood empty, except for a queen-sized bed, a lamp, opaque window shades, and a white Princess phone, but if anything, I thought the bareness of it, like a gessoed canvas waiting for its masterpiece, only added to the sense of impending glory. I loved to stand looking out my large, clean window at the bridge and the boats, feeling vindicated, feeling, for the first time in a long time, blessed.

Next, Corinne took me shopping on the second floor of Bloomingdale's, home to a maze of designer-boutiques. We tore through the racks, and I managed to spend practically all I had saved over the past few months on a summer wardrobe: designer bell-bottom jeans; fancy shorts; a formal-looking Ralph Lauren summer pants-suit of brushed cotton; a long, fitted skirt; several cotton and silk button-down shirts; a floral-print, chiffon blouse; a black cocktail dress; one midi-dress with dolman sleeves; the new cork platform sandals, and the dreaded high-heeled shoes.

I couldn't bear to have my new wardrobe sent, so together, Corinne and I piled the big Bloomingdale's shopping bags into a cab. With the help of the doorman, we got everything upstairs, where we heaped it onto the fluffy new quilt on my bed. The Bloomingdale's shopping bags sported that month's theme, which was a celebration of Mexico. Stick men in ruffled shirts, round women in bright shawls, and a childlike orange sun scrawled overhead decorated each of these magical packages. We dove into them, freeing the contents from yards of tissue paper, which we threw high in the air. We took turns holding the clothes up to my body.

"Well, pal, you're starting to get it together," Corinne said, her broad Cheshire cat face beaming at me over my shoulder in the mirror.

Finally, my mentor sent me to her upper-out-of-sight beauty salon on Fifty Seventh Street where they actually did make me over. The stylist performed his slight-of-hand miracle, snipping while we chatted in front of the mirror. He shaped my fine hair, layering it subtly around the face, introducing a long, wispy bang that thrilled me. Then he shooed me on to the colorist, who decided what I needed was streaks of tawny-blond, not so light that the outlines of my face would disappear, but fair enough to bring out the green in my eyes. Instead of a cap, he wrapped small sections of my hair in tinfoil that had been cut into strips, because, he said, it would look more natural. The two men consulted each other. They hovered around me and whispered.

"I think her brows need shaping," the stylist said.

"He's done a *marvelous* job on that baby-fine hair, hasn't he?" the colorist asked me, addressing my image in the mirror.

This was exactly the sort of experience that gave me the keenest pleasure, two grown men fussing over my hair, my skin color, and the angles of my face, which ordinarily I spent hours staring at all by myself. When they finished with me, my hair fell in rich, shiny tendrils down my neck. When I moved, it shimmered and bounced gently around my head. My hair was an asset! At last, a real asset! I understood then that beauty is nothing more than the expression of energy, someone's energy.

After Bloomingdale's and Frederico and company got through with me, I looked so well-heeled I had become a stranger to myself. No more picking at my fingernails, which were now a perfect rose pink; no more bare-faced afternoons—it was seamless and streamlined, this existence. I felt like a greased pig.

"Never mind, you'll get used to it," Corinne said. "Think you're ready to hustle?"

"Sure," I said, of course not feeling ready at all.

"This is in case you lose your book and every client in it, or you have to move to a new town; whatever the circumstance, you'll always have hustling to fall back on.

"First, you stake out one of the toniest hotel bars, the more conservative, the better. Then you go there, maybe carrying a shopping bag or two from Bergdorf's, dressed as demurely as is humanly possible. Then you discreetly, and I mean discreetly, hit on the likeliest-looking mark. But always watch your back. The house dicks work these places like jailhouse guards. They're out looking for trouble, and they don't want their nice, family-men-type guests to be exploited."

"What do I say to the mark? How do I open? And if I'm disguised as some super-conservative dame, how am I going to let him know I'm peddling my ass?"

"That's up to you. No two girls use exactly the same approach. Hustling takes some skill, I have to admit, but everybody finds their own gimmick eventually. You just have to figure out what yours is," she said.

So I learned how to solicit the visiting businessmen who dropped into the dark, cool, wood-paneled lounges during the afternoons at the cushier hotels on the Upper East Side. I never really enjoyed that end of the business, even though, as Corinne had predicted, I did discover a scam that worked for me. I would pick on the most happily married man I could find, the one who wouldn't dream of cheating on his wife, let alone paying for it. I would tell him that I could teach him how to give his wife more pleasure, that it was a sin for a married man to be so inexperienced. "The blind leading the blind," I would tell him. I tried to make him feel guilty. I was amazed this approach ever worked. Not often, of course, but even when the mark had no intention of buying, he never failed to find me amusing, as if I were another colorful New York side trip, like a visit to Chinatown on Saturday morning or a performance of *Oh! Calcutta!*

"Man is not monogamous," that was my line. I was just repeating what Corinne had told me. I remember with certain regret one shy man from outside Des Moines who had always been true to his wife until he met me. By this time, I believed so completely that practicing monogamy was living a lie, I saw nothing wrong in seducing him. In fact, I couldn't wait to enlighten the shy man from Des Moines.

Shortly after I moved into the Coventry, my old friend Whitney, a dance major from our alma mater, looked me up. I had not heard from any of my classmates since I had been kicked out of Pendleton, a college for budding libertines and aspiring dilettantes.

Traditionally, students had a hard time getting ousted from Pendleton. My friends thought I was a rebel to be admired; actually, I was usually too sick in the morning to get out of bed. Indeed, I was mortified that I suffered from acute anxiety attacks whenever I tried to enter the library, or that my crippling hangovers forced me to shun the classes of the very teachers who had offered the most encouragement. This is what drove the dean, finally, to ask me to leave. Immediately, I took off in the middle of the night with the reckless debutante Cynthia Austen White Andover Poole in her souped-up Thunderbird, the driver handicapped by a scared kitten crying and crawling all over her while she gunned the accelerator on the southbound thruway. As far as I know, neither one of us ever went back. Whenever I thought of that sanguine campus designed to replicate an old New England town, its open commons set high on a real New England plateau, I was filled with remorse and eager to put the whole experience behind me. I thought I had long since severed all ties with my Pendleton college chums.

As luck would have it, my college friend was in a hurry to sell her mother's tasteful furniture, enough to fill my little apartment. I gladly paid out three hundred dollars, the sum she had decided she needed to get across the country and establish herself at the ashram she was about to join in Colorado.

I had gone from knocking around like a stray on the backstreets to living in a fabulous big studio with a view of the East River, full of nothing but silky, varnished mahogany, fancy upholstery, and a walk-in closet very nearly jammed with clothes. Marvelous. And the best part was that I was sane, unassailably sane. Just as I suspected, money made the difference. Nothing like the grounding influence of *things* to keep me on track. I was shining with health and cosseted by all my possessions; for the first time in my adult life, I felt that I was a success.

The Comanche

I dropped into Felix's to show off the new me to Charlie Mooney.

"Look at you. Glossy blond hair and nail polish—and stockings and high heels. Well done. You're a knockout, Janet, too good for us. You're moving up in the world.

"Felix, come over here. I want you to see something."

Felix limped over. With his twisted body and his lopsided grin, he looked a bit like a toned and sun-kissed Quasimodo. "Yeah, yeah, Charlie. Can't you see I'm in pain?" he said.

"What happened to you?" I asked.

"A rough rugby match—an exceedingly rough rugby match," Felix said.

"I'm turning tricks now, Charlie," I said.

With his usual pomp, Charlie folded his arms across his chest and nodded, pulling in his chin in a parody of a fatuous authority figure. "Well, whatever it is, it's obviously good for you, Janet. I've never seen you when you had it so together."

Just then, a stretch limo pulled up in front of the saloon. The chauffeur scrambled around to open the door and everybody inside stopped whatever they were doing or saying to look. Who should step out, sheathed in a floor-length silver mink but the redoubtable Comanche (née Angelica), just the person I hoped never to see again. In she sauntered (for to call it a walk would in no way describe her Barbie-doll-gone-amok, hip-swinging glide across the barroom floor), until she was standing directly in front of the hunched-over Felix. She flashed him. She was naked inside her coat, of course. Then she grabbed Felix's nipple through his T-shirt and tweaked it hard.

"Want to fool around, Felix?"

"Ow, that hurt. No, I don't want to fool around. I'm in terrible pain."

"Whatsa matter, is it your back again, booby?"

"Yeah, it went out on me this morning, playing against those damned Irishmen in the Park. They're fiends. I should know better."

"But I can make it all well, I promise. My partner, Cissy, she loves to give back rubs (she also loves to suck cock). No, really, she's a genius at it. And we got plenty of pills. We got Dalmane, Percodan, Codeine #3, you name it, a full medicine cabinet. So come over, come in the limo."

"Go on, let the Comanche heal you. Go on," Charlie said.

Then she turned to me. "You look great, Janet. Why don't you come, too?"

I hadn't thought she noticed or recognized me, even though I was standing right next to Felix.

"We got speed—Desoxyn—OK, Janet? I know how you love that. And you'll dig Cissy. She's a gas," the Comanche said.

I have to say one thing for that old crowd of mine: crazy acting out, like banging wildly on a front door until the police come, was not a memorable offense.

"All right, I'll go if Janet goes. In my condition, I need a duenna," Felix said in his husky, raspy voice, made even huskier by the pain.

Soon we all piled into the limo, and I hadn't even had the chance to settle in when I realized where we were going.

"Why are we pulling up to *my* door?" I asked.

"You live here?" Angelica was surprised.

I nodded.

She squealed. "Janet, we're neighbors. What floor do you live on? Oh, we'll have great times. I get so bored waiting for the phone to ring. Are you working?"

"Yeah, I'm starting a book."

"Terrific. Cissy and I can turn you onto loads of tricks. We got more than we can handle. Hey, this is going to be fun!"

"All right, girls, it's very cozy and all that, but I got to lie down now," Felix said.

Angelica and I each took one arm and hoisted Felix into the elevator. She occupied a studio on the penthouse floor above me, and her partner, Cissy, lived in a one-bedroom a few floors below. We carried Felix down the hall to the one-bedroom, where a broad-shouldered, big-breasted, flaxen-haired farmer's daughter sat waiting inside, wearing a transparent negligee. She was glassy-eyed—the eyes of a body-snatched husk. Her legs were spread, and she absentmindedly dangled a limp hand between them.

"Cissy, you got to help this poor slob out with one of your super back rubs. This is Felix, and this is his chaperone, Janet. She's an old friend of mine and Michael's. We go way back, and guess what? She lives right here in this building, on the seventeenth floor. And she's in the Life now. Isn't that too much?"

Without responding, Cissy hauled a groaning Felix into the bedroom. Angelica threw her silver mink over a chair, even though now in the icy air-conditioning, the coat would have been more appropriate, and slipped on a silk kimono, which was left hanging open. She disappeared into the bathroom, and the next thing I knew, she was distributing pills and snifters full of cognac to her guests.

Felix groaned while the mighty Cissy kneaded his back. Eventually the medicine, whatever combination he had swallowed, began to work, and he became glassy-eyed.

"Oh, how can I thank you girls? I'm feeling no pain," he said.

"Actually, there is a favor you could do for us," Angelica said.

"Anything, anything."

"Well, I'm working on expanding my repertoire, and I need to practice something." Angelica hesitated a second, then she blurted it out: "We want to give you an enema."

Cissy's blank eyes lit up.

"Yeah, we would really get off on that. I got this trick referred to me, and I didn't want to have anything to do with it. I was going to turn him over to Cissy, but Mr. Fudge—" Angelica turned to me. "That's our man. Cissy's and mine. He looks after us, even while he's away. I can always hear his advice in my head. Anyway, Mr. Fudge explained it to us: 'Bein' a ho ain't no different than bein' a nurse. When you get one of 'em freaky tricks, you jes put on yo' nurse's cap. If you want to be a great ho, then you got to *de*tach. No body part, no bodily function, should disgust a good ho. Think

Judge Feinstein, what a cute old fart," she said, chuckling fondly over the memory.

"Can't keep her off the street no how, no way. You're a bad girl, Cissy," Angelica said.

"Where do you go?" I couldn't help blurting out. "I'm sorry, but I don't get it. You're supposed to be a high-class hooker—after all you live on Sutton Place—so why in hell would you want to turn streetwalker?"

Cissy stared at me.

"I thought there was more of a distinction between those two branches of the profession," I said a little apologetically.

"Nah, that's hype, that's what the civilians like to think. I throw on my mink and hit Fiftieth off Park, in front of the Waldorf Towers. The cops give me a hard time, obviously, but it's such a good strip to work, and it's open territory."

"Cissy means it doesn't belong to anybody else's pimp," Angelica said.

"I know, I know," I said.

"Well, well, get a load of the pro here. I remember you when you were giving it away, and pretty generously, too," she said.

"Now, Angie, nobody likes to be reminded of that," Cissy said. "Anyway, who hasn't given it up for nothing sometime in their lives?"

"Who out there isn't nowadays?" Angelica said.

"Yeah, with all the free pussy in the world, it's a wonder we're still in business. But you want to know why we are?" Cissy asked.

"Oh, tell us, great bwana, tell us your theory," Angelica said.

"Well, I know you've heard it before," Cissy said.

"A coupla times," her partner said, getting up to pour us all another drink from the blender that we were keeping in the refrigerator.

"OK, but Janet hasn't. Are you interested in hearing my theory about why we're still in business, Janet?" Cissy asked.

"And it's better than ever, too," Angelica said.

"Yeah, and it's better than ever, too. Want to hear?"

"Of course, of course," I said.

"The reason men go to hos is 'cause they like to pay for it, that's why. The money up front, that's what gets 'em. It's nothing we do, it's not even the sex; it's just that they like to pay for it, plain and simple," Cissy said, sounding triumphant.

"You know, that's really a brilliant theory. Brilliant. Once they pay, they're free. They don't have to say 'I love you,' don't have to raise the kid. But wait," I said, thinking a little more. "According to you it's even simpler than that. I get it. I remember now I read once in a men's magazine about an experiment where scientists put a vending machine in a cage of chimpanzees. When the animals pressed a button, they got a piece of fruit. The next thing you know, the males were exchanging bananas and apples with the females for sex. That proves what you're saying is true. Fuck it, I knew it! Oh man, that's wild, really, when you think about it. The customers *like* to pay. Well then, let's drink to whoremongers and caged monkeys."

"Knew you'd see the wisdom 'cause you're a smart girl. Isn't she a smart one, Angel?"

"Smart enough to be rich like us if she wants to. But you gotta find a good pimp, Janet, like Mr. Fudge, someone to manage things for you," Angelica said.

"Nah, there're too many gorillas floating around, pricks so dumb they mess up their own hos' faces. Not many gentleman players left like Mr. Fudge. I say you're better off on your own now," Cissy said.

"What about protection, backup? The street don't take too kindly to a girl out here by herself," Angelica said.

"Not if you discriminate. You gotta discriminate, Janet," Cissy said.

"Frankly, I can't see any advantage to having a pimp," I said.

"You don't know Mr. Fudge," Cissy said.

The two of them stared across the kitchen table at each other, their eyes locked in complicity, and smiled.

Bordello

"Wear jeans. That's all we ever wear here," one of the two madams, Felicity, told me on the phone.

Finally, I was going to see how the hip side of my generation ran things. I had been trying to build my own business. The problem was that I became extremely bored sitting around waiting for the phone to ring, so Corinne referred me.

"This whorehouse should be part of every girl's unsentimental education," she said.

The cab dropped me at a town house in Murray Hill that had a wrought-iron staircase leading up to the parlor floor. It was one of those sultry October days when the air is heavy with dawdling summer. A wisteria vine had twisted itself around the iron fence and hung off the landing. The blossoms had blown away months ago, but the brown stems were still covered with wispy green leaves. I felt as if I were marching up the steps of a real bordello.

A sullen-looking young thing in short shorts, thongs, and a halter top answered the bell. "Upstairs," she said, pointing to the back of the house.

We were in a big front room with high windows, empty except for a couple of couches. I started climbing the stairs.

"All the way to the top," the sentry yelled after me.

I passed a landing with doors on either side of it, then another one. I could hear Barry White on the turntable and, above his bass voice, women laughing. I followed the noise into a small room under the eaves, where three women sat on a built-in banquette around a large table. A stockpile of gleaming white cocaine had been heaped into a dish and set down smack in the middle like a centerpiece. I watched one of the women scoop what was at least a tablespoon of it onto a mirror. She started making lines with the precision of a jewel cutter.

"Time to wake up," the woman said, handing the whole thing to me.

I was so struck by her instant generosity, I beamed with pleasure.

"Is this for everyone?" I asked, horrified that I might otherwise expose my greedy nature right off the bat.

"See that pile? That is for everyone. What you got there is for you. You're way behind us. We've been doing this shit since...since when, Ginger?"

"Try last week," Ginger said.

"Did I just die and go to heaven?" I asked, snorting up everything with the short straw someone had passed to me.

They laughed.

"You're cute. My name is Ginger, and Mary Poppins over there is my partner."

"Hi, I'm Felicity, and this is Joey, our token jailbait," Felicity said.

"Who was that downstairs?" I asked.

"Oh, Marcy."

"No wonder she looked so miserable," I said.

"Yeah, we take turns manning the door. OK, I guess you can see how we run things here. Loose. You and Joey and Marcy are working today, and sometimes me, if I feel like it. Ginger here is getting married so doesn't get to turn tricks anymore. She keeps the guys amused if everyone is busy," Felicity said.

Ginger screwed up her face in disgust.

"Meanwhile, there's going to be work for you. Straight is fifty, half-and-half is seventy-five. If the john just wants a blow job, hit him up for fifty. Tell him you do deep-throat, it's your specialty," Felicity said.

"Know how to do deep-throat?" Ginger asked.

"I've never tried," I said.

"It's easy as hell, a gimmick, that's all. You let it in slowly and open your throat. Then, when you get used to it, just open and close your throat around his dick. He'll come so fast, you won't have a chance to gag," Ginger said.

"OK, the split is standard: sixty / forty. Sometimes I get a call from a hotel. I charge two hundred for that," Felicity said.

"Yeah, and lots of those calls are from famous rock 'n' rollers, like Ridley Stokes, when he's in town, or last week, we heard from Trip Oldman. We have fun with these guys. They like to get down. Plenty of good blow," Ginger said.

"Trip Oldman?" I asked.

"What's the matter, you sound bummed," Felicity said, laughing.

"Well, I mean, his politics. He's so passionately to the left. And then those plaintive, innocent love songs..."

"Oh, girl, you got a lot to learn," Ginger said.

"You Jewish?" Felicity asked me.

"Yep," I said, jumping at the chance to tell her, because it was obvious that she was Jewish, the first one I'd come across.

Felicity had long streaked-blond hair and slightly protruding large blue eyes; she wore diamonds in her ears. She looked like every elegant princess you ever saw on the Upper East Side.

"I could tell you were Jewish from your rap. You got a good rap. That might come in handy," Felicity said.

Ginger got up and stretched. She swiveled her hips and dry-humped the table. The oldest one there, in her thirties, she looked like she'd been around the block a few times. I couldn't tell what she was—Irish, Jewish, Italian—because she had that generic ethnic face, skin faintly scarred from teenage acne, dark wavy hair cut short. But she had flash. I wondered about the decent man who was planning to marry her.

"I'm bored," Ginger said.

"You're going to do great out there on the North Shore. Some housewife you're going to make," Felicity said.

"Don't let's talk about it. I still got a few months left. See my ring?" Ginger asked me, wriggling her fingers in my face.

The ring was a big diamond-shaped diamond.

"Who's the guy?"

"Oh, someone I met while I was filming *Prostitution and Drugs: The Intimate Connection*. His name's Kenyon Edwards. He's got a last first name and a first last name. Lots of class. He's a few years older than I am, but don't worry, he's rich."

"And he adores Ginger," Felicity said.

"So you're the one who got the Emmy," I said, almost starstruck. I'd heard her story.

"Yeah, I put the show together for PBS. Then I went to work for the mayor, helping him organize a task force to get rid of the pimps. I'm still on his payroll," Ginger said.

"Doesn't the mayor mind that you're here?" I asked. If I sounded naive, I was past caring.

"Listen, honey, didn't anyone ever tell you? Once in the Life, always in the Life," she said.

"But Ginger's much slicker than she's letting on. She's leaving for good, moving to a big house on the Long Island Sound," Felicity said.

"Dammit. I told you, don't remind me. I don't want to hear it," Ginger said, banging the table. The cocaine jumped in its dish.

"Watch it," Joey said.

"Oh, Joey, you really got my nose open, you know that? You are the sweetest little flower bud. Come here, baby, come to Mama," Ginger said. She went over to where Joey was sitting, leaned over the young woman's back and put her hands on her breasts. "Only seventeen, oh, honey, how'd you get so wise?"

"Quit it," Joey said, shaking off Ginger.

"Sassy, isn't she? But you should see her slit. It's perfect," Ginger said.

"Stop trying to shock Janet. You don't shock that easy, do you?" Felicity said.

"Well, for starters, I'm a whore, aren't I?" I said.

"Yeah, right, we're all hos," Felicity said.

There were men's voices on the stairs.

"Quick, hide the dope. We don't want these clowns dipping into our stash," Ginger said.

Felicity took the dish into a little kitchen across the way.

But the two men had brought their own mountain. They dumped a spoon of it onto a magazine. One of them started cutting lines.

The usual johns, a little younger and spiffier than my ambulance chasers and real estate salesmen, these were Wall Streeters, but basically the same. They threw off their jackets and loosened their ties like they were in danger of choking any minute.

"Joey baby, I came here just for you," one of them said. He sat down and pulled her onto his lap. "I dream of you. Did you know that?"

"No, I didn't know that," Joey said, her long brown hair falling over one eye. She sounded completely blasé, unflappable.

The john started bouncing her up and down as if she were a little kid. "Do you dream of me?" he asked her.

"Yeah, Henry, every night," Joey said.

"Who's the new girl?" the other one said.

"Want her?" Felicity asked.

"She'll do. Like sex?" he asked me.

"It's my life's work," I said.

"Come on, then, snort some of this," he said, handing me a little silver spoon.

After they had some scotch over ice that Felicity brought back from the kitchen, the two of them grabbed Joey and me like a couple of dashing pirates and pulled us downstairs.

Inside the bedroom, my john peeled off four twenties. He flopped onto the bed, still in his clothes, waving the bills in the air.

I snatched the money from his hand and stuck it on the mantelpiece. Then he closed his eyes and let his body go limp, like a puppy on its back waiting to have its belly stroked.

"An extra five for you, just between us. So do me good," he said.

The Gentleman Player

"Don't bother to take off your coat. We're going somewhere," Felicity said as soon as I got inside the front door.

"Where?"

"To the radio studio WWRN. You and me are going to do the talk show *Black Tells It Like It Is*. Know it?"

"No, never heard of it. What are we supposed to talk about?"

"There are a couple of issues we've got to cover. First and foremost is 'Off the Pimp.' That's the crux of what HONY is all about. I've even been known to cooperate with vice."

As it turned out, along with Ginger, Felicity was also an activist, the founder and leader of HONY, Hookers' Organization of New York. I hadn't realized it actually existed until she told me I was a member.

"You wouldn't believe what those thugs do. Last month, one of them sewed up his ho's pussy with a leather string. Can you imagine? And worse.

"We want to get the word out, let working girls know they can be independent. Also, decriminalization—not legalization, we don't want the government running things—just decriminalization. Prostitution is victimless, right? It's the oldest profession. Leave us alone.

"I picked you to come with me 'cause you can rap," Felicity said as she locked the door behind us.

"But couldn't you've maybe mentioned this a little sooner?" I asked her. My palms were sweating. I rummaged in my bag for a Dexamyl and swallowed it dry.

"It's better this way. You got less time to think. Also, I didn't want you to say no."

"What's your name?" Felicity asked me in the cab.

"Janet," I said.

"Yeah, but you gotta have a working name," she said.

"OK, how about 'Janet DeVille, Lady of the Evening,'" I said.

"'Janet DeVille, Lady of the Evening.' Good, sounds good—no, no, not that way, driver, through the Park. We want to go through the Park. OK?" Felicity said, yelling at the thick plastic wall in front of us.

"Hello, listeners. Thanks for tuning in on this cold Sunday afternoon, a good time to stay at home and listen to No-Jive Jocko here bringing you *Black Tells It Like It Is*. For the next two hours we'll be talking to Felicity Freed, the head of HONY, Hookers' Organization of New York, and another member of HONY, Janet DeVille, 'Lady of the Evening.' The issue we'll be dealing with today is 'Off the Pimp.' The two ladies will be glad to answer your questions live on the air. Just dial 727-WWRN. But first, let's hear what Felicity and Janet have to say. You are both active working girls is that right?"

Two hours? I frowned and looked at Felicity. I was trapped inside a glass booth for the next two hours, during which time I would be expected to sound off knowledgeably on a subject that I suddenly decided, in the grip of stage fright, I knew next to nothing about.

No-Jive Jocko peered at us over his half-glasses, waiting. He had a long and lustrous ponytail that made him look like an unreconstructed sixties hippie.

"Yes, we're working girls, and proud of it. We are independent businesswomen supplying a need, the oldest need in the book. We don't answer to anyone. We're free agents, and we're here to tell all the other working girls out there that it's high time you belonged to yourself, yourself alone..." Felicity went on and on, eloquent as hell, I thought. She inspired me.

"I turn tricks out of my own house, also the houses of friends of mine, madams. But whatever money I get, I keep. I don't have to have a man taking from me to make me feel all right about myself. My conscience is clear," I heard myself saying.

"WWRN. You're on the air," No-Jive Jocko said into the mike, his voice deep and sonorous, like a low, mellow horn.

"Girl, you, white girl, Janet: Your mama know what you doin'? Your white sisters know what you do? Ain't you got no shame?"

"Yes, but that's just it—that's why we're here, don't you see? To try and make you understand we've got no reason to be ashamed."

"Oh no," I thought, "do I sound patronizing?"

"Tell me your name, caller."

"Never mind my name...You're a fornicator..."

"Just your Christian name?"

"Regina."

"All right, Regina. You brought up shame, and I'm glad you did. Shame is the strychnine, the bitter strychnine, that causes working girls to give their money away, that makes them think they deserve to get beat. We have to get rid of the shame. That's the real enemy—the old double standard."

The phones outside the booth lit up. Jocko gave Felicity and me the thumbs-up sign.

"Janet DeVille, you got some powerful opinions. So let's hear from you out there. Should whores feel ashamed? This is No-Jive Jocko. You're on the air..."

"I'm a marine, just come back from 'Nam. I think Janet makes sense in what she's saying. Where would we have been without them sweet Saigon girls? Listen, you always got to pay for a good piece of ass, one way or the other."

That did it, a little encouragement, and I was off, ranting now.

"Here's the thing. You men can go away to kill each other, then come home and resume domestic life. But if I choose to be a mercenary, I am told I must never try to cross back.

"Well, fucking strangers is certainly not as bad as killing them as far as I'm concerned, and yet you're telling me I'm supposed to feel ashamed. No, no, if anything, I think they should pin medals on us for a change..."

Felicity smiled and nodded at me, perfectly happy to let me do all the talking now.

"WWRN. No-Jive Jocko at your beck and call...You're on the air..."

"Hello, my name is Lois," a tiny, halting voice said.

"Yes, Lois, what would you like to ask Felicity and Janet?" Jocko said.

"When I was twelve, my pimp pulled me out of my mama's house onto the street. He put me on the stroll. He say, 'You gonna work for me now. You don', I kill you.' I knew he was serious, 'cause he done killed my cousin Karen a month before. Shot her right up in the head. So I went to work, been his ho ever since. Now you two mean to tell me you don' gotta have a man? That mus' be some downtown thing. How you do that?" she asked.

After the show, Felicity took me down to a loft in Chelsea. In the big open living room, about six or seven very well-dressed African American men were sitting on a couple of big leather sofas. When they saw Felicity and me, they started to clap and cheer.

"Here they come, Felicity and Janet, *the* lady of the evening," one of them said.

"Step right over here, Miss Lady of the Evening, what will be your pleasure?" a handsome young man said.

I grabbed hold of Felicity. "Where are we? Who are these guys?" I asked.

"Pimps. I told 'em to listen," Felicity said.

"You what?" I recoiled in terror.

"Yep, all the players are here," Felicity said, smiling, calling out to several of them by name.

"This is like the lions and the jackals drinking at the same watering hole," I said to her, but she was already gone, locked in a circle of admirers.

"What'll it be?" the good-looking young man asked me, still holding on to my arm.

"Dewar's and soda, thanks," I said.

I had never actually come face-to-face with a pimp before, let alone a whole roomful of them. And after all those words I had just spoken so glibly for everyone and anyone to hear! What had I done? I was so scared, I was thrilled.

"Have a seat," he said, pointing to a long leather couch.

We both sat. I drank the scotch down in one gulp.

He smiled at me like an indulgent papa. "You were thirsty," he said.

"Listen, there's something I have to ask you," I said.

"Anything I know, you should know, too," he said.

What a beautiful, curving mouth. His hair was a full Afro framing his face. He was dressed in a flowing dark gray silk shirt, well-cut English trousers, and elegant Italian loafers. On his wrist, a thin gold bracelet dangled.

"OK, what I'm wondering is how come you're not mad at me, after all those things I said about pimps and offing the pimps?"

He sipped his brandy and looked me deep in the eyes. "Girl, those were brave things you said, righteous things. Felicity, she's a hell of a woman. I got nothing but respect for her. But I can see that you need to understand what I'm about, me and my confreres," he said, nodding in the direction of the other guys. "We are what you call gentlemen players. We are a dying breed, but we have a long history and a tradition. We don't pull hos, no, no, not interested. A woman's got to come to *me*, got to love *me*, beg me, even, to take her on. There's no shame in that. And the way I treat her—managing her career, never getting greedy—I can't turn her loose even when I want to sometimes.

"We are the lovers of this world, darlin'," he said.

The tone of his low voice was so intimate, I almost forgot to listen to what he said.

"I think I understand. You don't want me if I don't want you, right?"

"You got it, darlin'," he said, laughing.

I sighed with relief. I was convinced that no matter how great a man was in bed, even if he swooped down from the rooftops disguised as a swan and carried me off in the middle of the night, I would never be tempted to part with my hard-earned dough of my own free will. So I was safe.

As the bleak December sun fell outside, so early now, a party of sorts was starting to happen. Cool jazz, Pharoah Sanders, came over large speakers suspended on the wall. Tiny spotlights in the ceiling went dim. I felt self-conscious in my bell-bottom jeans, a sweater, and my platform shoes and socks, because the men were all dressed up. I sank back into a corner of the sofa. But my new friend, the gentleman player, brought me another drink, and we continued to talk. I found out that he was the son of a grade-school principal somewhere near Oakland, that he had graduated from college out there and then come to New York. He was a nice middle-class boy once, a dutiful son. It was an older woman, he claimed, who got him into the Life.

After this brief conversation, the gentleman player took me by the hand and led me up a narrow, winding staircase to one of the bedrooms where the men had thrown their overcoats. We did some blow from his dainty silver spoon, what they call a "one-on-one," after which he started to undress me.

"What's this about?" I asked.

"We're free. This is recreational," he said, unbuckling my platform sandal.

We snorted more big breakfast lines of cocaine off the surface of a magazine. Then suddenly we were sticking together, as if the friction were magnetizing our flesh. The scent of his Eau Sauvage poured off him now. He had no hair on his chest, only his lower belly. In that lullaby-soft deep voice, he whispered generic compliments in my ear ("Oh, baby, baby, fine, fine..."). He was smooth. Not one ungainly move during all the time we spent there—close to an hour. He was too smooth. I felt alone, thinking it had been a little over two years now since I had seen Michael.

Eventually, still strangers, the gentleman player and I came downstairs again. The crowd had grown and included several sophisticated-looking black women dressed in long, tight skirts and high heels. A man was playing a horn at the far end of the big room in front of the windows. Everyone was listening. I found Felicity standing by herself at the back of the room. She was staring at the horn player, with slits for eyes.

"Check him out," she said.

I moved a little closer, then I stood up on a leather ottoman, balancing myself by holding on to someone's shoulder. He was beautiful. Like the man I had just been with, the musician was khaki colored, lean, long fingered. And he played the tenor sax in a now blitzing, now whispering way, with a rhythm so subtle it escaped me. But even so, it made me want to follow it.

"What do you think?" Felicity asked.

I was flattered that she wanted to know what I thought, that she was treating me like a confidante. "I think he's hot, he's a dream," I said.

"Yeah. He's got my nose open. I'm going to get him," Felicity said.

Maybe it was because we were not far from Slim's Wide Missouri, or it could have been the way Felicity had her eyes trained on the horn player, but I was reminded of how I used to watch Michael pad around his old gin mill. I think the real reason longing finally overcame fear was because when the pimp and I were upstairs, I felt so damn free, it made me shiver. Afterward, although he wasn't unkind, it was as if he were shooing me off the plantation into the wilderness. There had never been any daddy, and now there was no man willing to look after me. I wasn't the type you even tried to own anymore.

Slim's Wide Missouri

There he was.

The ambiance was new, but the impresario without portfolio was not: Michael with his long hair, in his blue jeans and moccasins, sitting with his legs propped up on a chair in his new saloon—all's right with the world—on a Sunday night, one of his favorite nights, when the music played for the musicians and the straight world slept. My trepidation melted away at the sight of him. In fact, he looked downright homey and folksy compared to anything else in my life.

I hung up my Ralph Lauren fleece-lined jacket inside an unattended coatroom and went to the bar, which, because it was early, was nearly empty. This place didn't heat up until much later. The first set wouldn't start until after ten. I looked around. The bar, tables, and chairs were oak with a natural stain—everything was light and serene. Michael had ingenuously designed it so there was a window instead of the traditional back mirror, through which, from your seat at the bar, you could see the entire live act in the auditorium directly behind it. Huge speakers hung on either side of the window. This way, you never had to pay for the music. Other than this sixties touch, I was impressed by how much Michael's new place was in tune with the times, which had begun to celebrate sophistication.

The bartender was a stranger. I ordered my Dewar's and was about to put my money up when the man sitting to my right, who was very drunk—head-rolling drunk—said, "It's on me."

I turned to be sure I had recognized the voice. Yes, it was 4-H Jimmy, wearing a suit, but deep in his cups. His normally pink face was flushed crimson. I had never seen him like that, either the suit or the advanced degree of drunkenness.

"Guess you heard what happened," he said.

"I did. I was worried about you."

"Nah, nah," he said, waving a hand around, his elbow still attached to the bar. "I'm cool." He tried to focus on me, but he was too drunk. "OK, Janet. Good to see you," he said, and turned away.

And then Michael was standing there, as though we might have just seen each other yesterday. "Jimmy's been through a rough stretch. He's going to be all right, give it time."

There was no reference to the past, no airy "Where you been?" Not that I expected any conventional greeting like that from Michael. But it was spooky, his simply picking up as if in mid-sentence, and furthermore without the hours of scrutiny, without the preliminary judgmental distance I had expected. Nor was a single courteous reference made to my now streaked-blond hair or any other aspect of the polished new me. But that would have been out of character. Michael had often leered approvingly if he found me to be looking particularly hot, but he would never allow himself to become sidetracked by the trappings. And now it seemed his feral, moonbeam eyes were gazing into me, and it seemed, if I could trust myself at all, as if he were honestly thrilled I was there—for him thrilled, that is. I mean, he smiled. In spite of the slightly crooked teeth he never liked to reveal, he smiled broadly.

"It's really amazing you're here tonight. I got a friend of yours booked to play. Wait till you catch this band, the Backbrains, they call themselves. They probably won't live long enough to make it, but they're good," he said to me.

"A friend of mine? Are you sure?"

"Sure I'm sure. That's how he got to me, through you."

"Who is it?"

"You'll find out."

"But who would I know with a band that had a name like that? It sounds like heavy metal, the Backbrains," I said.

"Nope. They got a New Wave beat, but a real rhythm 'n' blues sound, straight rock 'n' roll. Go round to the front room when they start. Tell Willie I sent you," he said.

I was still in love with him. Why did this surprise me—hadn't I pledged never to forget? But it did surprise me. I was in love with him afresh, and not my worn-out delusion of him, but the corporeal here-and-now Michael. He just got to me. There was no one else who had ever so completely swept the doubts from my mind. I revered his face, his hands, his walk, that small voice, like a shy boy's, hiding inside, and his sense of the absurd. I believed in him. He was the real thing, an existential being. I imagined that everything he did, no matter how inconsequential seeming, he did deliberately, completely consciously. His very existence was an epic, I told myself. In his absence, the silver notes escaped me; I had become not color blind, but blind to color's radiance and its intensity. Without him, life lost its savor. A wave of sweet relief poured over me. I had always loved him, I always would, the way some men love the flag or even the truth. The wrenching loneliness I experienced next came from the realization I would never get the chance to speak my feelings out loud. I didn't dare to entertain the thought that he might feel anything even glancingly similar for me. He was like Jesus, asking not whom he loved, but who loved him. All right then, I loved Michael, loved him well enough for both of us.

Later that night, Willie the ticket taker let me in the makeshift auditorium, pointing to the back rows. The room was pretty empty, though, so I moved up close. Three young guys were sprawled over their guitars, feet wide apart. A drummer was hammering out the four-four beat with the precision of a galley slave driver. The rhythm guitarist pulled his head up long enough to look at the few people scattered in the seats. His eyes were pinned, tiny dots. It was little Eddie, little Eddie Carnivale, or, as he called himself, Eddie Apollo—Evelyn's beloved son. All grown up now, obviously. He leaned over his Stratocaster, slung just low enough to cover his genitals, and hit a chord. He was hunched over, his head hanging like a gorged spider. But a lot of the time, he played fabulously, pounding out some terrific licks, while the cunning boy up front growled into the microphone. Before they could leave the stage, I was calling to him, "Eddie, little Eddie!"

"Yeah," he said, already bored by stardom, not even bothering to turn in the direction of my voice.

"Eddie, don't you remember me? It's Janet," I yelled to him.

He spun around and his face broke open with glee. He came bounding down the aisle, stopping a little way in front of me.

"Janet, man, you look gorgeous. What a doll. I never woulda recognized you. Not that you weren't a piece of work before. I know what's good, but shit, you are fine now.

"What's up? You wanna join me and the boys out front? Cocktails on the house."

"Sure. Michael told me you were good and you are. Really good. I'm proud of you."

"Michael?" Eddie lost it for a second. He was nodding and scratching his face. He rubbed his now close-cropped hair. Then he remembered. "Big Mike you mean? Oh yeah, nice guy. Knows music. OK, let me round up the rest of those lowlifes back there. See you out front. We got a lot of catching up to do. Not that you or I give a hoot about my folks, those losers—ever hear from my mom?"

"Yeah, sure. I talked to her not too long ago, well, maybe it was a couple of months, but sure, we're in touch. I really dig Evelyn."

"She's a loser. It's too bad, but she is. I got another loser tagging along with me tonight, my sister, Ava. She's fucking Cornelius. He's the lead singer. He's an asshole, too. A perfect match. But then, Ava would fuck a snake. You remember my sis?"

"Of course I do. She was just a kid then."

"She's still just a kid."

I went out front, where, in the middle of a chattering crowd, 4-H Jimmy was asleep with his head on the bar. Michael beckoned me over to sit with him. Michael seemed changed—less paranoid, or more open, or something.

"Little Eddie, Eddie Carnivale. I never would have guessed," I said as I sat down.

"What's he now, seventeen? Anyway, you better watch out for that guy. He's trouble. He's a nasty little junkie," Michael said.

"Michael, you can't be serious. Little Eddie? C'mon now, he can't bother me," I said.

Just then, little Eddie, sporting a porkpie hat, came over to where we were standing. His fellow musicians were straggling in behind him. On the arm of the lead singer clung a moon-faced young girl. It was Ava, who'd grown since I saw her last. She was all legs with a long neck and a body like a grander version of her mother's. Maybe she would be stunning someday soon. It was the just-hatched look that detracted. Her tangled hair hung loose down her back. She was wearing no makeup.

Eddie pushed her away from the singer, Cornelius. "Go sit down. I'll be there in a minute. He turned to us. "Don't pay any attention to her. She's a bimbo. The band can't shake her."

"She looks fine to me," Michael said, coming to her defense automatically.

"I wouldn't know, I'm her brother, but Cornelius tells me she gives good head," Eddie said.

"A very redeeming trait," Michael said.

Eddie asked me to join him again, but this time I declined. Michael had never seemed as accessible as he did that night. He was practically voluble. I wouldn't have risked losing his company just then for anything.

Love in the Afternoon

Felicity and I were hanging out in Ginger's room like little sisters watching their big sister get ready for a date. Ginger was dressing for Kenyon, her fiancé, who was picking her up for dinner and the theater. Her room across the way mirrored Felicity's; it was the same kind of prosperous young matron's boudoir with its canopied bed and curved and draped dressing table. Except, unlike Felicity's bed-room, there were mountains of clutter: papers and books piled ev-erywhere, clothes hanging out of drawers.

Ginger was seated at her dressing table, while Felicity and I were sprawled on top of her rumpled quilt on the king-sized bed.

"I guess I gotta go with understated. Oh, God, a whole bland life of understated ahead of me," Ginger said. She was always complaining about her impending marriage.

"Lots of tennis, though, and golf," Felicity said.

"Yeah, and fuck you, too. Listen, Janet, honey, would you do me a huge favor and look through that pile on the chair for the black silk dress and lay it out for me? I'm running so late," Ginger asked.

The phone rang and Felicity picked it up. She talked into it softly, as if she didn't want the two of us to hear.

"Who was that—Lionel?" Ginger asked.

Lionel was the horn player from the party. Felicity and he had been seeing a lot of each other lately.

"No, that was Gunther. You know Gunther, don't you, Janet?"

I knew Gunther all right. He was handsome—honey-blond hair down to his shoulders, deep-set hazel eyes, about six-two, and Aryan to the hilt, with the possible exception of his wide mouth. He had a slight overbite, a parrot mouth. One of the house's chief connections, he dealt everything: coke, hash, pot, pills, even my old-time favorite, crystal methedrine. Sometimes Gunther would hang out with us upstairs for an hour or so, but that was it; he never took anyone downstairs.

"Gunther must be having problems with his girlfriend, because he actually wants to do a trade—drugs for sex. What do you think of that? Here was one guy I figured couldn't be had...Wants to know if anyone is working late tonight. I told him I was going out, but that you'd be around, Janet, and I'd ask you," Felicity said.

"That man is going to *pay* me to fuck him?" I asked, practically reeling from my own good luck.

"So, it's on, then? I didn't think you'd object. I'll call him back," she said.

Kenyon and Gunther arrived at the same time. Felicity went downstairs to let them in, and they stood like two gentlemen callers in the parlor, waiting.

"How do I look?" Ginger asked me, primping in the mirror.

"You look all grown up, you look glamorous," I said.

When we came down, the two men were exchanging a few polite remarks about the weather. Kenyon held a bunch of long-stemmed roses in one hand. He was tall, with a shock of white hair, and he was impeccably dressed in a dark blue pin-striped suit. In spite of that name, Kenyon, and what Ginger had told me, I still expected a swinging, greasy kind of operator wearing gold chains, the kind who would think nothing of marrying a whore. But Kenyon Edwards was what his name suggested: a distinguished-looking WASP.

Once again, I found myself measuring this reality against everything I had ever been taught. Adults lied, I decided. While she was braiding my hair Josephine used to chant, "Whistling girls and cackling hens always come to no good ends."

Genuinely frightened, I stopped whistling.

Now here was a supremely eligible man choosing Ginger, who may have been an award-winning whore, but who was a whore nonetheless, and not even a particularly young or beautiful one at that. No doubt about it, when the grown-ups told me to "be quiet," "let him win," and "he won't respect you after," they had all lied.

Right next to Kenyon stood Gunther. He was wearing a black leather jacket and a pair of worn-out jeans, his long legs disappearing into engineer boots. His thick dark blond hair just grazed his broad shoulders. A perfect icon of a man. His eyes kept following me across the room; he was glaring at me like he was angry.

"Want a drink?" Ginger asked both of them.

"Thank you, yes," Gunther said.

"Bourbon and branch," Ginger said, nodding at Kenyon, and then she turned to Gunther. "What'll you have tonight?" she asked, going over to the wet bar.

"Vodka on the rocks, please," Gunther said.

I was listening to the delicate clip of his accent. Just another client, I kept telling myself, but I felt that my obstinately eager face was probably betraying me. I tried to act cool. We all sat down there in the big, empty room. Gunther and I had not exchanged one word. Felicity, Ginger, and Kenyon were doing the talking. Finally Felicity said, "Well, go on, you two."

"Which room?" I asked.

"The first one on the right—our best—nothing but the best for an old friend like you, Gunther," Felicity said.

I poured myself a highball glass full of scotch and led my john up the stairs. Inside the room, he went over to the windows and looked out on the street.

"How do you want to get paid, all blow—I've got Peruvian flake—or maybe you are into something else?" he said, not looking at me.

After a long deliberate abstinence, I surprised myself by asking without hesitation, "Do you have any crystal?"

"Oh, yeah, I thought so. You like crank. I knew that. So do I. Want to do a few lines now? This stuff is pure. I had to cut it myself to keep it from melting," he said.

"How did you know I like speed?" I asked. After all, I didn't look very much like a speed freak anymore.

"Because I know you. I've known who you are for years."

"Years?"

"You are a friend of Michael's from the Traveling Medicine Show."

"Yes, do you know Michael?"

"Who do you think sold him the methedrine that made you crazy? I am the one," Gunther said with obvious pride. "I etherized that batch in my bathtub."

I couldn't believe it. This gorgeous Aryan was the wizard who'd cooked up that stuff that drove me mad! It was meant to be.

"All this time...How come we never ran into each other back then?"

"Listen, I keep a low profile. But I've observed you over the years. You never noticed me. I was just another customer sitting at the table," Gunther said, his slight German accent making him sound like a cross between a modern-day drug dealer and a man who should be wearing a monocle.

While he talked, Gunther tapped out long lines of that same gooey white crystal I recognized. We snorted up the lines with a short straw. Bam, I got a rush. My teeth started to chatter. "This time I can handle it," I kept telling myself. We were staring at each other now with our big black pupils like two ghouls from hell. I sucked down my scotch. He polished off his vodka. Still no action.

"I don't go with whores, you know that," he said.

"What happened to change your mind?"

"I always wanted to sleep with you, a long time before you turned pro...And then I just caught my girlfriend in bed with my partner, Gabe, Michael's dealer," he said.

I knew Gabe and I couldn't understand why she would do that. Gunther was a lot better looking.

"Well, I can make you forget for a little while anyway," I said.

"Yes, how are you going to do that?"

"Let me show you how," I said.

He poured a couple of grams of methedrine into a glycine envelope and handed it to me.

"Come here," I said.

"No, you come here," he said.

I went over to him. He started to kiss me, and I let him, soul kisses, while he ran his rough hands over my body. He was angry. He held on to me and looked me in the eye.

"Let's get this over with," he said.

A few afternoons later, Gunther dropped by. Joey and I were working that day. Without any banter, without so much as a nod at Felicity, he said to me, "C'mon, then," and we were back in the same bedroom. This time was different. At first his stroke seemed almost tentative, like a blind man feeling my face. I remember thinking when he was inside, 'This one fits. I have to have him. I want to marry him.' But I had said that kind of thing to myself before, whenever I got carried away, and I tried to ignore it. In spite of all my efforts, good sex and marriage—sex and true love—were still inextricably linked somewhere in a hermetic recess of my mind.

Back Gunther came on Friday, and the following Monday, and he kept on coming. Felicity just chuckled and let us use a room. By this time she was madly in love herself with Lionel the horn player, so she was in the mood.

"I guess I'm running a matchmaking outfit," she said.

But Felicity only knew the half of it; that is, she only knew about my daytime love life. At night, after a short nap, I headed down to Slim's Wide Missouri. There I stopped at the bar on the first floor just to check out that still iridescent, outrageous scene. Slim had hung his by now (more often than not) famous patrons' work, most of it huge canvases, all over the long, narrow room with its high ceilings. The paintings represented his profits, because Slim could never resist running a tab for the artists who hung out at his bar, both before and after they made it. As a result, he was driving his business into the ground. And he could not bear to sell those paintings, even though it would have saved Slim's if he had. He looked to me like an underground freedom fighter with his hooked nose and fierce eyes partially obscured by a shock of hair. He had a way of stooping over (he was tall) to listen to whoever was talking, as if he were really interested, which betrayed his naturally kind nature. In the petty, mean-spirited, nickel-and-dime world that is the restaurant business, Slim's largesse stood out. He seemed to have banished the very notion of lunacy, treating his most psychotic regulars with the same respect Sardi showed for his Broadway stage luminaries. Like his customers, Slim lived for posterity. He wanted to be remembered as a patron, not as a saloon proprietor. His real dream had been to attract the writers away from Irene's uptown, but instead, he drew artists and then rock 'n' roll stars, and that was the end of it. The bourgeois literati were not about to mix with imbecilic rock 'n' rollers.

So Slim resigned himself and hired Michael to turn the upstairs into a showcase for new music, what would come to be known as "New Wave," later renamed "punk" by the mainstream press. It began right there at Slim's, with a band of heterosexual cross-dressers who called themselves the Starlets; with Letty Jones, the brilliant poet-turned–rock 'n' roll musician, and her backup band, Channel Eleven; and the Dumb Generation, a wonderful dysfunctional group that heralded the nihilism to come. Michael booked them all regularly.

But the pièce de résistance of Slim's was the crowd with a penchant for fame that had put the saloon on the map. It gathered every night in a room downstairs at the back. The habitués there belonged to the most celebrated cadre of gay men and fag hags since Oscar Wilde: this was Andy Warhol's crowd. They yelled across the room at each other, calling each other every kind of fanciful, obscene name, and gave each other blow jobs underneath the large, cafeteria-style tables. Once in a while, someone who also hung out upstairs would invite me into the back room. I had always felt sad and rejected by handsome young gay men. My impulse was to try to seduce them, but knowing I could never convert them, it hardly seemed worth it. What was wrong with vaginas? I longed to ask. Admittedly, heterosexuality seemed tame by comparison, and this troubled me. I couldn't really defend it. I would have loved to attach myself to such a theatrical scene, but I felt like an insignificant, dull-feathered heterosexual in their midst.

After the occasional obligatory look at the downstairs, I went up to be with Michael. Recently, the East Village chapter of the Lucifers had become regulars. The Lucifers was a motorcycle gang whose local leader had dropped acid with Allen Ginsberg and then disarmed his followers, turning them into peace-loving outlaws. In the process, this leader, Hank was his name, had taught the other gang members to be archaically polite. They were gallant, pulling out chairs and opening doors for the ladies. Hank was about to marry one of Slim's more illustrious painters' daughter. The approaching wedding inspired so much speculation, it sounded more like the Junior League some nights.

The rest of the upstairs crowd comprised the local tattoo artist; a few downtown drug dealers; a whole array of stoned musicians and the hangers-on who wrote about them; very often music-industry moguls and their scouts; bartender friends of Michael's, and a larger-than-ever coterie of waiting women. The energy of the music and the serenity of the surroundings made it feel as though we were flying at thirty thousand feet.

In spite of all that was going on, Michael was loyal to me. Except on those dreaded nights when he went home to Roseanna and the baby (but really, I used to tell myself, that was only to crash), he stayed close. The Lucifers with their own supply of methedrine; the musicians and the rich record company moguls with lots of good Peruvian flake, not to mention the dealers themselves: all of these factions cut severely into Michael's draw. But a few of the more marginal types still responded to his waning charisma. I served as his hostess whenever he did condescend to invite a Starlet groupie or a rejected dealer's moll to go home with him. On these occasions, he loved to take the young woman back to my sumptuous apartment, which he showed off as if it were his. Usually, though, when we were together, it was just the two of us. We spent many early mornings by ourselves, feeling as if we were the only two people left awake on the island of Manhattan. Michael took turns settling (naked) into one or the other of Whitney's mother's chintz-covered club chairs, or sometimes he would just lie on my thick pile carpet with his back against the bed and stroke the pile around him with admiration.

Alone a lot, and possibly a little bored, we turned ever more playful. Our format evolved. Michael discovered he liked to watch. We were explorers, marveling over the mysteries of the vagina. In particular, its elasticity impressed us. We experimented by seeing how many vibrators I could comfortably stick up there, along with his penis, which took its place next to the hard plastic versions inside me like an unspoiled little brother shoved to the edge of the bed. I can still see his face bathed in reverence as, squatting and stuffed with hardware, I smugly held the pose. But in spite of our best efforts, our sex life, burdened with all its paraphernalia—the dildos, vibrators, and recent addition of handcuffs and ropes—was getting perfunctory. Michael, so accessible now, with his potbelly, his gripes about his job, the hair that was beginning to peek out of his nose, had become too real.

In public I was peaking, enjoying a little fuss upstairs at Slim's because, partly thanks to my speed-fueled lectures on the subject, hooking had achieved stature in that circle. Right after New Year's, Felicity and Ginger had declared 1974 to be the Year of the Whore. They were planning a big gala in the spring, and I had given Michael one of their posters, which was a drawing of an elegant forefinger on a clitoris. Below it a caption read, "Ball in the Year of the Whore: We Want Everybody to Come." Michael hung it proudly next to the bar. But in the midst of the hoopla, this brave cultural scene, I often found myself feeling despondent, because my obsession was losing its hold. Brute reality was busting my old dream, and I felt like a fool. I felt deflated, particularly on those nights when Michael chose to go home to Roseanna.

On a weekend afternoon around Valentine's Day, Michael and I decided to celebrate by taking in one of those classic underground blue movies that were being made in the seventies. We thought several of these were pure art. We cabbed it to the Universe, the theater that featured all the most intelligent porn films. This one was called *The Opening of Misty Beethoven*, and as good art is supposed to do, it triggered an important revelation. The movie turned out to be cathartic. A takeoff on the Pygmalion story, it featured a world-class sexologist (played by a future legit movie actor) and a Pigalle whore. The story went like this: One night, the sexologist and a friend, dressed in tuxes, are sailing through the Pigalle district in their limo when the hero makes a wager that he can turn any one of the mangy streetwalkers outside the tinted window into a high-class call girl. The friend takes the bet, and they pull some poor, unwitting slut out of the gutter into their magnificent car. The sexologist teaches her not only how to talk, walk, and dress, as in the more pallid version, but also how to fuck, suck, and cater to, in one memorable scene, four men at once. All the while, the whore has been in love with her mentor, who continues to ignore her, until the last scene, when both are dressed for a ball and suddenly he realizes how beautiful she is. Then he gently undresses her and they make love.

The catharsis comes when we see the stark contrast between the irrelevant jerk-off sex that has preceded it and the tender, intimate lovemaking itself, which is the opposite of performance. In fact, the man barely seems to move inside the woman. A private connection, so private even the camera could not invade it, was happening before our eyes. Besides being intensely romantic, the movie delivered a powerful message, especially to me that day. I sat there in the dark next to Michael, surrounded by the other men with their hats on their laps, and I recognized in that final scene Gunther and myself.

"Oh, so that's lovemaking," I thought at the time, quite overcome with the realization. I was recalling how much Gunther thrilled to be inside of me, how much my every quiver reverberated through him. It was love then. Unlike what I felt for Michael, my attachment to Gunther seemed to spring from a different chakra, from the heart rather than the head. With Michael, things were loose. Our partnership had come to be characterized in those days by an absence of feeling, a painlessness, which suited us both. And I still felt the lingering presence of the mystic whenever we were together. I thought maybe he felt it, too. But Gunther's passion was the lure of the earth. His warmth made me hungry and it fed me, filled me up. I was curious to see where this mortal thrall would lead.

Even so, I refrained from admitting to myself that Gunther was eclipsing Michael. It would be like admitting Michael wasn't really my other half, or like choosing Dionysus over Apollo. And yet by this time Gunther had won the supreme place in my thoughts with no more than the uncomplicated power of kisses and hugs. After the first strained encounter, Gunther and I began to open up to each other and were talking and laughing. Before long, our meetings took on the intensity of rapture: with openmouthed kisses we sucked in the breath of our mutual adoration and exhaled it into the rarified air fragrant with sex. Our feelings were in charge, and we both knew it, although as yet no words to that effect had been spoken. Gunther turned out to be exactly the opposite of the icy Aryan I had thought he was—generous with his affection and warmth —hugging me, covering me with kisses, and spooning me in bed afterward. This was unfamiliar behavior—it did not feel at all like that groove of pain I thought of as love but I managed to withstand it. Felicity wanted to know why our affair hadn't progressed to my house. I gave him my home number, but still, Gunther resisted. The whorehouse served as a kind of shelter for him.

On a slow Monday afternoon, Gunther swung me in his arms around the disheveled whorehouse bedroom to the strains of violins emanating from his favorite Moody Blues album. When the heartrending operatic chorus came on, "But I love you...oh, how I love you!" he dipped me back as if I were the most precious bit of cargo and cover my bared neck with kisses. Ecstasy.

On Tuesday, I proposed.

"Gunther, do you need a green card?"

It was snowing outside, the last snowfall of the year. The street was dead quiet. The house was empty—no customers. He lay there on his back staring at the ceiling without answering me. I had the eerie sensation of not knowing where I was or what I was doing there, in this strange big room, not my home, with this strange man, not even my man. We were players on a stage. Nothing mattered.

"Gunther, I asked you: Do you need a green card?"

"I heard you. Why are you asking?"

"Because if you did, then I'd be more than willing to marry you for nothing. I'd do it for nothing," I said.

"My mother is American. I don't need a green card," he said.

I turned on my side and faced him as he lay there, his eyes still fixed on the ceiling.

"Oh, well, how about this. In less than four years, I'm coming into around forty thousand dollars from a trust fund. Will you marry me?" I asked.

Nothing.

"Think about it, OK?"

Ever since Corinne told me no decent man ever marries a whore, I had been plotting, on a subterranean level, to get married. I didn't at all like other people assigning me a permanent place outside the pale. I refused to be branded. I was a nice girl no matter what, and it was my birthright to marry a nice boy if I wanted and settle down—any time I wanted. Nothing bothered me more than the idea that society still defines a woman by experience. Once she sins, there is no redemption. In other words, I was supposed to submit to being condemned and ostracized for life. No different from biblical times, was it? I did not have the same freedom to change, to rise above my past, to learn from experience as a man did. Only if I were willing to disown it, keep silent, live a lie, perhaps then I could reenter society. This is what Corinne meant by "no decent man would ever marry me." I detested that notion.

But also, I asked Gunther to marry me because I had fallen in love. The gravity of what I had done impressed me. I had never proposed to anybody before.

"So, just think about it," I said.

"Hello, Janet?"

"Gunther, is that you? You're calling me at home. This is my house, you know that?"

"Yes, yes, I know that. Are you alone?"

"I was on my way out, but I'm alone now."

"Please, I've got to come over. The DEA is on my case. They busted everybody, my partner, everybody. They are coming after me. I need someplace to go for a little while where they can't call me anymore. I'm sick to death of the calling, calling. May I come?"

"Of course," I said.

When he got there, Gunther found me changed into an oyster-colored satin negligee, an item of clothing I have never been able to afford since, but there I was in it, smelling of Chanel No. 19. He took one look around my fancy digs, at the glittering bridge outside my window, and then at me, and he did a classic double take.

"Janet, what a woman you are," Gunther said, closing in on me.

We didn't get out of bed for three days, except to go to the door when food was delivered. In the middle of it somewhere he said, "The answer to your question is yes."

A Short Engagement

Married? I didn't want to get married. What had I been thinking? I would lose Michael forever! And he had promised to take me to Felicity and Ginger's Hookers' Ball, a night I had been anticipating like a high school girl for months. Now it would never happen. And the illustrious Tommy Shelter had been coming around lately, minus his bodyguard. He had actually phoned me once or twice. And the Life! How was I supposed to leave the Life? I surprised myself when I realized I didn't want to leave it, just as Corinne and everyone else had predicted.

The first thing I did, even before Gunther had left to retrieve his clothes, was call Corinne. She was amused.

"Remember, let him decide who to vote for. You just take the checks. Get a joint account," she said.

Gunther and I giggled. As if anybody voted. As if anybody had any checks. But we did have some cash, and that happened to be a good thing, because his business was through. He was too hot now. And I was never to work at my trade ever again. My romantic husband-to-be was rescuing me from all that.

I took Gunther up the Hudson to Cobb's Wharf to meet Rayfield and his fourth wife, Betsy. When my father saw how Gunther doted on me, he approved, as did Betsy. By this time, Gunther loved me openly with abandon. I hadn't expected it, but once we got engaged, a torrent of love worthy of Schubert lieder rained down on me. He couldn't keep his eyes or his hands to himself.

"He loves you so much," Betsy said to me, sounding a bit wistful I thought. Rayfield's idea of affection was a pat on the head, a gesture he also lavished most democratically on his horse, the dog, and their three Siamese.

The second time we went up to Cobb's Wharf, my father sat us down in his slightly shabby Yankee-WASP-style living room in front of the big stone fireplace. The walls were lined with musty books, and the room itself was dotted with ancient American antiques, nothing but family hand-me-downs, really, which were teetering under back issues of *Car and Driver*. The whole house smelled vaguely of cat piss and pine needles. It was banked with towering old trees in front and a full acre of sloping lawn in the back. You could see the river from the rear windows. Ever since Highcrest brought my father and I together, I used to love to take the train up to this house once in a while for Sunday dinner. I would just sit by the hour, listening to the grandfather clock and watching the crows fly. The ambience suggested a hard-won, unruffled peace.

Rayfield said nothing for a minute or two. He stood by the fire and poked a few logs around. Betsy sat with her long, elegant legs crossed on a modest-sized club chair. Gunther and I were perched side by side at the edge of the stiff Duncan Phyfe Edwardian sofa, facing my father.

"Betsy and I have decided to give you a proper wedding," he said.

Then Betsy spoke up, and I understood immediately how much of this was her doing. She believed that life is better with a man in it.

"I've already talked to the local Presbyterian minister. It's true, I'm lapsed, but he seemed to welcome the business. He can't marry you in the church, of course, but he agreed that the chapel would be fine, and it's just down the road. He's a jolly man. I think you'll like him," she said.

Gunther and I looked at each other. A chapel, a Presbyterian chapel? Rayfield caught our expression.

"I was married four times: twice by a judge and twice by a minister. Believe me, when the ceremony is performed by a minister, it carries a lot more weight," he said.

After he got over the initial shock, Gunther thought it was a great idea. So, it was decided. We made an appointment to meet with the Reverend Webb.

By this time, I was dying to call the whole thing off. The reason I didn't, even though I felt myself sinking deeper and deeper into the most outrageous lie, is because I did not want anyone to think that I was not "a man of my word," that I had no sense of honor. God forbid somebody might discover I was capricious. No, I had only proposed once in my life, and I was going to stand by it.

One day, Maggie called. I had stopped talking to her again, as I did so often, shortly after I moved away.

"Betsy said that you're getting married. The least you could do is invite me to the wedding, Janet," she said, sounding genuinely hurt and trying to disguise it with anger.

"I'm really sorry. I've been meaning to call. Of course you're invited."

"What are you doing for a wedding dress? I hope you're not planning to wear jeans," Maggie said.

"I hadn't thought about it."

"Well, in that case, I want to buy it for you," she said.

"OK, thanks, Mom."

"And what about the *Times*? We have to let the *Times* in on it, on account of who your grandfather was. Frankly, it never would have occurred to me, but Betsy and your father insisted," Maggie said.

"Fine, fine, put it in the *Times*," I said.

"I've got to know something about this Gunther. Where did he go to school? What does he do?"

"He didn't go to school. He's a drug dealer," I said.

"I should've figured," Maggie said.

When the announcement appeared that Sunday, Gunther and I had no idea whom the paper was talking about. It's true, I had attended Pendleton until it kicked me out, but Gunther was definitely not studying to become an engineer. He had no intention of becoming an engineer.

"Where'd you get that one?" I asked when I called Maggie back.

"Well, he's German, so I thought 'engineer' had the right ring to it," she said.

"Sure, makes a lot of sense," I said, feeling resigned.

"How *dare* you complain, when the whole thing was just *dumped* on me? I had to come up with something, didn't I?" she yelled through the phone.

Now that my mother had gotten involved, my engagement took on a peculiar aspect. I felt as if I'd been herded and trapped by all of them, as if my family and Gunther were conspiring against me.

The two of us, Maggie and I, went tearing up and down Madison Avenue, in and out of the tony shops, screaming at each other. Finally, defeated, I let her pick my dress. She settled on an overpriced faux naïf number in off-white. It was decided that the groom would be outfitted the same way, in an off-white, hand-embroidered shirt and off-white pants. Great, we were now going to be married in a Presbyterian chapel disguised as Mexican peasants. Well, everything considered, it seemed appropriate enough.

Betsy and Maggie sent out announcements and invitations far and wide. I felt oppressed and ashamed to be suddenly exposed to legions of relatives and family friends. Fancy gifts from Tiffany and Georg Jensen—things I felt that, being an imposter, I didn't deserve—were piling up unopened in the corner on the floor of my studio apartment. Often, I found myself gasping for air. I kept wishing that Gunther and I had snuck off to city hall, or, better yet, that we had decided to simply live together. It had gotten way out of hand.

The only bright note is that Felicity had decided to throw Gunther a bachelor party. A bunch of us was planning to leap on him and ravage his body. But Gunther didn't go for it. He was genuinely hurt.

"You're all I want, Janet," he said.

We killed the last week of our single lives awake on Gunther's notorious etherized speed, flitting from saloon to saloon, saying good-bye to all my old friends. Gunther had gotten it into his head that he was stealing me away from these people. He imagined that all the men were in love with me. I didn't bother to enlighten him.

One night, when we were both drunk as hell, I tried to call the whole thing off. First Gunther burst into tears, said he'd kill himself if I left him. Then, as if to emphasize his point, he slapped me so hard, it was almost a punch. I went flying across the tiny studio room, smack against the wall. After that, he cried some more. The next morning it was like it never happened.

Michael, in particular, had gone out of his way to befriend my fiancé, to emphasize that there were no hard feelings. He offered him work repairing the duckboards behind the bar upstairs at Slim's Wide Missouri. The two of them agreed that Gunther would start work there right after the honeymoon. Everybody on all sides was taking him into the fold. I was the only one, apparently, who harbored doubts.

Covenants

On the eve of our wedding, we crashed. That was a big mistake. If you've been up for five days, you're going to need at least two days to crash. It wasn't like we didn't know any better. We slept through the alarm, coming to at a little after eleven. We were supposed to be exchanging vows at noon. It took forty minutes up the Saw Mill River Parkway just to get to Cobb's Wharf. We had planned to change at Rayfield and Betsy's house and then march down the road to the chapel.

Panicked, we ran out of the apartment and jumped into Gunther's Volkswagen. Only after reaching Cobb's Wharf did we realize we'd left our wedding clothes behind. The simple solution was to hold the reception first, sans groom, while Gunther raced back, got the clothes, and returned in time for the ceremony.

Quite a few of the guests had already arrived and were sitting around waiting in the local historical society building, where they'd been told to gather before the wedding and where the reception would be held. Now I had to walk into that place alone. It was hell.

The German Jewish side of my family had commandeered the corner nearest the punch bowl. Next to them, but keeping a discreet distance, was my father's kin: children by former marriages, an unfamiliar cousin or two. Across the room sat Gunther's folks, all in a row. It seems that none of them were speaking to each other, let alone to strangers. His marine colonel aunt had chosen to wear her uniform. She looked out at the rest of us as if she were planning a dawn raid on the premises. Gunther's barmaid sister had come dressed for work in her uniform, too, a bright orange-and-black T-shirt with the words KARL'S PLACE: COLD BEER, WARM HEARTS scrawled across the front of it. Her five kids were running up and down, upsetting the chairs, throwing ginger ale at each other.

Then a limousine pulled up out front. A few of us went outside to see who it was. The chauffeur, whom I recognized, came around to open the car door. Into the hot sun stepped my grandmother. She leaned on the chauffeur for a second, taking deep breaths while she accustomed herself to the open air. After that, she rose to her full height, all five feet of it, and looked around. She was a miniature tiger of a woman. People stood back while she stared at them like the Empress of All the Russias surveying her troops. The chauffeur took her by the arm, led her inside, and pulled up a chair for her smack-dab in the middle of the room. The grand widow herself, in a powder-blue suit to match her eyes, and wearing a hat with a little veil, sat there casting withering glances at the rest of us. "Riffraff," I actually heard her say.

"Grandmother, how kind of you to come," I said.

"Wouldn't've missed it. Who are those people?"

"The groom's relatives," I said.

"I see," she said.

Meanwhile, her own children had gathered around and were falling all over each other to get her some punch and make her feel at home.

"Where is the groom?" my grandmother asked.

"We forgot our clothes. He had to go back and get them," I said.

"I see," my grandmother said.

All of a sudden, in blew my crowd, my bridesmaids. There was Corinne, wearing a very wide-brimmed chartreuse hat that nearly covered her eyes and one of her dated, flowing outfits that made her look like a well-fed Blanche DuBois. Right after her came the rest of the gang: Felicity, who had dressed appropriately in a beige silk pantsuit, and Joey, who had not. Joey was wearing a miniskirt that barely grazed her crotch. She looked as if she were hoping to pick up a little business sometime during the long afternoon. Behind them, Ginger, the dogged rebel in her tight linen dress and high heels, seemed to be hanging back, as if weddings were contagious. Unable to postpone it any longer, she was slated herself to get married in another month.

"Are these your friends?" my grandmother asked, staring at Joey.

I didn't bother to answer. "Is there anything else I can get you?" I said.

"I'm just fine, as comfy as can be," my grandmother said, with a vicious twinkle in her eye.

After I ran the gambit, I made a beeline for Felicity. "I need to wake up," I said.

"Felicity brought you some coke, and I've got a bottle of Jack Daniel's right here," Joey said, patting her big straw purse. "Don't worry, we're going to help you make it through."

"Is there someplace we can go? I'll turn you on," Felicity said.

But before I could load up on coke, which I sorely needed right then, Maggie made her entrance. She was already half in the bag. She walked right by me and over to the refreshment table, where the bowl of ice was melting in the by now intense heat. There was no air-conditioning in the Cobb's Wharf Historical Society building. The lettuce in the little sandwiches had wilted. Maggie picked up one of these and threw it down again. She poured herself some punch. Then she came up to me, glancing at Joey in passing.

"Leave it to the WASPs to make you suffer. Lousy punch. Where's Gunther?"

"He's coming," I said.

"That would be the best thing that ever happened if you got stood up at the altar." She looked over at Gunther's sister, who was yelling and shaking a dirty kid. "Who are those people? Oh, hello, Mother," she said, going over to where my grandmother sat surrounded by family.

"You've been drinking," Grandmother said.

"So what if I have? It's not every day your only child gets married."

The Reverend Webb came up to me. He was mopping his flushed, sweaty face with a white handkerchief.

"I have to talk to you. Would you join your father and Mrs. Chace in the corner over there?"

I followed him to where Betsy and my father were standing. They had grim expressions on their faces.

"As I explained to your father, I am afraid I won't be able to marry you now until around three this afternoon. You see, I have two other ceremonies scheduled today. June is my busy month, you understand. The next one will begin shortly; the other is at two," he said, looking at his watch.

Rayfield just shrugged his shoulders. "We'll have to try and keep everyone entertained until then. That's all we can do. I'll make an announcement," he said.

"I am so sorry for this big inconvenience, I am truly sorry," the Reverend Webb said. He shook our hands. Then he nodded at everyone and trotted out the door.

It was not quite one o'clock. The old room was stifling. My prissy little cousins had found Gunther's nieces and nephews. They were running in a pack, smearing each other's faces with food.

Rayfield went over to my grandmother and whispered something in her ear. Then he spoke to the room: "There is going to be a delay, about a two-hour delay, in fact. If anybody wants to go for a drive or something, that might be a good idea. One way to pass the time."

Nobody moved, except the kids, who by now were being ignored. My cousins' little white shirts and little pink dresses were covered with grease. They were all shrieking. Otherwise, silence, stone silence. It was really too hot to make an effort. People walked outside, seeking the shade of the big sycamores in the garden.

Finally, Gunther showed up. He walked into the hall and held our clothes, slightly wrinkled from the trip, high in the air.

"Here I am," he announced.

He looked radiant. Well, no wonder. The bastard had gone and gotten high on crank without me, I thought. Everybody clamored around him, as if somehow his presence were going to make it all right.

Grandmother took one look at him and started to grin. She loved handsome young men.

"Come here, young man," she said.

Gunther threw our clothes over a chair and then leapt to her side. "You must be Janet's grandmother," he said, taking her hand and kissing it in a way that I found unctuous.

But Grandma beamed. She was a sucker for that sort of con. "I think I like you. Please don't take it personally if I go now. I'm too old to sit here for the rest of the afternoon. Now that I've seen you, I can give you my blessing, and I can leave," she said.

"Well, I wish you would stay, but I understand," he said.

Of course, Gunther didn't understand; he couldn't. He didn't even know yet that the wedding had been postponed for two more hours, but he kissed the old lady's hand again. "An honor to meet you at last," he said.

"I have an idea. Are you handy around the house?" Grandmother asked.

"I could build a house single-handed, if I had the materials," he said.

"I thought so. I'm going down to Palm Beach early this year, in September, and I need a man around the place. Of course, there's Fritz, the chauffeur, and the old gardener, but I need someone to run things. I want you and Janet to join me for the winter. My house is beautiful, gardenias in the pool. What do you say?"

Gunther looked ecstatic. I knew what he was thinking: He'd be giving the slip to the two officers in the Drug Enforcement Agency who were still harassing him. He'd also be getting me out from under all my bad associations. Nobody was bothering to consult me. I was just the wife now. This was going to be even worse than I thought.

"I'd love it, and I'm sure Janet would, too. It sounds like one long honeymoon," Gunther said.

"A honeymoon in paradise," Grandmother said. "Janet, please go to the car and get Fritz. Tell him I'm ready to leave now."

On the way back, I grabbed my bridesmaids. "Let's get me changed. And let's, by all means, get me high," I said.

The rest of that day passed in a murky blur. I remember the men consuming the beer and the whiskey that Rayfield had supplied. They took off their ties and jackets and opened their shirts. My uncle Jack proceeded to get very loud. He was yelling at Maggie about something. She started to yell, too. Other people pulled them away from each other. A little while later, she came over to me.

"Janet, why isn't your father talking to me? What did I ever do to him, will you tell me that?" she said. She was good and drunk.

"I can't imagine," I said.

Betsy came up and steered her away."Don't worry, Janet, I'm going to suggest that your mother rest at the house for a little while," she whispered to me.

Gunther's sister went and laid her bulk down on the grass outside. The old ladies from the neighborhood whom Betsy had invited sat along the wall on the porch there in the sun and fanned themselves, shaking their heads in open disapproval. The kids were running in the road by this time. Nobody paid any attention to them. It was just too damn hot.

I avoided Gunther and instead spent most of the time hiding out with my friends on the second floor, where, ostensibly, they were getting the bride ready. I was getting ready, all right. I was snockered. They had to shovel coke up my nose toward the end so that I could walk a straight line.

When I finally got up to the altar, it occurred to me that Gunther was just as afraid as I was. Immediately, albeit temporarily, I felt reconciled to him. We were the only two people here in this particular circle of hell after all.

I couldn't look up above me, and neither could Gunther. We stood there, our heads bowed, feeling the eyes on our backs like hot branding irons. Everybody was expecting something big now after the long wait. I think the preacher sensed this. He stood there quietly, waiting for the crowd to settle down. Finally, he launched in by trying to read the John Donne poem I had given him, "The Undertaking." The lines I particularly liked:

If, as I have, you also do
Virtue attir'd in woman see,
And dare love that, and say so too,
And forget the He and She...

He mangled it. How could he have? "And forget the He and She." What's so difficult about that? It was as if the very sentiment of the poem itself were an anathema.

After that, he got on with the traditional ceremony, sermon included, which we had agreed to let him do—to keep in the spirit of the thing, we decided. But we had had no notion, not an inkling, of what that man was suddenly hurling down at us from his pulpit, the force of the Protestant Almighty behind him. He bellowed, he intoned, and then he let the silence of eternity descend on the gathering. As he did so, he raised his hand and looked over our heads as if he were saluting a platoon of avenging angels. Then he hit us not only with vows but with covenants. Loads of covenants we found ourselves making. The irrevocable binding weight of them smashed right through the gauze of booze and coke. It decimated Gunther's carefully crafted speed high. We started quaking. This fellow, the Reverend Webb, wasn't kidding, apparently.

When he finally finished, he abruptly shifted gears, as if he were coming out of a seizure. He leered at the two of us.

"Just kiss her, Gunther," he said.

The ordeal was over. The bride and groom, sweating in the heavy cotton of their Mexican costumes, and the drunken, disheveled guests stumbled outside once more into the scorching haze. Someone took pictures with a Polaroid. The kids began shrieking again until they were hauled off in cars.

It was over. Gunther and I spent the first night mainlining speed, something we rarely did, with our new set of honeymoon works in a motel on a traffic island in the middle of the New York State Thruway. Sheets of rain were drowning out the sounds of all but the biggest trucks. Where were we? I thought I had been taken hostage. I was spooked. When my new husband reached for me, I flinched.

"We can still make love, even if we are married," Gunther said.

But he had hit on it. I felt there was something obscene about having sex with a relative. For all of the next year that we stayed together, that feeling never left.

Casa Pacifica

"Janet, Janet, that was the second bell for lunch. I know you heard Katherine ring it. She came right out by the pool. I will not tolerate lateness. Gunther, you can stop work now and wash your hands. Luncheon is served," my grandmother said, standing in the doorway of the breakfast room.

I dreaded moving out of the sun to go inside and eat a heavy meal. But Grandmother lorded over us with the will of a white man in the jungle gone psychotic. From the day we arrived, Gunther had been reduced to little more than her zombie. I was the zombie's consort. Well, I had tried to tell him, but he didn't get it. He thought that family is family.

Now he was swooning in the late-summer semitropical sun, trying to finish the wall-to-wall bookshelves so that he could go on to the next big task, retiling the kitchen floor. He was working in the shade of the patio adjacent to the pool. I lay nearby, occasionally breaking to swim among the gardenias floating on the calm turquoise surface. Even if Gunther had had the leisure time to dive in with me, he was a weak swimmer, pounding the water with flailing fists. So he spent the mornings hammering and sawing inside the patio, his hair wrapped up in a red bandanna, the sweat pouring off his face and down his T-shirt.

Palm Beach, and Casa Pacifica in particular, never failed to bring home to me that the ultimate luxury is misery. To feel nothing but despair in these lush surroundings appointed with such marvelous lapidary touches of exquisite beauty—from the hidden statues in the tropical orchard, to the giant koi lazing at the bottom of the man-made waterfall, to the hand-painted mosaic tiles on the wide front stairs—was the limit of self-indulgence. All the more because there was no one in the world to pity me. If I cried out in anguish, no one would emerge from behind the beach plum trees surrounding the pool to comfort me. Rich people, or even poor people surrounded by riches, are not entitled to feel pain. But in spite of the sensual intensity, in spite of the elaborate melodies of exotic songbirds and the host of fragrances and colors competing for my attention, I had plunged into a torpor of self-loathing.

The three of us sat at one end of the long glass table in the breakfast room, while Katherine scurried back and forth with the obligatory courses: cold lemon vegetable soup, cheese soufflé, salad, finger bowls, and melon balls for dessert.

"Don't you think Janet would look better with her hair off her forehead? Even girls who are not great beauties should at least show their intelligence, if they have any," Grandmother was saying by way of conversation. "And while we're on the subject, I think it's high time you got a haircut, Gunther. Only factory workers wear their hair long like that; company presidents do not. Don't you want to be someone?"

"Yes, madame," Gunther said. He had begun to address Grandmother as "madame" the way the servants did.

"I'm so glad you agree with me. I'll call Roberta at Elizabeth Arden and get her over here this afternoon. I wish Janet responded to suggestions as amenably as you do, but unfortunately, Janet is just like her mother, difficult. Well, you'll see. I hope you won't always give in to her," my grandmother said.

I was sitting right by her side, but she often referred to me as if I weren't there.

The sunlight bounced around the glass-enclosed room, flirting with the yellow roses in the wide vase in front of us and shining directly in Gunther's eyes. He shielded them and looked at me apologetically. He could not defend me. Gunther was overwhelmed, had been so since the moment we arrived.

"My Gott, *scheiss*! It's so beautiful. My Gott, Janet," he said, walking around in a circle when we got there, staring up at the cathedral ceiling that soared high above the giant living room. I ran up the hand-painted tiled steps to the balcony, where I stood looking down at him.

"Janet, Janet!" he yelled. "You are my princess, you know it? My princess!"

Grandmother joined Gunther in the living room.

"I'm glad you like it here at Casa Pacifica. We think it's beautiful, too." Then she called to me. "Janet, you're not to go in your usual room. I don't want you staying in the big house. Too much work for Katherine. Besides, I'm saving the guest rooms for guests. You and Gunther will share the apartment with Fritz over the garage."

I wouldn't have minded sleeping over the garage next door to Fritz, the chauffeur, if grandmother had not treated Gunther and me the same way she treated her servants, which was lousy. I mean lousy.

Right after we settled into our tiny room with the linoleum floor, the clumsy, protruding wardrobe, the noisy fan and the creaking double bed, the old woman presented Gunther with a page-long list of jobs he was to do. I protested, but Gunther was stoic.

"Janet, that is no way to talk," he said.

"She is my flesh and blood, you know," I reminded him when we were alone again.

"Nevertheless, we have to make the best of it. Don't create trouble. Kiss me now. We're together."

He tucked my head underneath his chin, where it did fit rather nicely we had discovered, and held me there.

"I love you so much," he said then.

Right after lunch, Grandmother arranged for Roberta to drop whatever she might have been doing and come over to cut Gunther's hair. At least we wouldn't have to go out "motoring" with the old woman in the powder-blue Lincoln Continental, the three of us squeezed in the back, Fritz driving up front, with all the windows shut and no air-conditioning because she detested drafts. Roberta could have put hot straws underneath Gunther's fingernails for all I cared; at least I was escaping that.

As it turned out, Roberta did a smashing job, layering Gunther's honey-colored waves so that they framed his dreamy face. He could not have looked more handsome. When we walked down Worth Avenue later that same day, a rich young matron stopped him on the street. Would he mind helping her with her packages to her car? I was left standing there while he went off with the woman, into the store and back out again, in and out. I was in a rage, chiefly because Gunther was so oblivious to his own power to attract. He just thought he was being a gentleman, until the moment, of course, when, he later told me, she asked for his number while they were leaning, heads together, under the hood of the open trunk.

Meanwhile, I was already mad at him for other reasons. Before we came down to Casa Pacifica he had made me give up my Sutton Place apartment and return every stick of Whitney's mother's furniture to Whitney, who had to fly east to retrieve it. Now we were stuck at Casa Pacifica with no place else to go. I didn't like feeling as though a big chunk of my recent past had been confiscated and since disappeared without a ripple. I managed to hang on to my clothes, but Gunther claimed the furniture and the Sutton Place apartment would be constant reminders of the Life, which all of a sudden he wanted to obliterate. Gunther had assumed a different role now that we were married. I was his wife now: *his wife*.

If it were not for the satisfaction it would've given my grandmother, I might have left him the first month after we arrived in Palm Beach. My love for my husband was dying. Still, I felt bad for him, and I blamed myself. Meanwhile, obviously frustrated and confused, he withdrew from me—wouldn't say peep a lot of the time. Or if he did, it was just to snipe at me. Once or twice, he got as capricious as a big bad cat and cuffed me on the back of the head. I said something like "fuck you" then; I still wasn't out-and-out afraid. All I knew was we were no longer allies. The only experiences we openly shared were our drunken nights.

We decided to use the time in Florida to clean up, with the exception of alcohol, of course. After all, liquor was legal. We wanted to kick the other stuff, the speed and the coke, the quaaludes, the reefer, and the hash. But because booze was still OK with us, on our first free afternoon, we took the Volkswagen over to West Palm Beach and, using the last of our wedding money, loaded up on a case of scotch, rum, and vodka. The problem was, since we shared the garage-apartment kitchen with the not entirely trustworthy Fritz, we had to find places to hide all the bottles in our small bedroom. Also, we decided, we were going to have to learn how to drink moderately and quietly. At first, we managed to do that, sipping a cocktail or two before dinner and maybe taking a quick snort before bed. In the beginning, Gunther was so exhausted he usually didn't even want a drink at the end of the day. I did, though. I would sit by myself in the cast-off old armchair underneath the window, gazing at the blotchy stars, swigging scotch from the bottle.

One night, Gunther and I, Katherine, and the cook, Marie, stood in the driveway waving to the Lincoln Continental as the taciturn Fritz drove Grandmother to a dinner party the toothpick heiress was throwing. Everybody would be there, and although Grandmother had little use for the vapid rich widows who ran this town, she loved to see what they were wearing, the bugle-beaded gowns and chinchilla wraps, the face-lifts and the waxed bony knees. Grandmother, a suffragette, didn't even own a pair of high heels, short as she was. Her idea of dressing up was to put on her floor-length white silk *schmatta* that Katherine had made for her and a little pink lipstick. But she did adorn herself with her sapphires on these occasions. She was not that big of a prude.

Dusk settled over the tropical orchard. Before he left, Fritz had turned on the spotlights, which focused on the web of roots at the base of the banyan tree, the fronds of the traveler's palm, and the masses of orchards surrounding the silver water in the long pond at the bottom of the dormant waterfall. The spirits of the woods were being summoned to the footlights. Katherine and Marie retired to their rooms behind the kitchen in the main house to pray silently, privately, on their knees. Gunther and I went back to the garage, where we filled up a big soda bottle with rum, laced with a splash of Coca-Cola.

The night was ours. We came back to the orchard, sat on the swinging bench by the water, and took turns with the rum. In the darkness, birdsong gave way to a wall of sound charging out from the crickets and the tree frogs. There was nothing crawling around or flying in the air. All the salamanders had disappeared with the sun, and there were practically no insects, too close to the ocean. In a moment like this, I could admit that the sheer comfort of this queerly stagy version of the outdoors, a little patch of manicured jungle, had always suited me. I thought Casa Pacifica, and especially the orchard, was supernaturally beautiful. From earliest childhood, I compared this place with the hill my WASP father's family owned in New Hampshire, and while I was quick to acknowledge that the other rugged country was the real one, the authentic country, it did not otherwise appeal to me any more than this. In fact, even when I was blue, I had come to prefer this spot, this construct of heaven, to any other on earth. When I was still a child, feeling slightly guilty for choosing the dulcet-toned Palm Beach over the harsh, bright mountains, I reasoned that if I were a fairy, for instance, I would have automatically chosen to haunt this twinkling, enchanted wood, this ineffable mixture of electric light and moonlight.

Gunther did not seem at all to fit here. He got up from the swinging bench and began to roam. Like some poor Caliban who had lumbered unbidden into the territory, he scrounged around looking for evidence of the world as he knew it. He found a scrap of paper, a broken gardening tool, a cigar butt. Each one he held up, saying, "Aha."

"Come here," I said to him, patting the bench.

"No, you come here," he said to me, laughing.

It was a reference to our first encounter, our little private joke now. But he did join me on the swinging bench. We began to nuzzle each other, then paw each other. Finally, giddy now, Gunther and I stripped naked. We ran around, skirting the spotlights. I pretended to chase him, laughing louder than the crickets. When Grandmother and Fritz came home promptly at ten thirty, they discovered us lying in the missionary position under the banyan tree, on the dark side, but the soles of Gunther's feet were caught in a spotlight.

The car door slammed and we scrambled apart, taking refuge against the wall at the back end of the orchard. We were still naked, having shed clothes all over the place, so we just stood there, covering ourselves as best we could with our hands, while we watched the old woman pick her way in and out of the lights. She stopped about ten feet in front of us, holding on to the trunk of a kumquat tree, shaking all over. Then she let go and began to thrust her fingers in wild, stabbing motions through her upswept hair.

"I will not have it. I will not have it," she said. "Janet, you are the embodiment of evil."

She turned and stomped out of the orchard. We had crouched down, where we now remained, giggling.

"It's not like we're not married. What's the big deal?" I said.

But the next morning, when Grandmother emerged in public at about eleven, after her usual breakfast in bed and a bath, she marched over to the patio to tell us that we would have to go if she ever caught us in flagrante again.

"You must think of the servants. It won't do. I can't harbor a pair of animals in this house," she said.

"I'm sorry, madame, I don't know what came over us. It won't happen again, I can promise you that," Gunther said.

And it didn't, nothing like it. We were trapped, hemmed in by dinner bells and airless car rides, Fritz snoring next door, the interminable round of stifling days and nights with no release. We would have left on a dime if there were anyplace to go. The more oppressive it got, the harder it became to think of a way out. Gunther couldn't take it. He began to drink more, to sneak it in the morning, too, sometimes. One Sunday, when everybody was off at church, except for Grandmother, who was resting on the balcony after her facial, Gunther started to slap me around our bedroom. I forget what we had been fighting about. We were always at each other by this time.

"You are a little whore," he said calmly as he whacked my face with the back of his hand.

"Fuck you!" I screamed, and spit at him.

"So, you want to play?" he said.

Then he punched me. I fell clean off the bed onto the cold linoleum floor, where he began kicking me with the toe of his engineer boot around the kidneys, across the small of my back and on my behind. But I sensed by the way he paused each time to take aim with his foot that he was still in control of himself.

'He won't kill me,' I kept thinking.

In spite of the fact that I was getting kicked hard by someone who was a foot taller and outweighed me by seventy pounds, it didn't hurt, because I was too afraid. My body went into, if not actual physical shock, then some equivalent state of numbness. And the crescendo of rage that was triggered inside of me with every jolt up my spine was a relief. I actually felt grateful.

'Finally, I can leave you, you son of a bitch, you motherfucker. That's it. I can get out now,' I almost said out loud.

After what seemed like a very long while, he said, "You're disgusting," and walked out of the apartment, slamming the rickety screen door behind him.

I threw all my clothes in the big suitcase, pulled it down the stairs and out onto the street. I dragged the thing a mile into town. My eye was starting to close, I could feel it. People stared at me from their cars, but no one on that Palm Beach boulevard stopped, needless to say. I kept trudging along through the heat that was coming off the sidewalk at me in waves. When I got to a phone booth, I called Rayfield and told him the whole story.

"Don't worry, I'll wire you the money to come home. Do you have a place to stay in town?" he asked me.

"Yeah, Mother's I guess. Or no, this time I think I can bunk at a friend of mine's. Anyway, I'll be fine as long as I can get out of here. It's hell, Dad," I said.

"I know, I know. I thought the whole idea of Palm Beach was a bad one from the start. I'll call your grandmother and tell her what happened. You'll be all right. Just take the first plane you can get, darling," he said.

It was the only time I could remember that my father had ever called me "darling." His sudden tenderness took me by surprise. I started to cry.

"I never hit a woman, you know."

Silence.

"Go to Western Union now. It's going to be all right, don't worry. Well, good-bye, pet."

The marriage was over; I had my father's blessing. No one could blame me. Oh, thank God. I wasn't mad at Gunther anymore, not at all. Instead, I wanted, deep in my gut, with all of my aching body, to tell him I was sorry.

The Mohican

Rayfield sat across from me in the dark barroom dressed as always in a turtleneck, this one light beige cotton. He hadn't had a tie on in decades. He was a stubborn misfit. But, as always, with his silver temples and his black arched eyebrows, he managed to look distinguished. We were down in the fish restaurant in the tunnel at Grand Central Station eating our supper at breakfast time, around ten, because we were both on what they call the lobster shift, he at his daily newspaper where he worked nights as an editor, and I as an employee at the Sultan's Retreat, the best massage parlor New York City had to offer. My father, oblivious to the hot May day above him, ordered his usual, a wintry oyster pan roast, while I stuck to the raw ones. I let him pick them for me; he knew them all—the Chesapeake, the Golden Mantle, the Wellfleet, two of each. I piled horseradish and hot sauce on top and sucked them down, trying and failing not to eat them too fast.

But I was hungry. Busy night at the Retreat. A small band of coke smugglers who came up from Florida about once a month and took over the joint had descended the night before. They were gorgeous outlaws. My favorite customer was the wiry, intense leader. The two of us soared on his high-quality cocaine all night long. From the minute this pirate walked into the waiting room and nodded silently in my direction until my shift ended hours later, there was no way to distinguish it from an abiding passion, except for the wad of cash he threw at me up front. This time, we broke away from the orgy in the Karma Sutra Suite. He pulled a massage table out of one of the small trailers. The two of us on wheels, sailing from one end of the long, empty corridor to the other, banging against the red flock walls as if we were on a bumper-car ride.

I sat ramrod straight, sipping my Bloody Mary, buzzing, as usual, maybe slightly more than usual. My father chose to ignore the frenzied light in my eyes, or if he did notice, he simply thought I was full of energy. The only kind of high he knew how to detect was drunkenness. So his perky daughter, just as bright as a shiny penny, was not stoned by his definition.

I think my father had a pretty good idea of what I was doing. He let me know that reading porno and watching blue movies around Times Square were secret hobbies of his. I didn't really approve of my father. I didn't approve of him tacitly approving of me to be exact, but that's the way it was. I would bait him, tell him secrets, try to get a rise out of him in a futile attempt to turn him into a normal American dad.

"Don't worry, you and I will never make love," he once said, his green eyes jumping with tiny lights, revealing that the thought had obviously occurred to him.

I was the one who invariably ended up shocked.

That morning, I told him I could no longer meet him like this, because the place where I worked had changed my shift. I was being promoted to the ten A.M. to six P.M. slot.

"I'll miss these breakfasts of ours," he said, banging his unlit Player's Navy Cut cigarette against the edge of the table.

"Oh, me, too. After this when I see you in Cobb's Wharf, I guess we'll have to revert to our father/daughter roles."

We sat there for a moment.

"Say, Pop, tell me something. I just don't get it, you know, why people put up with it, why they keep trying to organize themselves into these little constricting units—one man, one woman, babies. Why? I mean, what are they after? I mean, Pop, I just don't get what it's all about, the whole family thing."

"The truth is neither do I," he said.

When he answered me, he looked deep into my eyes, as if his intention were to bore a hole through the bewildering muck of civilization, as if to acknowledge that, finally, we were no longer strangers.

Michael had welcomed me, this time without any hesitation. It didn't occur to me that he might have been upset by my marriage. I wouldn't fully understand that until later. In the meantime, I delighted in how openly glad he seemed to have me back again.

The scene had changed during the time I was married. I started out freelancing at a few of the larger cathouses, but massage parlors were all the rage just then. It was Michael, naturally, who suggested that I case massage parlors for a steady job, especially the Sultan's Retreat, the one with the best reputation. And Michael was also the one who, treating me like an escaped refugee after my hasty return from Palm Beach, right away found me a place to live. He turned me onto a residential hotel, a few blocks north of Slim's Wide Missouri, called the Mohican, which was a poor man's Chelsea, if that's possible, a rotten, falling-down old thing that cast its lurid shadow like the shameful block-buster it was over the neighboring town houses right on Gramercy Park.

I took a suite of two rooms and a bath on the seventh floor. From both my windows, I could see the squareheads trotting around the park's tall iron fence, exercising themselves like apartment-house dogs. The inside room held on to the remains of a kitchen, while the other room was furnished with a club chair, its stuffing long since ground into dust; a sagging double bed; and a funky bureau with a cracked mirror hanging above it. I draped blankets across the windows to block out the sun and brilliantly shaded paisley silk scarves someone had given me over the bedside lamps, and I was home.

Now Michael had two of his women conveniently housed at the Hotel Mohican. The other contender, and moving up every day it seemed, was, of all people, Evelyn's daughter and Eddie's little sister, Ava. She had matured some, but she retained a doggedly passive air, as if she were an amused child watching the silly grown-ups. She said very little. At the same time, Ava possessed her mother Evelyn's earthiness. She had a wry sense of humor, a way of laughing at human folly that made her seem much wiser than her years. I can't say I ever resented her presence. On the contrary, I invited it, because all three of us reveled in play. Our threesome was Euclidean —a balanced, even plane —an equilateral triangle that floated through the night. Together it seemed as though, like black magicians, we could defy gravity. We read a translated version of Baudelaire ("Be Drunk") and William Blake. "The road of excess leads to the palace of wisdom" was one of Michael's favorite bits of poetry, while mine was from "The Question Answered":

What is it men in women do require?
The lineaments of gratified desire.
What is it women do in men require?
The lineaments of gratified desire.

We took turns reading out loud, hovering close to the sultry light of the paisley-scarf-covered lamp like children around a campfire, a prelude to the elaborate sexual concoctions Michael would cook up to keep us entertained.

Michael had gotten hold of a Polaroid camera. He usually preferred to watch us and take candid snapshots than to actually participate. This is perhaps why no one felt left out. Ava and I experimented. I climbed on her. She was big and sturdy, her body a pale tabula rasa, her limbs immobile as she lay loose but inert underneath me. Her pleasure was secret, her orgasms still private in spite of the circumstances. I understood why so many men loved girlish modesty. Ava was sweetly obliging, easy to use.

On my days off, we convened at my place, because I was the parlor boarder. My apartment looked out on Gramercy Park, and my bed was the newest. But four days a week, my lobster-hour shift prevented me from joining them, and I was so preoccupied with my work at the Sultan's Retreat, so intent on doing a good job, I could easily ignore the fact that Michael might be on the floor below with Ava. He'd burn out on the youngster soon enough was how I figured it.

Then I started working the day shift, while it was Ava's turn to work the lobster shift at an all-night coffee shop in the East Village. Michael and I found ourselves awake and alone yet again. He would spread my grandmother's thirty-year-old abandoned silver mink coat over the dusty club chair, which he pulled close to the bed so he could prop his feet up. I lay on the bed naked and he sat nearby naked reading magazines. It was a study in fur, the mat of black hair on his chest framed by the silver mink. Every so often, he would wriggle his behind deeper into the chair, as if he were sticking it to my grandmother.

We were constantly surrounded with music coming through the two big speakers right next to us. I can still remember that we were listening to Bob Dylan's *Blood on the Tracks*, in which finally he had become so musically and lyrically sophisticated, he tore himself out of the genre he loved. Joni Mitchell's disillusioned silver siren voice, Van Morrison's aching, melodic poetry, Al Green's songs of innocence, Tom Rush's expressive ballads, and, of course, always, out of loyalty, we listened to the Rolling Stones, who were currently in a slump, stuck in the shallow end of the genre they were pretending to disdain. Taken together, this music was our private swan song, a lyrical farewell to an era, because every night at Slim's the piercing death rattle took over. Not that we didn't love the final rush, that last burst; it could be argued that the New Wave produced some of the finest music of all. But the righteous anger and the anarchy portended the death of the underground. It was a gasp, a spasm of defiance. And when the final set was over, Michael and I preferred to retreat to the bosom of old time rock 'n' roll.

Music was not a casual, in-the-background kind of pastime. We listened to a few albums at a time over and over for days, until the melodies and the lyrics had sunk in far enough to become the medium through which we experienced the world. Michael never stopped seducing me; I don't think he knew how to stop. The songs we played were love laments. There was always the promise of love hovering around us. It had me confused; my head would sometimes unexpectedly jam up with the static of thwarted desire, and I would have to talk myself down. "This is all there is," I would have to tell myself.

Inside the sound, we were silent, unafraid to sit awake saying nothing for hours. I thought it was the essence of revelry, this deliberate exclusion of the outside world. Like every room Michael inhabited, the old one at the Mohican was hallowed. As high on speed as ever but more reverently now, that is to say more cautiously high, I would eventually drift into an alpha state, at last free from the noise of my mind.

But along with the serenity, there was a dead-in-the-water sense to the time we spent together. Occasionally, I found myself feeling embarrassed for both of us, the nights were so pointless. Very often, we did not even bother to have sex. Once in a while, he dragged out a vibrator, or on occasion we did make love, our no-surrender version of love, but it was more for something to do than anything else. Early one morning, I became preoccupied with the troubling thought that we were the ones who were played out. I decided, after much agonizing, to talk about it. I pulled myself up on the bed, covered myself with my kimono, and crossed my legs underneath me. Then I leaned over slightly toward Michael, who sat facing me in his mink-lined chair, and I asked him what was wrong between us.

"You know what the problem here is? You don't think I feel any pain," he said abruptly, as though he had already given the subject a lot of thought.

"OK, I admit what you're saying is true. You're sort of a father figure to me, so of course, I won't let myself think of you as vulnerable or hurting. Too scary. You're supposed to be invincible, and I know that's probably a strain."

His silence seemed to confirm this.

"But I mean, what is it you're trying to say here? Are you hurt? By me? I can't believe it. What did I do?"

"Why don't you think about it and get back to me."

"Why don't you tell me, for God's sake?"

"I would think it's obvious, Janet."

"Well, it's not. Meanwhile, Michael, while we're on the subject, you always do know when I feel pain. That really is obvious because I don't know how to hide it, but since when did you care? It was never about how I felt. And after I married Gunther, it got worse."

"Did you want me to wait around?"

"What is that supposed to mean? Have you left me?"

"In a manner of speaking, yes. I'm already gone."

"I hadn't noticed."

"You will one of these fine days, you will."

"Are you leaving me, Michael?"

"Were we ever together, Janet?"

"Yes, I mean, OK, it's an unconventional relationship, but it does exist. What am I saying? Of course we're together, practically every night. And I want us to stay together."

"Then why did you get married? Why did you become exclusive—exclude me? I never would have done that to you."

"I had no idea you cared one way or the other. I had no idea you even missed me."

"I'd rather have someone put a gun to my head than to hear them say 'I love you.' Owning is the opposite of loving as far as I'm concerned. But what happened in this case is you cut me out altogether. You made yourself inaccessible."

"Haven't you ever done anything like that?"

"No. I have never done that."

"What about Roseanna and the baby?"

"What about it? She wanted to have the kid. I couldn't stop her. Anyway, nothing changed. I didn't marry her, did I?"

"But my marriage is over now. Tell me we can survive—OK, OK—survive my mistake. Because, really, I can't imagine life without you."

Silence.

"Michael?"

Silence again.

"Maybe we're like one of those patchwork quilts they just keep adding pieces to," I said.

"That'd be quite a patch job."

One evening, I came home to find Michael still in my suite where I had left him that morning. He was on my bed with Ava. They were rolling on the ancient, greasy bedspread with their arms around each other, locked in what looked like a desperate kiss. They were making out, something I had often reassured myself Michael didn't know how to do anymore. When they saw me, they sat up abruptly like two kids who had been interrupted by their mother. Then Ava stretched out and sunk down onto one elbow. She lay there facing me, her long brown hair parted like two sides of a wavy shawl, falling in tresses over each bosom. Michael was right behind her, also on his side, framing her. His own dark hair, still long, hung wet and loose about his shoulders. Right then I felt hot tears on my cheeks that came out of nowhere. I wanted to give them my blessing; it seemed as if they belonged together. Ava had a particularly implacable look on her face, as if she were saying, *Keep away: he's mine.* And the message that came to me from Michael was plaintively clear: *Please let me go.*

Island of Women

It was Tall Ships Day, the long-anticipated bicentennial on the Fourth of July 1976. My coworkers and I were sitting around freezing in the too generously air-conditioned receiving room of the Sultan's Retreat, still the most prestigious massage parlor on the Upper East Side. I was spacing out on the red-on-red velveteen wallpaper, a gold sateen pillow propped over my bare stomach to keep warm. Other girls were watching the giant boats sail up the Hudson on the tube. It was, as always, dark inside the massage parlor. The bright blue sky outside flickered live on the screen. There was no business, but the girls were not discouraged.

"Look at those hot pieces raggin' in the wind," one of them, Penny, said, pointing to a medium shot of a man hanging off a jib. "Any time now, I'm going to be rubbing that sailor's cock, any time."

"This place gonna be overrun, overrun. I can feel it in my clit," Molly said.

"Listen, kids, I don't know how to tell you this, but those guys aren't coming in here," I said.

"Why not, they're sailors, ain't they? Don't we always get the ships in here? Look at 'em, hundreds of 'em," Lorelei said.

"Yeah, but you're not going to see them in the flesh," I said.

Nobody paid any attention to me. They just kept gaping at the set.

"Man, I got me extra rubbers. I'm up for this. Bu'ness been slow as a dry turd lately. C'mon, boys, c'mon down," Penny said.

"I'm telling you to forget it," I said.

"Since when are you such an expert?" Molly said, turning her milky-white body over so that she could curl up in the corner of the couch. It was cold in there.

"You don't have to be an expert to know they're not those kind of sailors," I said.

"Sailors is sailors," Cleo said.

A chorus of "yeahs" and "right ons" followed. I wasn't getting through. I decided to drop it.

We could have been a troupe of June Taylor dancers on a break, all fifteen or so of us outfitted exactly alike in our halter tops, diaphanous sultan pants, and spike heels. But one look around the big anteroom, its red flock walls lined with gold sofas covered with waiting women, and you'd have to notice the variety. Each one of us was a different type. Pretty clever on the part of Max and Sam, the two managers, the way they had stocked their stable, something for everyone.

We were all white, except for Cleo and Jasmine, who was Puerto Rican.

"It's what the traffic will bear," Max said matter-of-factly.

The Sultan's Retreat might very well not have employed any women of color, at least in the daytime, seeing as how neither one of the managers had to answer to either the law or a liberal conscience, but Cleo was too good to pass up. She was probably the classiest whore in the place. Her hair was always perfectly coifed in a relaxed, soft flip, and her skin was her trademark. She was constantly swabbing her legs and her arms with perfumed lotions. Cleo could also be depended upon at some point during the long afternoon to deliver a lecture on nutrition. She knew exactly what wicked foods would block the colon, as well as what best promoted white teeth, shining eyes, and supple joints. As for Jasmine, she compensated for her Indian-brown skin by behaving at all times like the decorous lady. She was the only one of us who eschewed foul language, even referring to the johns as her "clients."

My best friend's name was Anita. She pronounced it "Anida." She was a gorgeous young Irish-Italian woman from Bedford-Stuyvesant, a real lowlife from a long line of lowlifes, easily the most popular one in there, besides me when I had a suntan. Anita was tall, with slanty green eyes just like mine, only hers were extremely wide-set in a cat's face. She wore her light brown hair long, parted in the middle, nothing fancy. Anita was a no-nonsense type of broad, with a highly developed sense of justice. Men are only after one thing, well, OK, they were only going to get one thing. No frills.

The john would say, "What's your name, sweet thing?"

"Anida," she'd say, sullen, pouting.

"Anita, that's a pretty name," he'd say.

"You wanna get on with it or what?" Anita would say, growing impatient.

She had no use for any of them.

The great part about the Retreat was the lack of overhead. This is what attracted women from all over the world, women like Colette from Marseilles, who was saving up for a beauty parlor in Queens; Lorelei, originally from West Berlin; and Rachel from Tel Aviv, who planned to go back, buy a big house on the water, and marry a professional man. I couldn't figure out Rachel's scam to save my life. She was a large, stocky woman with oily skin. In other words, she was homely, but somehow, she did a pile of business, all regulars. Michael had a theory that it was the nice, assimilated Jewish boys who had married shiksas.

"They like to sneak back home once a week for a little of Mama's old-fashioned chicken soup," he said.

But even Rachel was sitting around on her billowing behind with nothing to do on Tall Ships Day.

"Well, I know Charlie'll be here. He needs me," Cally-Ann said. She spoke with an Ozark drawl: "he naids mah."

"I don't see how you can stomach those zits all over his body," Molly said.

"I don' even notice 'em, pooah man. He's the loneliest critter on this earth. I feel so sorry fer 'im. You know, Jake is jes after me and after me to quit the Life, but I cin't, not so long as there're pooah boys like Charlie comin' around, naiding mah so," Cally-Ann said.

"Yeah, and if you quit, where's Jake gonna come up with his fig? He don' want you to get out, I don't care what kind of pillow talk he's talking. You're the best thing ever happened to that gambling deadbeat," Penny said.

But even the zit-riddled Charlie was taking a powder. Things had never been this dead at the Retreat. At last, the women lapsed into silence, watching tall ship after tall ship crawl up the Hudson. The sky on the television screen turned a deeper, more brilliant blue. We watched the sailors hugging their wives and children, boys in the crowd mugging for the camera, faceless potentates waving from terraces high above the river. All of us sat there in the dark, watching and waiting. No one came at all.

PART III

Eddie Apollo

It was late August 1976, five years after I turned my first trick. Ava had moved away and Michael with her. I found myself feeling lost. I couldn't make sense of things anymore. In one fractious, lucid moment, I looked around and discovered that I was sick and tired of casual sex. Without my Svengali around to supply an audience and cheer me on, hooking suddenly lost its appeal. I felt like Titania in *A Midsummer Night's Dream*. One morning I woke up to discover my life was wearing a donkey's head. Without Michael around, being a prostitute was no longer a gorgeous metaphor, no longer a Baudelaire poem.

In spite of my disillusion, I had a hard time giving up the Life. I was accustomed to the everyday adventure of how much money I could bring in and the friendly competition with the other members of the harem; beyond that, just as I had been warned, blue money was easy money. In little more than a year I would be coming into $40,000, the principal of the trust fund my grandfather couldn't rescind, and as it was, I had close to $10,000 saved, rolled up in a wad of fifties and hundreds in the top drawer of my bureau at the Mohican. But I kept telling myself I needed to go out and turn tricks. I had become a garden-variety capitalist coward. I was too used to having and getting easy money. I didn't want to stop.

Sad and restless, I started to wander around downtown after my day shift ended. I was drawn back again and again to a hoary old saloon in the West Village. It was the logical place to go, the Alamo, because drinking was a serious business there, and drinking was starting to appeal to me more than ever, in a new way. I was fed up with speed and even with cocaine. I was fed up with staying awake. I had been awake for years now, and it occurred to me I might be missing something. What drew me especially to this hangout was that most of the old beats there were also burned out. These people lived to drink; the mirror behind the bar seemed to suck your face into its murky brown depths; the floor was coated with a millennium of solid dirt, which could have been sacred seeing how undisturbed it was. The denizens, mostly men in their forties and up, were honest-to-God left-over bohemians, which means they were ex-marines who knew Jack Kerouac and Neal Cassady personally, and who could recite whole poems by Edna St. Vincent Millay. They were given to drunks that lasted days. And they went out of their way to ignore me.

My first friend there, Horace, was a senior editor at a very old and dying independent publishing house. The token gay man in that otherwise homophobic Alamo—the kind of homosexual who chose the company of straight men for some masochistic reason, but maybe also because he was getting a little long in the tooth and, like the rest of these old warriors, preferred to drink without the harsh interruption of sexual challenges—Horace explained to me why the regulars were so hostile. There were a couple of reasons, he said:

"To begin with, they don't appreciate strangers. A very provincial crowd down here, you've got to understand that. An outsider is like someone who comes to the theater so late, he misses the first act. They think it's rude of a young person such as you to break in on their lives, especially when you consider that for all intents and purposes those lives are over.

"But maybe more important is that you're a woman. They don't like women, you see. Oh, I don't mean they don't fuck them—of course they do when they can get it up—but they just don't like them."

Horace waved his hand like he was shooing flies.

"Now that I've made you feel thoroughly welcome, have a cocktail on me," he said in his high tenor voice, with its very clear diction. No matter how in his cups he got, Horace never slurred. He slumped, and his face folded up like an abandoned beach ball in the rain, but his talk never got fuzzy. It was a point of honor with him.

Every boozehound had one, I discovered. Some of the regulars prided themselves on being able to sit very erect like good schoolboys at attention. Others made a show of going to the jukebox, stiff-legged, walking a maniacally straight line; still others never talked at all, but sat demurely in the corner, as if to show that drinking themselves quietly to death was their own damn business.

The music behind the bellowing and the free-floating monologues that passed for conversation was still vintage jazz, classic cuts by Duke Ellington and Billy Strayhorn, a little Zoot Sims thrown in. "I've Got It Bad and That Ain't Good" was a song you frequently heard.

There were only a few other women who drank at the Alamo besides me—real camp followers they were. One had been a lieutenant in the navy, which meant she was the highest-ranking officer in the joint. And with her perfectly knotted bun, stockings, and heels, she was dignified, too, always accorded a respect, at least to her face, the rest of the women were outright denied. Most of them had supported one or the other of the guys over the years, when the guys were still young enough to get away with pretending to be musicians or writers, and now, as often as they could, these old dolls, their wide rumps spread across the barstools, were content to hang out alongside their exes until closing time. Usually, they couldn't. Once they got soused, they liked to yell at the incorrigible old bums, the erstwhile loves of their lives, until Arthur, the scowling Irishman behind the stick, his drooping mustache wet with beer foam, glared at them with a baleful look of world-weary disdain and banished them out into the street. For it was the females who unfailingly got eighty-sixed, never the males. A self-evident truth at the Alamo: women were the troublemakers of this earth.

Naturally, I felt at home. Lately my version of feminism amounted to drinking with men, whether they liked it or not, until all hours. And it took only a couple of nights to get over on Arthur, the tall, rugged-looking bartender with his doleful mustache and his flashing, angry black eyes.

It was a balmy September evening when I walked into the Alamo with Arthur, and who should be sitting there in the midst of a crowd of adopted fathers doing his silly Bing Crosby imitation—"Bohm bohm, bohm bohm"—to amuse the old folks, but the snide rock 'n' roller himself, little Eddie Carnivale.

"Hey, Arthur, my man, you're a sight for sore eyes. What's the matter with this dildo behind the stick? I been here for *days* and he won't buy me nothin', not even a draft. Tried to tell him you got a buy-back policy, but I don't think he gets it," Eddie called out.

"C'mon, Eddie, you been practically drinking on the house all day," the day bartender said.

"When'd you blow back into town?" Arthur said, acting not surprised or happy to see little Eddie, but willing enough to acknowledge him all the same.

"My mom had enough of me," Eddie said.

"She had enough of you going through her purse," Arthur said.

"Yeah, something like that," Eddie said cheerfully.

I just stood there, waiting for him to recognize me. Finally, I gave up.

"Hi, Eddie, how is your mother?" I asked him.

"Janet. Janet, man, what are you doing in this dive?"

"I live here."

"Nah, don't tell me you're doing this scene now. My crib is just around the corner, so I *gotta* drink here, but what could possibly be your excuse?"

"I'm with that guy."

"Who you talking about, not old Arthur?"

"Yes, old Arthur."

"That's a shame," Eddie said, and he sat there, leaning on both elbows with his back against the bar, looking at me. First he stared at my breasts, which were naked underneath my translucent peasant blouse, and then he lifted his head slowly until he was peering right into my eyes. "That's a real shame."

About a week later, I was coming out of Chester's, which was the other hangout, a few blocks away from the Alamo. People bounced back and forth between the two bars all night long. There was a constant wobbly stream of drunks cutting through Abingdon Square, turning up Eighth Avenue one block, and then walking east on Jane to West Fourth Street. I did this myself when Arthur was working. Chester's had a different, more civilized ambience. For one thing, a woman owned it, Donna Vickers.

Anyway, I was careening out of there around two in the morning, on my way back to cause a scene with Arthur at the Alamo, when, in passing, I heard a couple of guys on the stoop next door talking. One of them spoke my name. It was Eddie and his young buddy, the cook at Chester's. Eddie was wearing what looked like a Sherlock Holmes hat. They were passing a joint.

"See that chick? She's got a crush on me," I thought I heard Eddie say.

What? C'mon, really. Here I was, wearing my new sea-green cashmere sheath, with its own little hood bouncing behind me. The dress stretched over my body to about the middle of my calf, meeting the tops of my stacked-heel tan leather boots. I had tied back my streaked-blond hair in a ponytail to show off my neck. Since when did hot numbers like me go for juniors, for little punks like Eddie Carnivale?

Then one night in late October, when the sudden chill of autumn was kicking in and the city takes on an expectant air, as if it were winding itself up, I was turning the corner on Bank Street. Eddie came out the front door of his building. He was wearing nothing but a black T-shirt, black jeans, and white sneakers. It was a little too cold for that. All the same, he looked at home in his tight boy-body, his biceps jumping as he braced himself against the gusts of wind that were now charging off the Hudson River. And he looked alone. I don't mean simply all by himself for that moment, but really alone. Eddie was fine, very fine. I was seized by a whim, a pure and captivating whim. I went up to him, held him by the arm, and turned him around until we were both facing the open door leading to his lobby.

"It's cold out here. Let's go inside," I said.

His junkie friend Louise was crashed out on the floor next to the bed. Ignoring her there, Eddie poured us tumblers full of scotch, which we downed like Gatorade before the big game. When eventually we got around to having sex, we used the presence of that inert body right below us to measure our oblivion. We thrashed and pounded, slamming against walls, drunk and wild, raping each other. Blood from my period smeared all over the sheets. Nobody came. Too much at stake. It was an assault, a street fight, no kidding around.

"You're not going to turn tricks anymore. Never. Never again. No more fucking around. No more seeing Arthur. I'm going to stop you, Janet, I'm going to stop you right here," Eddie said.

His words stoned me. I adored him. The next day, I stuffed my huge wad of bills, the almost $10,000 worth, into my pocketbook, packed up my clothes, paid up my bill at the Mohican, and swooped down on little Eddie, Eddie Apollo, who sat waiting for me for some unknown reason in the dark in his apartment on Abingdon Square.

Gravity Knife

"You don't just stab a person and leave," I said.

But that morning, little Eddie wanted to split. He sat up in his bed, which was a cot really shoved next to my cot, and pulled the old, scratchy sheet up to his chin. Eddie stared straight ahead at himself in the cracked mirror on the far wall above the bureau, his smoke-gray eyes wide. He looked like an animal caught in the high beams crossing a country road.

"I don't believe what I did," he said.

By this time, more than a year had passed and we were back at the Mohican, three floors directly below my original suite.

The day Eddie went out and bought the knife, I knew that he meant it for me. I was with him, as a matter of fact, when he picked it out: a gravity knife with a blade about eight inches long, thin and double-edged. The whole time I kept shaking my head and telling him it was dangerous to carry a knife when we were both so drunk and stoned and generally violent, but it was his birthday.

It was the winter of '78, a lot of snow on the ground. The routine now was to go down to Avenue D, cop six bags of heroin for a hundred dollars, cab it back to the Mohican, split the glycine envelopes, three each. First Eddie cooked up his three, and after he got off, he cooked up mine. He hardly used any water at all. He liked to boot it forever, which is why I preferred to have him get me off instead of doing it myself. I wouldn't have had the guts to boot three barely diluted twenty-dollar bags of dope into my arm, over and over, until, as often as not, I swooned and sometimes overdosed. (The longest I was out was two hours once: Eddie hauling me, dragging me back and forth to the bathroom, throwing me in the tub, slapping me around, while my lips turned Kool-Aid electric blue and then dulled to a dead-leaf magenta.) He never missed either, never pierced the vein through to the other side. He had a touch; he knew the angle. Eddie was a master, he was a dope genie. And he was fervent, a purist, a passionate junkie. It was like living with a Talmudic Jew, or some other kind of religiously dedicated male, who has his purpose bent higher than love, higher than the mortal, petty concerns of everyday men.

I tried to be as single-minded as he was. For instance, I had come to the conclusion that it was immoral to read. Many people in the ghetto didn't know how to read, so it wasn't fair that I actually enjoyed it. I used to read with shame. That was the only thing I did in those days that made me feel ashamed. It was a bourgeois pastime, a luxury, like being a liberal or going to a Caribbean resort. If Eddie caught me with a book in my hand, I'd throw it down and say I was sorry. Otherwise, my policy was the standard street credo: never apologize.

And to whom would I apologize? To my father, poor, stoic Rayfield, who was now dying of cancer in the hospital a few blocks away? To my father, wheeling the saline solution plugged into his nose on its metal stand into the visitor's room, while the puss oozed through the gauze bandage covering his tracheotomy, to join me so I could have a cigarette? I remember the day the pain was so bad the tears were streaming down his face, while I sat there trying not to nod on him. Should I apologize for that? I was his favorite, he told me so on his deathbed. Well yeah, I was the only one of his kids he even vaguely knew. But Rayfield and I understood each other. I think it was because, finally, I learned never to demand anything from him he couldn't give. I sensed in the end that you had to be kind to Rayfield. He was a depressive. I didn't try to get blood from a stone.

I happened to call, which is how I learned that Rayfield was right nearby at a local hospital. Watching him give me the slip once and for all, I felt the old unrequited longing kick in, but I just sat there by his bed, sometimes holding his hand, nodding on the dope that Eddie had minutes ago pumped into me. He never cried out. All the hair on his legs had disappeared, from the chaff of his riding boots, he said. I recognized my legs; we had the same-shaped legs, along with the same black eyebrows and the same wide-set green eyes, which were deeply set, belonging to two brooders, two solitary dreamers. My father, Rayfield, Ray, and me—he drifting on the fresh inroads of his morphine injection, I awash in cheap Mexican brown dope—in the twilight, that agonizing time of day in winter, when everyone in the city suddenly discovers that he or she is alone, abandoned. While we communed like this, the man with two stumps for legs in the wheelchair across the way poured forth an elegiac wail of curses, on and on, until it ceased to have meaning. Toward the end, when it hurt Rayfield to talk, he wrote slowly on his yellow pad in his meticulous backhand script, "Don't worry, pet. We're all waiting to die."

That was part of the routine in the winter of '78, checking in with my father, when I could make it, for a couple of hours. But those hospital visits ate up my high. I came out of there stripped and starving. I would join Eddie and we would hit the first bar on the corner on the way across town to the West Village and the refuge of Chester's, where we passed every night drinking ourselves blotto, sometimes scoring a gram of coke and splitting that in half and shooting it all up in one shot, and then back out into the night, the after-hours joints, sometimes making love, too, maybe on very cold nights, or in the morning when the combination of withdrawal and a hangover made every nerve sing. That was the routine.

I can't say I loved my life, but I loved Eddie so fiercely, it compensated; it was like being happy all the time, to love someone that obsessively and be able to hold him to you. Thanks to the money, I thought. Once I came into the $40,000, I had him. It didn't even matter really whether he loved me. He used to love me, before I got the money. He loved me once, and now it didn't matter. Oh, not to say that I wasn't always whining and crying about it to him and everybody. In the middle of Chester's I suddenly broke down.

"He only loves me for my money," I wailed.

"That's right," our bar chums nodded agreeably.

"What money?" Eddie scowled. "You call those few lousy bucks you got money?"

On that bitter night in February when he stabbed me, we had been yelling, or I had, in Chester's. I used to shake my index finger at him and harangue him. But why? We won't ever find out now. No one remembers. We were at Chester's. And then he just took a powder, silently slipping out into the night in his black leather jacket and his noiseless PF Flyers. Mid-sentence gone. It was too cold to look for him in the other gin mills, in the shooting gallery on Seventh and B. So I cabbed it to the Mohican. I'm sure I was really upset by that time, because I hated to lose him, even for a minute. He was so young and cagey. Graceful the way only streetwise boys can be. I missed him, I realized as I searched for my keys.

When I pushed open the door, he was hiding behind it, hiding there in monkish silence and had been for I don't know how long. He jumped out, pushed me on the floor facedown, and stabbed me to the hilt in the back of my thigh, right up into the muscle. Pinned with my face to the floor, I felt, of all things, neutered. What I remember most was the humiliation. I remember thinking it would have been better if he had stabbed me in the stomach, so I could have contracted, thrown my head back, and fainted. Some dignity in that pose at least. This way, I felt like a kid in a schoolyard. It was funny how little blood there was. All gristle there, I guess. Didn't hurt too much either, not a sharp pain, more like an ache.

The next day it was hard to walk, but after I convinced him not to leave me, Eddie held me up, and we made it over to Dr. Schrein's office around the corner. Dr. Schrein, a man of true Aesculapian calling. Once my trick, now my friend, he administered vitamin shots and scripts for Dexosyn on a weekly basis. In the meantime, he continued to get fatter and fatter and suffered from gout. But he treated everything that came his way, like a good country doctor. He attended to the old, the outlaws, actual sick people. When I told him that I had been mugged, he simply nodded over his receptionist's squeaky objections.

"Make her go to the police," the properly horrified young receptionist said.

I think she wanted to hear me confess, but Dr. Schrein told her to mind her own business.

"She's a big girl. She knows what she's doing," he said.

He put a bandage over the hole in my leg, told me it was clean, and lent me a cane.

For as long as I hobbled around, Eddie hovered by my side, solicitous. "I got to hand it to you, you got guts," he said with love in his eyes. He walked me to the hospital, where he sat by himself in the lobby reading *Creem*, the rock 'n' roll magazine, while I went upstairs to see my father. Eddie ran me hot bubble baths. We lay in our old sagging beds at the Mohican at night, attached to each other at the lips for hours, not moving. Funny what bonds you to someone.

All during our first year together, we had celebrated in public, staying very much on view, as if we were an enviable couple, paragon lovers. We wined and dined each other across Hudson Street, at Chester's, where we ran an endless tab. Eddie could do that. He was the most disarming con man I'd ever met. He would stand at the bar, thumb hooked into the waist of his jeans, one leg on the brass footrail, and rub his face and the top of his close-cropped curly hair like a man who needed to feel something. He had a guileless way of getting intimate, as if he and the mark (which was anyone else) were on the inside track, hip to some kind of sacred knowledge that the world was not privileged to share. "Life's tough," he used to say. He had compassion.

Then, he rarely if ever lied. He would tell someone like Donna—the owner of Chester's, who knew how to swagger like a man, with a real black beauty mark on her un-made-up face—he would tell her how he beat so and so out of such and such, and until the day he cleaned out her cash register in front of a pack of regulars two deep at the bar, she persisted in her belief that Eddie would never do that to *her*. Because Eddie was her friend. So, when he finally did take people, it had the effect of seeming like retribution. They had not heeded their neighbor's misfortune.

Eddie was a marvelous master of betrayal. After years on the street, I still had not cultivated that kind of loner mind that distrusts and cons equally all of humanity. I tried to determine whether this was a skill that could be acquired or whether one had to be born with it.

"I just tell people what they want to hear, that's how I get over," Eddie would say.

He couldn't explain how he did what he did because he was a natural. Grifting was all he had ever known. Eddie had one distinct advantage over most of us: he was born and raised outside the law.

That first spring, the spring of 1977, found us both out of work, my trust fund only months away. It got manic. He began to lend me his clothes: shirts, hats, scarves. My favorite article was the red-and-white broad-striped T-shirt, which I wore over his black jeans. He convinced me to dye my hair even lighter, which I did, but the cheap over-the-counter shade was too orange I decided. On top of the dye, then, I stripped big swatches of platinum. I was blond-on-blond.

Rather than try to resist each other, we stoked it, our neediness, the killing dependency. We twinned, merged with a vengeance. Eddie insisted that we smoke the same brand, said it would be cheaper that way, and we both switched to Kools. I let him take me over. I liked his taste in music. I stopped wearing makeup and heels. If we could mirror each other—better yet, become each other—then there was a chance we would stay together. Eddie's gift for betrayal did not extend as far as our relationship. He gave and he demanded total fidelity. I began to warm to this other philosophy, this foreign ethos. When two people are willingly, enthusiastically monogamous, the result can be exciting, erotic. A revelation to me.

The first time I saw Eddie shoot up in the bathroom around Thanksgiving, he'd been clean (off heroin, anyway) for over a year. I watched him pass out, fall backward, banging his head on the porcelain sink, then the toilet, then the tub, before he hit the tile floor.

It was a *petite mort*, the most erotic surrender I had ever seen a man make: total. His swollen lips, his eyes like empty white satin jewel boxes that had been robbed of their contents, and his prostrate, limp body reminded me of paintings I'd seen of a saint's final passion. I couldn't bear anyone getting higher than I did or Eddie going so far away without me, so I made him cop me a bag. Right away, it wasn't enough.

After Michael and I split up, I assumed that I would have to destroy myself by myself. Apart from a certain animal hesitation—an appetite that would feed itself—the lower I fell through my haze of drugs and alcohol, the lonelier it got. Then, when it seemed as if the bottom were rising up to meet me, I found Eddie. He was like a benighted cleric who longed to perform last rites. Michael had been content to stand by and watch me drown, but Eddie was the whirlpool itself. He sucked me under with no warning and no regret.

Hopheads

On bright mornings and rainy mornings, come what may, at least three times a week, I took a cab uptown to my branch of Banker's Limited at Fifty-Seventh and Park, where I would first have to see Ms. Greyson, VP, to get her to OK the checks I cashed for $500 each. I had no other identification besides her brisk, urbane signature. She did not make it part of her business to pass judgment. She dressed in suits with tight skirts and high heels. Her nails were short and bright red. Her hair was frozen in an irreproachable upsweep. She had known me all of my life. She smiled from the other side of her desk like someone handing the potential suicide victim the rope.

"There you go," she always said as she returned my check.

It would never have occurred to either Eddie or me to resist. The money I came into—lucked into—on my thirtieth birthday, the trust fund that couldn't be rescinded, was like blue money. It had to be spent, and it had to be spent on dope. We went about this inexorable business, this joyless ritual, with the air of two bowed workers on a tough and boring mission, two bullocks yoked together in the rice paddy. Bad enough to be handed the unearned dough, money you didn't even have to con someone out of, but to revel in it, that would have been too much. Eddie and I suffered from an aching conscience, which we defied with a teeth-clenching sense of purpose. We were exploring this groove. It would never have occurred to us not to follow it down. Anywhere, so long as it was down.

While I was out there hooking, I stayed free of pimps. I was a maverick, screwing for kicks and running away. I was too slithery, too wide-awake to be worth the bother. Now it had caught up with me. The other side: sooner or later you search out the balance. What had I been selling anyway? The lure of open cupidity. The humiliation that comes from knowing you're the mark and still you can't resist. Lascivious pleasure—one-sided, intense pleasure—the essence of anonymous sex. This is what men crave. The whore's contempt teases below the surface like scratchy sackcloth. Satisfaction runs correspondingly deep.

Jasmine, the redheaded Hispanic from the Sultan's Retreat, understood this. She was soft-spoken, calm, ever the lady, even when she was jerking off that young Japanese boy while several of us stood around and watched. He lay on his back on the massage table in the tiny cubicle like a patient about to go under the knife. We stood there because he had paid us all. She pulled on his penis (too hard, I thought, making it difficult, surely) and repeated over and over again, "Come on, honey, come, come. You can do it. Come on, baby..." *Hurry up,* in other words. And he held back, out of fear, out of pleasure, out of shame. That's what it was like, that second year with Eddie. Responding to his quick friction-stroke, I took his passion, even what might have been his uncertainty, for impatience. I heard Jasmine: "C'mon, baby, c'mon, you can do it."

Disgust, contempt, self-loathing, and, under that, curiosity. Where does this go? Where will it take us? Is it irrevocable, the damage we're doing? So much the better. Make it count, make it tell.

But in the flat, still hours before dawn, when the bravado had vanished like the illusion it was, Jasmine's stone cold rhythm would haunt me. I couldn't shake the image of us standing around the boy lying prostrate on the massage table as if he were some kind of ritual sacrifice. When this and other stark memories muscled their way in, I would reach for Eddie, throw my arms around him, lock myself against him, stripped of everything but need. Eddie always turned and faced me and hugged me back. He'd stroke my face, look into my eyes, and whisper, "It's OK, doll. Everything is OK. Go back to sleep."

He understood; he knew about demons. After comforting me, he'd lie there staring into the darkness as if he'd been awake all along. We'd lie there together in some kind of vigil, staring at the old cracked-plaster ceiling becoming visible in the dawn light.

When I turned thirty, he was a month away from twenty-four, after all this time still so young. I was captivated by that. I have an image of Eddie: his shining junkie-white skin, his heavy-lidded eyes, his full mouth drooping. On the nod, he is sitting with his back against the wall in the dust on the floor of our suite at the Mohican, plucking at the steel strings of his Stratocaster—temporarily out of hock—which he never bothered to plug in.

Or Eddie wheeling around the room in hophead mode searching for our works. The windows are covered with blankets. The bedroom is dark and hot and airless. Eddie is oblivious; he is about to get off.

"Here they are, honey, on the windowsill."

He never called me "honey" except in that heightened moment of anticipation.

Heroin was the most glamorous drug I ever did, in the sense that death, sister of the night, is glamorous, because it truly was a sojourn with the sacred dead—it was incandescent silver-blue forever twilight on the horizon of nowhere: painlessness. Speed was a Western escape. It vivified; it enhanced everything. Heroin was an Eastern good-bye to even the light. The drug put you on the other side, beyond speculation.

And meanwhile, I had descended into the pool of disease, into bloated flesh and uncharacteristic summer pallor. I was glistening white, with rippling flanks and, for the first time, a weak belly. When I looked at myself in the old, flaked mirror of the Mohican, I saw this buried thing. The eyes peered out of watery flesh, as if I were a baby at a christening wrapped up and bewildered inside blankets. Eddie's body grew flaccid and weak as well. But his green tone seemed to belong to him. I understood that he owned it. He might not be passing through as I was. I was always just passing through.

"You're so young," he said to me on the street one day, when he caught me laughing, still laughing.

He took my open face in his hands and looked into it as if my expression had betrayed something, a basic soundness, a wholesomeness that nothing, no punishing detail of this sordid life, could completely smother.

"You'll always be younger than I am," he said.

And it's true that Eddie indulged me, played with me, as if I were a child whom he was being paid to keep amused. He led me into strange bars that suited his whim. Sometimes he deliberately took me to gin mills in unfashionable neighborhoods, devoid of any kind of appeal, except the allure of old men drinking boilermakers. Worse even, we would go to some obscure Chinese restaurant in midtown and pour down sweet, warm vodka martinis.

I thought that he must be ashamed to be seen with me, who wore rags now, ill-fitting unfashionable clothes that were a far cry from the all-black uniform of jeans and T-shirt of the winter before. I had begun to dress myself in a methadone-clinic-waiting-room series of outfits: khaki cotton pants from Hudson's Sporting Goods and acrylic T-shirts in those cheap opaque shades of acid green and yellow, a canvas pocketbook, dirty sneakers. The pants might be too tight, the crack of my ass showing through the heavy, shiny material, or they might be too loose, hanging down at the crotch. My haircut had lost its shape, and I parted it in the middle, tucking the wisps behind my ears. The bleached patches were starting to break off now in strange places. I looked poor, and the worst thing about looking poor is that it renders you invisible. But I was nodding, on the nod; my eyes were delicate pins. I might be invisible, but then so was the world.

The Rescue

Later that summer, Eddie and I decided to make a real home together. We rented a U-Haul and dragged Eddie's old furniture out of its cool vault and piled it into the van. I couldn't see the point of it.

"Come on, Eddie, really, let's chuck the junk, take the van back, or better yet, go for a ride in the country now that we got wheels. But let's forget about this junk. Why can't we do it like other young couples starting out? Buy things piece by piece, things we care about? Let's just dump this garbage, let's, c'mon, Eddie. Please. New furniture for our new life, our new beginning."

"Janet, you've got a bourgeois streak a mile wide, you know that? Who here would be willing to cough up the bucks for *furniture,* for Chrissake? I'm not shelling out any dough for furniture. Anyway, we've been over this and now it's too late. What's wrong with what we got? We're not moving to Scarsdale, you know. You think you got to impress the neighbors on East Sixth Street? Get hip, Janet."

"We'll keep the bed, of course. That's OK. But the rest of it stinks! I don't want to live with that crap."

"Fine, fine, then don't. I'm getting my furniture out, and I'm moving to Sixth Street, and you can go fuck yourself."

Eddie disappeared inside.

The apartment Eddie and I had found was formerly a storefront, a floor-through, with one window in the back that looked out on a concrete courtyard. Next to it there was a door, its faded coat of black enamel paint unsuccessfully hiding deep gouges in the wood. There was only a sealed showcase window in the front, which was wide and bare, but an ancient glaze of soot filtered out the north light and afforded some privacy from the street. And if we opened the front and back doors, we figured, we would get a cross breeze, a real luxury. Our immediate neighbors, on both sides of us, and for most of the way up and down the block, were Indian restaurants. 'Indians are law-abiding and they mind their own business,' we thought. What we didn't get is that five or six little kitchens attract industrial-sized vermin: roaches as long as your arm, rats and the spraying toms that follow them. These animals had us pegged for chumps, for the same kind of shiftless interlopers they were. In the back, our one window had bars but no screen. Wild alley cats immediately reclaimed their turf, stinking up everything: clothes, shoes, the armchair, our double bed. The roaches, too big to kill, occupied the walk-in closet a former tenant had installed during a previous era, when the block had still been inhabitable. The hot water boiler sat right underneath us, in the basement. It was like living on top of a furnace in the middle of a desert. Once we moved in, we just lay there on our reeking double bed until the sun went down. It was too hot to move. We lay there, awake but motionless, steeped in this perfect hell.

But it was hard to admit that we had screwed up. In spite of all the evidence to the contrary, for a long time we insisted to our chums in the local gin mill a few blocks away that we had plans for the place. We were going to build a wall here, put a couch there. When winter came, it would be fine. The cats would die of the cold; the roaches would retreat.

In the meantime, there were a few unexpected benefits. We were suffering too much to fight. Victims under siege, we began to draw closer to each other. I sweated off the winter's bloat. It was good for that, too. The most we ever ate was a few slices of plain pizza, or we'd split some kind of meat sandwich from the old Jewish deli down the block.

In the early morning, as the sun came up, we made love in a new way. Not exactly kissing tenderly, but sometimes into the act a gentle caress would creep. Someone might hold someone's hand. We lay there with our faces pressed together, our eyes open, as if this were intimacy. Intimacy is torture, just as we had always suspected. Torture. To prove it, we lay there like that for hours at a clip.

Evelyn's budget whorehouse was not far away. One weekday afternoon, when presumably business was even slower than usual, she decided to pay us a visit. She tracked us down at our local hangout, the Monterey Bar and Grill. She wore a sleeveless leopard-print sheath, which clung all the way to the middle of her calves, and gold sandals. Her toenails were bright red. So were her fingernails and lips.

She walked right past Eddie, who seemed not to notice, and over to where I sat at the end of the bar.

"You look awful, Janet. You look like you could get eighty-sixed from the women's shelter. What did you let him drag you down for? Don't you know any better than that by now? Never let a man take you down."

"Hello, Evelyn, how's tricks?" I said.

She sidled up close and put her arm around my shoulders.

"Janet, you and I used to be friends, sort of. I'm appealing to you now as a friend, capiche? As a friend. He's no good for you."

"Want a drink, old friend?"

"I didn't come here to drink. Talk to me."

"I love your son, Evelyn."

She backed away as if she'd been slapped.

"You're too old for him, Janet," she screamed at me from the middle of the empty barroom. "Why don't you leave him alone?"

"All right, Ev, darlin', calm down," Eddie said.

He took her by the arm and led her outside. Evelyn stood facing the sun, shielding her eyes and barking at Eddie. He turned and walked out of my view. I saw her chase after him. A few minutes later, he came back inside alone.

"She won't bother us for a while."

"What did you say?"

"I said she wasn't going to get the chance to exploit your tender, little body anymore, that I was looking after you now."

"Eddie, that's kind of unfair. After all, your mother never really exploited me. She was good to me."

"I told her I thought you were beautiful just the way you are, because I do. I told her to beat it."

"You said that?" I asked, incredulous.

"Well, it worked, didn't it?"

Eddie ordered another bottle of cold beer, then went over to the window, where he stood guard. The jukebox played on. It had a rich sound in the sweet silence of the vacant summer afternoon.

Still not yet ready to give up on her son, Evelyn sent her two emissaries. They appeared at our hangout on St. Mark's Place the next afternoon. They were there, in fact, when Eddie and I arrived at the cocktail hour. It was one of those late-summer days when dirty clouds block the sun and every foul odor hangs undiluted in the thick air. Eddie was restless and probably looking for trouble, I thought. Except when he saw Michael with his sister, Ava, standing together by the jukebox, he stopped inside the door, pivoted on one boot heel, and walked back outside.

"Eddie!" his sister yelled.

He just shook his head.

He was gone. I remained on the spot, pulled in both directions. I watched Michael come toward me across the barroom floor. It had been two years. His stomach protruded a little more than before under the familiar off-white cowboy shirt that he wore with the shirttails loose. His temples were gray. Michael, my north star—Michael the überman set down among us for our possible salvation—Michael to whom I had always so freely gravitated—my other half! Well, perhaps not. He had lost the light. I compared—dared finally to compare—that punk outside with my old flame, and by God, I loved Eddie more. Eddie's tight body, his streetwise prowl, those smoky eyes flickering with dark mischief—it really was Eddie. I turned to follow him. Just then, Michael reached my side and grabbed my arm.

"Janet, you know you're killing yourself."

I shook his hand away and kept moving.

Eddie and I waited behind the window of the secondhand record store across the street. We watched Michael and Ava come out and look around, presumably for us. Finally, they turned and began to walk west. They were both so tall. Ava in profile looked serenely beautiful, her dark hair pulled back in a luxurious ponytail. Then I saw Michael, in a few quick steps, scoot around her to be next to the curb. He was protecting her. They fell into an easy stride. I thought of how, in contrast, when we walked down the street, Eddie seemed always on the verge of pulling away. But I had chosen now for good. I watched Michael and Ava disappear in the St. Mark's Place crowd, after which Eddie and I went back inside our gin mill, and I quickly got drunk.

Then right after Labor Day, which Eddie and I had celebrated by getting particularly ripped, my mother wrote to me with a proposition. I think she could smell my misery. It must have wafted all the way uptown to the Park Avenue co-op. She offered to take me away to Montauk for a week or maybe even two. Under other circumstances, even circumstances like the Mohican in summer with its Gramercy Park illusion of a breeze, I might have had the character to refuse. You don't just desert your lover to go off with your mother, become her not-so-well-paid companion when it suited her. A lover is a grown-up, respectable thing to have, while a mother is not. But she had a hook: hotel reservations by the ocean.

At nine in the morning, an old Cadillac limo pulled up in front of our storefront on Sixth Street. Little children scattered like pigeons, while the elderly men on the stoop at the end of the block turned their heads in the direction of the car, watching its slow progress until they were sure it was not a politician coming to disturb them in the sun. The chauffeur, dressed in a tight light brown uniform, his tie loose, came around and opened the door in an absentminded way, looking off across the street, as if the whole charade were beneath him. Maggie climbed out, wearing a long fake-denim cotton shirt over lavender pants, big, thick prescription sunglasses, and old-lady sandals. She tossed her head and looked up and down furtively, as if she expected beggars or muggers, or both, to leap on her from the sun-drenched doorways.

I stood at the encrusted window and watched her. When had my mother decided to become old?

Behind me, Eddie lay asleep on the other side of the musty old curtain surrounding our bed. The night before, he had helped me pack. He even washed out some underpants for me and hung them over the tub. He was so jealous of my beach trip that the feeling had collapsed, imploded, into one of abject self-sacrifice. He certainly did not blame me. It was every man for himself in this world. He would have done the same thing. In fact, he would go to visit his own mother out on City Island. He would swim in the bay there. He would think of me every minute. He would get by somehow.

"Don't screw around," he said. "Promise me, Janet. Even you can be faithful for two weeks."

"Oh, I promise, I promise. I'll miss you like crazy," I said, covering him with kisses.

But I felt like someone who was about to be sprung. I thought of Maggie as my savior come to lift me up from Hades, to rescue me from Pluto and his red-hot underground. I watched this unlikely knight of mine in her fake blue-jean-blue shirt with its incongruous ruffle and her clunky open-toed sandals swagger up to my door. She banged against it.

"I thought we agreed you would be waiting for me out on the street. You know this neighborhood makes me nervous," she said as soon as I let her inside.

"It occurred to me you might want to see where I live."

"Why would I want to do that?"

She did look around, though, her eyes squinting in the dark. She pulled back the curtain. "Oh, hello, Eddie," she said.

He turned under the sheet. His morning hard-on poked up through it. "Hi, Maggie, what time is it?" he said, rubbing his eyes like a little boy.

"Time for us to get moving. Come on, Janet, where's your suitcase? Let's go. The chauffeur is waiting out there."

"Say hi to the chauffeur for me, Maggie," Eddie said, turning his face to the wall.

I leaned over and kissed him. He grabbed me with one arm.

"Don't cheat," he said.

End of the Line

And I planned to be faithful. It was all I could think about for at least the first hour. Gliding past streets of stunted row houses and out onto the open highway next to Maggie in the backseat, who rattled on and on about how much the trip was costing her—the motel, dinners for two, and so on—I dreamed out the window about Eddie. The hangover had sanded my nerve endings to an extravagant pitch. I felt wave after wave of tender pity for him as I pictured him lying back there, under a sheet, in our hot box.

Once the car started hitting the potato fields, however, the specter of a drained and sweltering Eddie began to pall. Almost alone on the road on this weekday morning, we drove through the small resort towns on the South Fork, where big, fat oaks and glamorous copper beeches were planted at considered distances. On the central greens, willows dipped into the still ponds. Hedges and flowering bushes set off gabled, freshly painted houses. Maggie lit a cigarette and opened her window. Air swept in, gala fresh. She asked the silent chauffeur (whom she had tried to engage in conversation earlier, but who had cleverly refused to bite) if he would mind turning off the air-conditioning. Reluctantly, apparently against his principles, he obeyed. A sweet breeze blew against our faces. I began to feel prodigal. Why had I forsaken the bourgeois life? Order, refinement, design. By this time, I couldn't stand to think about that melting asphalt netherworld and that pale, blank-eyed loser sunk in his circle of hell. He reminded me of those transparent animals, the ones with no coloration at all, who live in the heart of caves. My stomach heaved with disgust. I was free now, returned to my world.

Maggie shifted around in her seat. Silences made her nervous, suspicious. She felt conspired against. I could tell that she was casting about for some topic.

"Did Eddie get a job yet?" she asked me.

Of course, Maggie couldn't care less whether Eddie worked. In her moral lexicon, work for work's sake didn't count as a virtue. Blue-collar outdoor kinds of occupations blurred as one. Besides, Eddie had been job-hunting since the day we met. It was a rhetorical question.

"Let's agree right now not to talk about my love life," I said.

"Why, you two breaking up?" Maggie asked.

"No, no, but the subject just gets us going," I said.

"What is there to talk about? Everything I bring up is taboo. No matter what I say, you fly at me."

"That's because you're always looking for a way in, a way to get to me. Let's just stick to impersonal things, you know, like the trees, the beach, what's on *Masterpiece Theatre,* stuff like that."

"I don't see what's so personal about wanting to know whether Eddie's working or not. Seems like a pretty ordinary question to me."

"Forget it, OK?"

"Fine. We won't talk at all then. We'll just pass the days like the Dominicans. It'll be good for the soul," Maggie said, turning to look out the window.

Perfect circles of sweat had formed under the arms of the chauffeur in his miracle-fiber short-sleeved leisure shirt. He carried all four bags at once up the flight of stairs, where he deposited them just inside the door of our motel room. Maggie pulled her usual routine of "Just wait a second! I have to find my purse," followed by endless rummaging until she located her wallet, then the long examination of its contents, the fingering of money, the contemplative look. Finally she tipped him—not enough, I thought.

It was a snazzy motel room, the kind at the time I liked best. All-American, with no individual character to intrude on the tactile experience of comfort: two queen-sized beds, a twenty-one-inch color TV on a swivel stand, a refrigerator, and a terrace overlooking the ocean.

I wanted to go out right away, have a beer, swim. Maggie insisted that I unpack first. She pulled off the bottom part of the hotel hangers and threw them on my bed.

"Now you do this or you can go back on the next train," she said.

"All right, I'll go back on the next train," I said.

"That's fine. I don't know why I brought you here. You're not fit company anymore anyway. Help me with this bag, will you? I can't lift it," she said, dragging her big suitcase across the room.

I did that, also helping myself to ten dollars out of her wallet. It had not eluded me for one minute that I needed a drink. I put on my bikini, which didn't look half bad since I had sweated all the bloat away on Sixth Street, and covered it with one of Maggie's beach jackets, the one with pockets. I excused myself and split, before she had a chance to object.

We both used to love the ocean, but ever since Maggie's eyes went bad, she preferred to swim with her glasses on and her head above water in the motel pool along with the little kids. I walked across the street to the beach by myself, where I dove under the surf and swam parallel to the shore. I had the energy of an escaped convict.

Later that afternoon, I found myself sitting in a dark bar looking hard at where my life had gone. I couldn't exactly blame Eddie. I knew, I took comfort in the fact, that he had never sunk so low before either—not on a day in, day out basis. We were like spelunkers. That's what I told myself, spelunkers exploring the depths. I couldn't leave him any more than you could leave a partner dangling from a stalactite under the earth. Nevertheless, something had to give.

Sometimes you throw your hands up in despair and it works, which was probably why Maggie seemed undeniably cheerful when I walked into the room. She was getting ready to go out to dinner. It was as if the question of whether she would be eating with me were beside the point. I was safely peripheral now.

"You're home early," she said.

"I thought we had a date for dinner," I said.

"Since when did that matter to you?"

"Well, I'm here aren't I?"

"And you're drunk again, just like every other day so far this week. So what?" she said, arranging a white silk shawl over her shoulders. The skin sagged under her arms. I wanted to tell her to keep that shawl around her. She was wearing a sundress underneath it with one of those built-in bras that stands up by itself.

"I'm not drunk," I said.

"Hurry up and put on some clothes if you want to eat," Maggie said.

My impressionable mother never forgot the book she read years ago on the subject of alcoholism, the one that counseled the wives of alcoholics not to enable their spouses. This meant that she could contemplate leaving Rayfield in good conscience. To stay would be to *enable* him. It was a new idea at the time. She fitfully resumed the studied air of detachment she had learned from the book whenever it occurred to her. I recognized the old 'you can't get to me' attitude. Forced as it was, it had its effect.

I went to the closet and pulled out a cotton dress that I had found at the Goodwill. It smelled like its previous owner, but I didn't mind. The previous owner was obviously wealthy, and her odor was that of a cautious, contained woman. A kind of subdued sweat smell. Probably better than mine, I thought. This dress made me feel beyond reproach. It was seersucker, with its own real leather belt and little capped sleeves, which made me feel coltish and inspired me to assume poses. I stood at the mirror over the desk next to Maggie and applied lipstick in a very controlled way, only reeling slightly.

"I'm ashamed to be seen with you," Maggie said.

"Ditto," I said.

"What have you got to be ashamed of? I'm not drunk," she said, gazing into the mirror and yanking up her bosom by the straps of her shiny cotton sundress.

"No, but you look tacky and that's worse," I said.

"Thanks. Thanks very much. Just for that you can sit here and starve for all I care. Or go back to those bums in the saloon. I've had it with you," she said, picking up a hairbrush, then slamming it down. Maggie was really pissed now, shaking with anger.

Naturally, I immediately felt the old remorse. It was as though I had spoken for the sole purpose of reminding myself of what heel I was. "I'm so sorry, I didn't mean it," I said.

"What's so tacky? The dress? It's just a sundress. Everyone wears them out here. It's comfortable." She was smoothing the front of it, looking down at herself. "Is it that awful?" she asked.

"Of course not. Don't pay any attention to me. Plus which, as you so wisely pointed out, this is Montauk. What could be more appropriate?"

Maggie stared at herself in the mirror, sucked in her cheeks, her stomach, and then threw back her head. "Not bad for an old girl," she said.

We walked away from the ocean, down the main road that led to the harbor. The land was so flat it created the illusion that the house lights in the distance were far below us. It was dark on the road. Maggie made me take her hand because she had night blindness. Even though we were walking on a sidewalk, she was afraid of tripping and falling and, for all she knew, being left there on the pavement to die. So she clung to my limp hand as cars flashed their brights, illuminating this spectacle of two women who looked like stumbling refugees fleeing from a war-ravaged town.

"Stop walking so fast. You know I can't see," she said, squeezing my hand until it hurt.

"Would you loosen your grip, please? What do you think, that I'm going to run away and leave you out here? You've got all the dough, remember? And I'm hungry," I said.

She relaxed immediately and chuckled. "That's right, isn't it?" she said. "I know I'm safe with you as long as you need something."

To the left, a lake shimmered, reflecting the twinkling lights that were hanging from the branches of the trees. We turned off the main road and gingerly made our way along a sandy path to the Grey Swan Inn. There was a half-hour wait. The main room was packed with tables like a dining hall in a dorm. Babies in high chairs were screaming at their mothers in their lobster bibs. I suggested we go to the bar, a relative oasis. Strangely enough, Maggie was receptive to the idea. It was agreed that I could have one drink there and then only a carafe of wine with dinner.

"I want to get home tonight," she said, still afraid of losing me and being left stranded in the dark.

Maggie was sitting inside the motel room on the token chair in the corner, gripping the armrests and staring at me with a look of angry consternation on her face like I was someone she had never seen before. Her eyes were blown up to the size of hens' eggs by the magnifying lenses of her bifocals. I couldn't stand to look at those conspicuous eyes. They reminded me of how, practically overnight, she had stepped into the guise of old age, with a vengeance it seemed, as if this were her last great role and she was going to play it to the hilt. The purple muumuu she had on, plastered over with a chunky purple coral necklace, did nothing to dispel the image. It sent spasms of guilt through me just to look at her.

"Where were you all night?" she asked me.

"Your guess is as good as mine, but I can tell you where I found myself this morning."

"Where?"

"On a boat, a fishing boat I'm pretty sure. Anyway, it certainly smelled like it. God, I was sick."

"By yourself on a fishing boat?"

"Did I say I was by myself? There was a guy next to me, oh yeah, probably a fisherman," I said, as if I had just deduced this.

"Janet, I'm sorry to have to bring this up now of all times, but I've been thinking a lot about it, and I believe it's a question of survival—my survival. I can't take it. I really can't. I don't want to see you anymore when you're like this."

"Fine, fine with me. Is that why you've been sitting here waiting for me, to tell me that?"

"No. Your stepmother called. She tracked us down out here. Janet, your father is back in the hospital. How awful—and I dragged you out here—of course I never would have if I thought there were any chance he would be going back so soon. He didn't get much time at home after all. So sad. Poor Betsy. Apparently, you did tell her we were going to Montauk, but that's all. Betsy said she spent the whole morning phoning one motel on the beach after the other...said she asked you before you left the name of the motel where we would be, just in case something like this happened, but you couldn't remember. Obviously, you couldn't be bothered to find out either. And you promised to call Betsy and your father when we arrived. Obviously, you forgot.

"Janet, are you listening to me? Really, Janet, under the circumstances, you'd think you would make a point..."

Suddenly, my mother's tone changed, from one of stern reprimand to despair. Her anger, a feigned emotion to begin with, collapsed. Her face crumpled. No. She was crying. Not that. *Pretend to be mad at me. It's much better when you do.* Out of nowhere she said, "Where is that adorable, elfin little girl running toward me with her wild hair blowing in the wind? Where did she go? Am I never going to see her again?"

I had a mad impulse: I longed to pat her fragile little head, to hold her hand again on the dark street, but gently this time. I wanted to hug her—my mother—and just be with her forever. I loved her that much. Too much. I was terrified I would disappear inside that love. Consciously and conscientiously I courted my fear, because if I lost it, I might tumble in for good. I would be like a stillborn, without a life of my own. So I held on tight and said nothing.

Maggie took off her glasses and rubbed her eyes with the heel of her hand. She put the glasses back on and tugged her muumuu farther over her knees. She stayed still for a minute just trying to compose herself. Then she recaptured her indignant posture.

"Well, never mind, forget it, Janet, your father is back in the hospital. Betsy says it won't be long now."

They had let Rayfield go home for a while, mainly because he refused to die. Under the circumstances, since he'd endured the maximum radiation therapy a person was normally allowed and there was nothing more they could do, they had to let him go. He actually rode his horse a few times that summer. Someone had to put him in the saddle, but once he was up there, he did fine, apparently.

One of the last times I had been to see him before he went home, I heard him whispering in his delirium, "Dixie, Sinbad, Clover..."

Alarmed, I moved my chair closer. Those were the names of former pets of his, the border collie and two Siamese cats. All three of the animals had died. In spite of the numerous wives, children, and wars, what did my father cling to in his waning hour but his dead pets. A strange man indeed.

"Don't worry," he said to me, coming to, "I know they're dead."

But then he slipped back into his doped reverie and continued to call out to them in his hoarse whisper: "Dixie, Sinbad, Clover..."

I thought I could sense his spirit rise up and leave his body for a moment. Surely he was close. Instead, they sent him home a week later.

Now he was back, and I knew that if I didn't hurry, I would miss the chance to say good-bye. I had to see him.

I wanted to be his daughter at least this once.

Maggie loaned me some cash, about a hundred dollars, which was surprisingly generous for her in those days. I threw my clothes in my suitcase over her protests ("That's no way to pack, Janet") and, without bothering to check the timetable, took a cab to the train station. It turned out I had an hour to kill, so I left the suitcase on the empty platform and walked over to the local gin mill, the Big Clam. The place was nearly empty. I did manage to catch the last train.

Foxhole

When I got to our apartment on East Sixth Street, I found that the frontdoor had been left unlocked, but Eddie was gone. The place was unbearably hot and airless, as if nobody had opened the back window in days. Not a good sign. His things and mine were there, though, strewn around the same as when I left. I figured he must have just stepped out to the corner or something, so I found a piece of paper—an unopened month-old Con-Ed bill—and wrote a short note:

> *10:30 P.M.*
> *Dad back in hospital. Have gone over to visit for a minute. See you later.*
> *Love,*
> *Janet*

I locked the door, wondering whether Eddie had bothered to take his keys. Well, serve him right. You're not supposed to leave your front door open in New York City.

It was no cinch getting past first the man at the front desk, then the big-chested, old night nurse on duty on Dad's floor.

"He's fast asleep," she said.

I repeated the speech I had delivered in the lobby: "Listen, I came all the way from the country as soon as I heard. I know he's dying. I just want to say good-bye. I got to. It's my pop," I said.

"Yes, Mr. Chace doesn't have long. All right then, for a few minutes," she said.

He was alone, because the inordinately devoted Betsy was too sick herself to make the trip that night. He was not asleep. My father was sucking the air, trying to breathe. When he saw me, he mouthed, "Morphine, morphine," over and over.

The tube trailing from his tracheotomy gurgled, and the air around his bed reeked from the excess of chemotherapy mixed with galloping cancer, from the foul odor of rotting, burning flesh.

The big nurse was reluctant at first. "I gave him his last shot two hours ago."

"But he's suffering. He's in terrible pain. I know the guy, he wouldn't be asking if he didn't need it," I said.

I was wild. What kind of country was this that you had to beg to relieve a dying man of his torture?

Finally, she agreed.

After the morphine took, I watched his drawn, sweaty face relax. I mopped his brow, but it scared me. His skin was so clammy and cold, it felt like touching a cadaver. His white hair, what was left of it, sprouted from the top of his skull like the hair on a shrunken head. I kept thinking, "Damn, if it weren't for the chemotherapy, he'd still have his gorgeous mane. Rayfield wasn't meant to go bald." I almost wished, for cosmetic reasons alone, that people died the way I imagined they used to: quickly, naturally.

I sat with him in the semidarkness for as long as the nurse would let me. It wasn't very long, however, before she came and stood in the door, her massive shape blocking the light from the hallway.

"You'll have to leave now," she said.

"Don't worry. I'll be here tomorrow," he whispered. He patted my hand. "Old soldiers never die; they just fade away."

As soon as I hit the street, it occurred to me that I had about seventy dollars cash on me. I meandered through Stuyvesant Square, pausing for a moment underneath the tall trees to listen to the leaves rustle and get my bearings before I walked over to the Monterey Bar and Grill on St. Mark's Place. I figured Eddie would be there.

But there was no sign of him. I decided to wait, of course. Various regulars offered opinions about where he might be. Most of them suggested the shooting gallery on Seventh Street and Avenue B. It did seem likely. Meanwhile, I was pouring down shots of Jack Daniel's and chasing them with short beers. Soon, Eddie's whereabouts no longer seemed like a big deal. I had a place to crash; that was all that was important.

The Monterey Bar and Grill was a misnomer: there was no grill. The bar itself was a thing of beauty: wide, semicircular, and polished to a high gloss. The Ukrainian owner obviously cherished his place, but he was too practical to try to discourage the onslaught of kids that had taken over the joint. In fact it was he who had renamed it after the famous music festival in the hopes of attracting them. He didn't protest either when they offered to fill up his old jukebox with the Stones, the Sex Pistols, Television, the Talking Heads, and Elvis Costello, along with a fine selection of rock 'n' roll oldies, like Buddy Holly's "Not Fade Away" and "The Girl Can't Help It," by Little Richard. It was a hip jukebox, cutting edge, a philosophical statement, evidence of a shared worldview. But this guaranteed that his once-loyal customers would desert him, which they did; friends and neighbors of a lifetime cleared out forever, preferring now to hang at small taverns, such as the Blue and Gold, on the side streets.

Sometimes in the late morning, I would catch a glimpse of the old man through the window. He'd be sitting alone at the end of the bar with his head bobbing on his sunken chest, snoozing. The nights were too much for the poor geezer. Still, he didn't dare leave the place alone, because he thought, and rightly, that everyone working for him was a thief. He was always there, dressed in old-fashioned suit pants, hitched high on his waist, and white nylon short-sleeved shirts, through which you could see his cotton undershirt. He winced when Sid Vicious hit a particularly raucous chord, the wonderfully hideous noise of it blasting over the crowd. For hours, he would pace slowly up and down at the back of the room, looking sadly to me like a fish flopping on the sand.

Now the old grandpa made his way through the small cluster of people at the bar and tapped me on the shoulder. "I tink your boyfriend has got trouble," he said.

"What else is new?" I said, throwing back a shot. "Have a vodka, Doc."

We all called him Doc.

"No, no tanks, later maybe. But you listen what I tell you," he said, shaking his finger.

"OK. I'm listening," I said.

"Some colored boys was in here asking for him. I tell them I don't know nothing. They go away, but they say I should tell Eddie they was looking for him. I don't like it," he said.

Doc lived in fear of the black and Hispanic population. No matter that his saloon catered to second-story men, dope dealers, and every other kind of lowlife vermin. The point is they were white.

"Thanks for telling me, Doc," I said.

Fat Jack sidled up next to where I was sitting on a tall barstool and pushed his good-sized belly, which hung out over his jeans, into my thigh.

"You look gorgeous with that tan, Janet, like a *Penthouse* foldout. Since Eddie is nowhere around, Red and I was just wonderin' if we could turn you onto some rock, dynamite stuff. We'd be perfect gentlemen. Whaddya say?"

Fat Jack pursed his pudgy cupid's bow mouth, then he licked his lips. His jolly, open face, with its quizzical expression, might lead you to believe that here was a nice guy, until you witnessed one of his bar fights, during which Jack would think nothing of breaking a beer bottle against the wall and then going after his victim with the ragged edge.

Fat Jack had been a mail carrier on Long Island before he got busted for the sauce. Once upon a time, he had total health benefits, a little bungalow in Malverne, the promise of a life. His buddy Red was an albino who was as tall and stringy as those punks from Queens, the Ramones, but without their charm. How he got his nickname was a mystery to me. I thought the two of them were loathsome as toads, beneath contempt. For the past month, they had been breathing down my neck, traipsing at my heels, staring after me when I walked along St. Mark's Place.

"That's a fine woman," they said to Eddie.

"You shoulda seen her before I got to her," Eddie said.

"Where's Eddie? He isn't shtupping someone else? C'mon, Jack, tell me the truth," I said, suddenly seized with dark suspicion.

"Nah, Janet. You know better. Eddie don't care about pussy enough to fuck around. You know what he's into," he said.

"Dope."

"Yeah, he managed to get into a real jackpot during this last week while you were away. I don't think you should ever leave him alone, Janet. He started working for these young kids on Fifth Street and Avenue B. Got some kind of a super deal going down, where they fronted him ounces, and he was supposed to step on it once more, break it up, and sell it off, bag by bag. Imagine, he conned those niggers into *fronting* him, a white guy, ounces of smack. A good thing, a really good thing, but he's already blown it."

"What do you mean, blown it?"

"Janet, Eddie is such a fuckup. Thinks he can get away with anything. Thinks he's so sly and so tough. The kid's heading for a big fall. Believe me. Not only is he lifting huge amounts of smack off the top and cutting it to nothin', but he's braggin' about it all over the place. Worst of all, he's trying to beat those black kids. Hasn't paid them a cent so far. What's his problem, anyway?"

"Is that what's going on?" I asked, grateful it wasn't a woman and horrified, too.

"You better not even go home tonight. Those niggers are looking for him all over. They're pissed. Come upstairs with Red and me, why don't you?" he said.

"OK," I said.

Once upstairs in his nearly empty railroad apartment, I almost regretted my decision. The floors were so thick with dirt, there was a path worn onto it where Jack walked from room to room. The furniture consisted of a claw-footed bathtub in the kitchen, a bare mattress in the far room, and a few foam pillows scattered around. Red got out a new set of works and mixed up some cocaine with water.

We took turns getting off. I was too drunk to be uptight about doing myself; I didn't miss. I even booted it the way Eddie would have done. The steady drip from the faucet in the sink began to ring, to chime like bells. The world stopped moving. Everything got very clear and still and made perfect sense. Bam, I booted it one last time. The air sang, the floor dropped out from under me. I reeled. A hand caught me.

"Drink some of this whiskey," Red was saying. At that moment, he looked to me like a holy man, bathed in an eerie white light, wearing shades.

We sat on the pillows and passed the bottle for a while. In spite of my drunkenness, in spite of the lingering effects of the cocaine, I was so disgusted I felt physically ill. It occurred to me suddenly, as I closed my eyes, that this was no fun anymore at all. In fact, it had not been fun for a long time now. I had sunk much lower than I could have imagined. My dissolution had taken on a life of its own. I actually experienced the sensation of gravity pulling me down at an accelerating speed, deeper and deeper. "Fuck it, too late to care. You're under the rock now for good," I told myself. "Only a matter of time now... Don't fight...just go with it...All over soon," I thought, as I turned my face into the dirt-black foam pillow behind my head.

After a few more minutes of this, I insisted the three of us return to the Monterey Bar and Grill. I was starting to miss Eddie.

"He been here looking for you," Doc said.

I knew I better go by Sixth Street, in case he was stuck outside with no key. I ordered one more shooter for the road, on Fat Jack, and spun out into the crystal-still street, still buzzing from the coke.

Sure enough, Eddie was waiting there, sitting at the top of the stoop of the brownstone next door, his elbows on his knees, his chin resting in his hands. He came down the steps quickly when he saw me. We met under the streetlight. He was very high. His face was chalky, with black shadows underneath his eyes that made him look like a sad Pierrot. His face was not unlike my dying father's, I thought, haunted looking, and his pupils were tiny black dots. When Eddie's pupils contracted like that, it always seemed to me as if he were concentrating on something, as if his mind were far away, but he took me in his arms, held me, smothered my hair with kisses.

"Oh, baby, baby doll, I missed you so much," he said.

"I missed you, too," I said.

He kissed my hands. "My little monkey, my little monkey. Don't leave me again," he said.

Eddie was really stoned.

When we got inside, I asked him why he left without his keys, without locking the door. I sounded belligerent because I was pretty drunk, but Eddie was way beyond me, in a dope-chilled world of his own.

"There was business to take care of. I was in a hurry," he said.

"Fat Jack tells me you're in some kind of trouble," I said.

"Yeah, which reminds me. When I came around there, Doc told me you left with Fat Jack and Red. What were you doing with those two scumbags?"

"They had a little blow. We just went upstairs to get off," I said.

"Oh, well, in that case. Still, I don't like you hanging around with them. They're real lowlife scum, Janet."

"I know, I know...So what's the trouble you're in? Don't I have the right to know what's going on?"

At another time, Eddie would have leapt at the word "right." He liked to deny that I had any rights at all. He could be depended upon to deny it, in fact. But now he was impervious.

"Don't you worry about a thing. I got it under control. There's no trouble, no trouble at all...A slight misunderstanding between me and my new business partners, but I got it all sussed," Eddie said.

We had been standing in the back room. Now, he lifted me up, carried me to the front, through the curtains, and deposited me gently on the bed. It was so private, quiet, and safe lying there, surrounded by the rough muslin curtains we had bought at the fabric store on First Avenue. (Eddie's natural modesty had ensured that we would conceal where we slept and made love, at least, from the bare showcase window, which was not far from the foot of the bed.)

"Everything was great for a while. We could've had money, all the dope we needed, but good things never last...You woulda been so proud of me, doll, I scored big...Never mind, something else'll come along."

"From what I hear, you're lucky you didn't get killed," I said, still bucking for a fight.

"What? Don't listen to idle bar gossip. That'll get you nowhere in life. Forget it, OK? It's just you and me now, c'mon."

Eddie was determined to be tender, so I gave up. He kissed me. We opened our mouths and let the hot breath from the bottom of our chests pour into each other. I felt really bad about the Montauk mistake with the fisherman, but I decided to put that behind me.

Our kissing became wilder then. We pulled each other's hair, grappling the way we did when the sex was good for us. Eddie yanked off my clothes and his. He looked at my brown skin and poured himself over it, hands, mouth. He was discovering new levels of passion, going somewhere he had never been before, and so was I. We were afraid of the intensity, but that didn't stop us. We rubbed our sweaty bodies together until it was unbearable, and Eddie slipped into me. The friction was so sweet, we would thrust together and pause, shuddering and trembling in the dark. We stared into each other's eyes with alarm. We could see there where the ecstasy came from: beyond the skin, from our palpable, meshing souls. On the edge of consciousness, I felt at the same time as if I were being returned to myself, as if I were touching down on a deeply familiar but rarely visited place. We settled into a rhythm I hardly recognized, because it was neither too fast nor too frustratingly slow. This was Goldilocks love: at last, just right for me. I opened up all the way. I kept giving more and more of myself; I couldn't give enough. When I came (an orgasm that started at the base of my clitoris and nipped along like a fuse until it exploded inside), he stayed with me, letting me spend it, but he was right on the edge, and he could hardly move. When he came, it wasn't in his usual stealthy, controlled way. This time he yelped, sounding surprised, like he'd been shot. And for once, I wasn't jealous, didn't resent the exquisite sensation of fluid bursting, didn't feel aroused and abandoned. Instead, I was coming with him. He belonged to me; I was satisfied.

A lucid break in the general scheme, that was all. An unaccountable night of genuine intimacy. Quixotic as I was (under the circumstances), I had been long searching for it. Our connection was an oasis of grace.

Eddie and I stroked each other, laughed quietly. In the dread first light sifting through the curtains, we peered into each other's eyes. We were close. It was uncanny how close we were, in spite of ourselves, like the only two soldiers left alive in the field, grateful for not just all of our moving parts, but for each other.

Blackout

I woke up the next afternoon, startled by the sudden recollection of my father lying nearly dead across town. I threw myself into the shower, pulled on my shorts and top from the day before, stepped into my sneakers, not even bothering to tie the laces tight enough, and hit the street, which was tranquil and gray beneath low clouds. Overripe and exhausted from the long, dry summer, the tall, rare elm trees in Stuyvesant Park drooped with their burden of leaves. I was starving, so I grabbed a couple of dirty-water hot dogs at the far corner of the park before ducking into McCann's for a quick shot and a beer. When I reached into my pocket to pay the hot dog vendor, I discovered, to my horror, that Eddie had already stripped me of forty of the fifty bucks I had left from the night before. After I got over what should not have been the surprise of it, I was grateful he left me the ten.

This time, I walked confidently past the nurse's desk to the last room on the left at the end of the corridor, where I knew my father was lying in the first bed. The door stood wide open. Against the starched white hospital sheets, I saw black skin. A black man occupied my father's bed. It was surreal, the kind of trick your dreams play on you, when one economical picture tells the whole story. I broke down standing there, staring at the stranger. I couldn't move away. Sobbing, I covered my face with my hands. A young nurse not at all like the one from the night before came up and put her arms around me. She steered me gently into the back room, sat me down across from her at a round white table, and made me some tea. I so rarely cried, and I felt ashamed. I apologized for my outburst.

"It was just the shock," I said.

She assured me that it was the best possible reaction. Some people did not know how to grieve, she said.

Rayfield had died, finally, a few hours after I left.

"But he promised not to, not just yet," I kept thinking.

The first thing I did was to march into the empty saloon down the block from the hospital and announce to the bartender, who had never seen me before, that my father had just died. My hands were starting to shake and I was hoping he would buy me a drink. He didn't; embarrassed, he offered me his perfunctory sympathies. It occurred to me that even huge quantities of booze might not help much that night, but it was the best I could do. I decided to go over to the Alamo, where maybe the dour Arthur with the drooping mustache, who was a practiced mourner, would let me run a tab for old time's sake.

Then there are a few hours missing. I don't know how, for instance, I got back to Sixth Street. I was in a blackout. I only know that when I came to, my key still in the door, I was watching the profiles of a couple of wiry-looking young men in the far room; one of them was holding a gun. When they heard me, they turned their heads and the gun, for the flick of a second, in my direction. Out of the shadows leaped Eddie. He knocked the gun from the one kid's hand. It spun across the bare floor.

"No one pulls a piece on me in *my house*. No one," Eddie said. His voice was oddly calm. He sounded to me very Sicilian, completely in control.

The two young men were caught off guard. They looked at me, then they looked at Eddie, then one of them ran after the gun with shaky hands. But Eddie had already scooped it up. He pointed it at both of them, who stood frozen in place, way across the apartment.

"Don't say nothin' to no one. You never saw us. Got that? Otherwise, we come get you. Understan'?" one of them said.

I noticed even at that distance that the one talking had many teeth missing; also, he was still just a kid.

They started to edge toward the back exit, which opened on the courtyard, all the time facing us, pointlessly waving their knives.

"You, you little cocksucker, we definitely comin' fo' you," the other one said as they turned and ran outside, sprinting over the low brick wall.

When I was sure they were gone, I walked over to Eddie. He was standing there, marveling over his right hand, as if it had independently summoned the courage to knock the gun to the floor.

"Did you catch what I just did? Can you believe it?" Eddie asked.

Somewhere mixed up in there with the booze and the terror was the pride I felt. What guts he had. But then it came to me that nothing was finished. Those little thugs would be back.

"Eddie, you gotta get outta here."

"Whaddya mean? Forget those little slimeballs. They're never going to bother you or me again, I'm tellin' ya. Anyway, they were full of shit. I proved that. Didn't you see what I just did?"

"Eddie, how do you know what they're gonna do? You had no business bringing them here in the first place while I was gone. They don't take you to their cribs, where their old ladies live, do they? Of course they don't. Because the home is sacred, Eddie. It's sacred. You do not shit where you eat. Anybody on the street knows that. Disrespect me, you disrespect yourself. This is my house. It's sacred! You blew it. You blew it!" I screamed at him.

Then I went and sank into the only chair we had. He cornered me there, leaning over and thrusting his hands on my shoulders.

"I just saved your life, you bitch," he said.

"Saved my life? What were those two creeps doing in my house to begin with? Get out! Go home to your mother. Leave me the fuck alone."

"Fuck you, you cunt. This is my house, too. I ain't leaving. I ain't going nowhere," Eddie yelled at me, and he slapped me hard.

"My father just died," I said, speaking quietly now.

"Baby doll, why didn't you say so? No wonder you're upset. Come here, come to me. I'll be your daddy now." He pulled me out of the chair and put his arms around me.

I shook him loose. "That's got nothing to do with it," I said, turning away.

"Sure it does. You just lost the only pop you're ever gonna have. Don't worry, little doll, I'll take care of you. Don't turn your back on me. He's dead and gone, but I'm alive. Here. Look at me. Don't turn your back on the living."

"'The living'? Is that what you call yourself, you suck-ass little junkie?"

He looked at me. "Sorry, baby, but it's your grief talking. Come to bed now. It's over; come to bed. You need to rest." He reached for my hand.

"Eddie, will you get out of here? As long as you're around, I'm not safe. I need for you *to leave*." I was screaming again.

He sat down. Very cool, like an exercise in cool. "Calm down, will you? I know what's good for you now. Sleep, that's what you need," he said.

"Eddie, I am calm. I am very calm. Listen to my voice. I'm not going to bed until you leave," I said.

The truth is I had no intention of going to bed at all. I needed a drink. Well far along on my bender, I could see withdrawal coming at me at sixty miles an hour, and it was unyielding; it was bigger than I was. Tremors, ringing ears as loud as sirens inside the head, sweats, darting hallucinations, nerves so raw the light felt like a thousand jabbing knives—no, I wasn't ready yet. Add to this a new sorrow and it's easy to get why I would have done just about anything for a drink. That was one reason, perhaps the only real reason, I wanted to get rid of Eddie. So I could go out again and drink.

"OK, doll, let's discuss this in the morning," he said.

Of course, Eddie wasn't about to split in the middle of the night. If I had been rational, I would have asked him to go in the morning. Not good enough. I was scared and sad, irremediably sad. I was aching for a drink.

"No, no. You gotta go now. What if those guys come back tonight? No! I don't wanna get killed, understan'? Get out. *Get out!*" I was screaming again.

Eddie walked away finally. "I'm not going anywhere, I'm tellin' ya. You get out," he said.

"Right, that's exactly right, OK. But I don't want to see you here when I get back," I said.

"Janet, baby doll, my baby, Janet, don't go. Come on, you're upset. Come back! I'm sorry, I'm sorry. Hey, I mean it, hey! Janet!" Eddie yelled after me as I ran off down the street.

The bar I was headed for on the corner of Avenue A wasn't our usual hangout, although God knows we'd been there enough times. Its only drawback was we couldn't run a tab. I decided to go there anyway because I couldn't deal with the prospect of Fat Jack and Red leering at me just then, and they were sure to be at the Monterey. This other place stayed open late, usually until after five in the morning, and I thought maybe, magically, in the few hours I had left, I could hustle some drinks. The front room was empty except for the man behind the stick, who was sipping a rum and Coke and listening to the jukebox play "96 Tears." He was thumping the bar, pretending it was a drum.

"Hi, I need a drink, but I'm broke. Can you help me out?"

Then they were there, crowding in the doorway. The two little punks who had just left our house, plus another big guy with shining black skin and dreadlocks. I kind of recognized him from around. And someone else—a Puerto Rican guy wearing a tight suit and inexplicably a green carnation in his buttonhole. And then an unfamiliar white guy appeared, a pasty, pudgy Irish-looking guy. They didn't belong together, this crew, but there they were. And they didn't come inside. They just stood in the doorway, blocking the streetlight. The bartender said, "Get in or get out. Don't crowd the doorway."

The big African American guy answered him, but he was looking at me while he spoke. "We want to buy this woman a drink."

We? The whole damn gang?

He stepped up to the bar. Then the rest of them walked away, out of sight.

"Anything the lady wants. And I'll have a Black Russian."

His diction was clear. He was clean-shaven and his T-shirt was spotless. Not that I trusted him. The scene gave me the creeps. But before he could change his mind, I ordered.

"Bring me a shot and a Heineken. Make it a double shot," I said.

When the bartender put up my drinks, the guy grabbed the bottle of Heineken. He waved it in front of me. "Come outside," he said, smiling. His teeth shone white against his African-black skin. He put some money on the bar. The bartender walked away.

I wanted the beer—and the short glass full of whiskey he was holding in his other hand—very much. I can't tell you how much. I followed him, past the oblivious bartender, out the door. All the time, the guy was dangling the bottle of beer, the Heineken. It looked lovely, the green glass dripping cold in the muggy air. There was no breeze and the street greeted us with a blast of foul smells from the overstuffed garbage cans, their contents spilling out, pools of urine stagnating on the pavement and the occasional fresh explosion of vomit.

When we had gone far enough and he was sure the bartender could no longer see us through the window, the leader called out to his buddies.

"Let me have my drink," I said.

They shoved me along the pavement.

"Not till we get where we're going," one of them said.

The leader was jostling me down the street.

"Just give me the drink. Give it to me."

They pushed me down into a basement. The two punks went and stood guard at the door. They were silent. The white guy and the Puerto Rican threw me onto the wet concrete floor. The African American, the fake Rastafarian, took hold of my arms and yanked me along on my stomach up to where he was now sitting against the wall. The top half of my body straddled his thighs. He opened the fly of his jeans and pulled out a long, fat penis.

"You don't have to be so rough," I said.

"What's that you say?" He slapped me around the face, across the head, hard. "Shut up, pork, and swallow this," he said, shoving it down my throat.

Someone else pulled the rest of my body out straight, so that my legs were spread wide on the floor, just my head raised, gagging on the huge penis, which the ringleader kept thrusting against the back of my throat. Then one of the two men behind me put his full weight on his hands, pushing down on the small of my back to hold me still; the other one tore off my pants and reamed me. It felt like he cut me open. The pain was searing, fierce. I almost fainted; the pain brought me around. I kept trying to summon a whore's detachment, to loosen the sphincter muscles so I could take it better, but whoever it was back there didn't want me to take it any better. He liked ripping into me, liked hearing me cry out each time he did it. Meanwhile, I looked up at the man in front of me, expecting to see his face hooded with pleasure; instead, he was staring back, his eyes wide with outrage. His eyeballs were the color of yellowed ivory; the sweat dripped down, but he did not blink. He stifled my screams with his penis, jamming it in deeper and harder until I stopped making any noise. He cursed me, called me "slut," "hole," "pork." Then he grew quiet, too; at least I think he did. All I could hear or see was pain, endless it seemed. It felt like I was being punched in my throat and stabbed up the ass over and over. "When are they going to come?" I kept praying for them to come. I thought it would be the finish, that their orgasms would save my life. But what I failed to appreciate is that coming had nothing to do with it. This was something else.

All of a sudden, for no apparent reason, the ringleader pulled his still-erect penis out of my throat. One beat later, the guys behind me scrambled to their feet, the Puerto Rican kid pulling his swollen prick back into his suit pants. I gasped for air and collapsed, splayed out like a dead animal. But I was feeling triumph. "Nobody got their rocks off," I kept thinking. For some reason, this was important to me. I lifted myself up on an elbow and turned my face around in time to catch the Puerto Rican kid zipping up his fly. The green carnation, a little brown around the edges, still hung from the buttonhole of his suit jacket. He was shivering.

"We got a message for your boy. You tell the little scumbag we're going to ice him. And he won't have to wait long," he said.

The two punks turned and stared at me. They looked terrified. Then they ran out of the basement, almost as if I were going to come after them. The fake Rastafarian leader didn't rush. He was the last one to leave.

"Takin' care of my business. That's all it was, pork," he said.

I lay there, amazed to be out of pain. When I was sure they were gone, I spit at the damp concrete wall in front of me and then tried to yell after them, "I'm still alive, you motherfuckers. Get it? I'm still alive!" But I was too hoarse to make myself heard.

Park Bench

I had to get back to Eddie fast. They were coming for him. It was hard to walk. I started to worry about how I was going to be able to move my bowels when the time came. But compared with the ripping agony of a few minutes earlier, what I was feeling as I walked slowly home was negligible. In fact, the first thing I felt after emerging from the dark basement would have to be described as pleasure. My whole body had gone numb, and I was experiencing this irrepressible lightness of being. Waves of gratitude swept over me for every scraggly braced-up tree, for the undisturbed quiet of that private hour, and for the gentle blessing of the wan morning light. Then after a block or two, exhaustion hit. The only thing that kept me going after that was Eddie. I was praying I would make it home in time.

When I got back to the crib, Eddie was gone. God, I hoped wherever he was, he was safe. I realized I couldn't look for him now. I was beat. I needed to get clean. While I dragged myself through the empty streets, besides worrying about Eddie, I had been dreaming only of sinking into a hot bath.

Unfortunately, the bathtub at Sixth Street, coated with filth, had never been used for its intended purpose; it was simply the place you stood when you took a shower. So I would have to make myself stand up under the water for as long as it took to get clean, if I ever could. I wasn't too sure about that. It wasn't until I started to undress in the bathroom that I realized my shorts were wet with blood. I threw all my clothes in a pile in the corner and climbed underneath the shower. After a while, I leaned over until the feeble jet was hitting me between the cheeks of my behind. I watched the water, pink with blood, disappear down the drain. I collapsed right there, where I stayed for a while curled up into a ball. I think I slept. Finally, I climbed out of the tub and went over to the mirror above the sink to examine, as best I could, a place that was stinging on my head. I discovered a cut on my scalp, right above the temple. Slapped backhand with a ringed finger. I combed my broken hair very gingerly over the spot where the blood had congealed. Then I got scared. Maybe they had already killed Eddie. Maybe they had come back while I was under the shower. This time to kill me. For a minute I just froze. Finally I worked up the courage to leave the bathroom.

I pulled on a pair of big cotton underpants that I rarely wore and stuffed them with toilet paper. At the bottom of a pile of clothes in the dark recesses of the walk-in closet, I found an apple-green circle skirt I had bought for a few dollars on the street. It was way too big for me now. I rummaged through the pile until I found a dirty silk sash from an old kimono. I tied the skirt around my waist with that. Then I put on a fresh black T-shirt, taking a minute to decide, even then, whether it would look better worn tucked in or hanging loose. Either way, it was a hideous outfit, I thought, but I should at least wear a skirt if I wanted to pass unnoticed when I went uptown to Park Avenue. And it had become obvious to me that this was where I must go. I needed to be safe, and I needed someone to take care of me; even Maggie would do.

I had an easy time catching a cab on First Avenue. There seemed to be a fleet of them charging north on their way to pick up the uptown people bound for work. I found my voice and told the driver, an old-fashioned taxi driver, a Jewish grandpa from Brooklyn, that he would have to wait a minute while I got the money from the doorman. He didn't object, seeing as I had given him a Park Avenue address. It occurred to me that I didn't really have to beg for cab fare. I might very well still have a few hundred dollars in the bank, but I wasn't sure. I never read those damn statements; they made me cringe. In the meantime, I fully expected to walk into the Fifty-seventh Street branch of Banker's Limited one day soon and have Ms. Greyson tell me that I was broke. Not today, I decided. We cut over to the FDR Drive on the East River, and I sat back and watched the morning sun bounce across the silver water. The familiar spectacle of the gutsy, lively river, actually managing to look fresh as little waves skidded over its surface in the false hope of the early-morning breeze, never failed to lift my spirits.

When we pulled up in front of Maggie's awning, the doorman Oscar ran out, swiveling on his arthritic hips, and opened the car door for me. I had known Oscar nearly all my life.

"Miss Janet, welcome home," he said.

"Will you wait a minute? I'll just get the money from my mother," I told the cabdriver.

"I'm waiting," he said.

"Just a minute, Miss Janet, I'll have to call upstairs. It's seven in the morning. I'm not sure your mother is awake yet. I'll have to let her know you're here," he said, sounding apologetic.

Something was wrong, and I could feel the blood seeping through the toilet paper in my underpants. I needed to get inside soon.

"Since when do you announce me, Oscar?"

"Since your mother left strict instructions. I'm sorry, Miss Janet," Oscar said.

He rocked from leg to leg over to the house phone inside the front door. I followed him, preparing to take the receiver if there was any trouble. It rang for a long time. Finally, I saw him nodding into it, saying, "Yes, missus, yes, missus." Then he hung up and turned to me. He shrugged his shoulders.

"You're not to be allowed up today. I'm sorry," he said.

"Whaddya mean? Let me talk to her," I said, sounding a little frantic.

Oscar turned back to the switchboard and pulled down one of the levers. When he heard Maggie at the other end, he handed the phone to me.

"Mother, I need to come up. I've been raped, brutally raped," I said.

"Forget it, Janet, I don't believe you. You can't come around here with your stories any time you feel like it and disrupt my life. I've had it; I just won't stand for it. Why can't your boyfriend, Eddie, look after you?"

"I don't know where he is. The guys who raped me, they're going to kill him when they find him if they haven't already," I said.

"Janet, this sounds like more of your drug-induced hallucinations. I know I can't help you by giving in. You have to check yourself into a hospital. Meanwhile, I told Oscar to call the police if you refuse to leave. That's all. Good-bye." She hung up.

It occurred to me to mention that Rayfield had died, but what if she didn't believe that either?

Oscar and I stood there staring at each other.

"Now what?" I said.

"You're in some kind of trouble, aren't you?" Oscar asked.

"Yeah, I guess I am," I said, realizing as I said it that this would have been the ideal time to turn on the tears, maybe in the process win Oscar's broadest sympathy, get him to appeal my case. Except I had forgotten how.

God, I needed to lie down, I really needed to lie down. That was all. If only I could lie down someplace, everything would be all right, I knew it. In the meantime, I didn't know what to do, so I just stood there.

Oscar had stationed himself a few feet away in his blue summer uniform and his little blue doorman hat, torn between all that costume meant to him and helping me, the bright-eyed little girl he had watched grow into this wasted specter of a human being. In spite of my suntan, I must have looked ominous to him against the backdrop of that pristine, gleaming marble lobby, my body swimming inside the big skirt, the blond-on-blond hair sprouting from dark roots. It was obvious he wanted me to go away, but he didn't have the heart to call the police. Then, as if he had been debating it, he suddenly reached into his pocket and pulled out a twenty.

"Here, take this," Oscar said, pressing the bill into my hand.

"Thank you, Oscar, I'll pay you back," I said.

"I know you will. That's a good girl, go on now," he said.

He walked me back to the cab and opened the door for me. Once I was inside the car, he leaned over and peered at me through the open window. "Where are you going to?"

"Tompkins Square Park, the southeast corner," I said.

Oscar leaned farther into the cab and gave the driver the address.

I was hoping to find one or two of my drinking buddies from the local bottle gang still sitting out on the bench from the night before. Sometimes these old guys shared their Wild Irish Rose with Eddie and me, letting us chug back their wine while they regaled us with horror stories about their days in Sing Sing or their dirt-poor childhoods in the South.

Sure enough, Whitey was there and one or two of the others. Whitey was the porter for the Monterey Bar and Grill. He was very fond of Eddie and me. On several occasions, after he had finished mopping the floor and tying up the garbage, the three of us would convene to this very spot to continue drinking.

"Hello, girl, you up early this morning," Whitey said.

He was wearing, as usual, a T-shirt gray with age and a pair of heavy greased-up dungarees. He looked like a workingman out of the countryside.

"I gotta lie down, I just got raped," I said, and collapsed on the bench next to his.

The few men who were there wanted to know what happened. I felt ashamed to tell them, but I sensed their concern was genuine. Without going into too much detail, I got the main points of the story across. Someone slipped a folded-up nylon jacket underneath my head. Someone else threw a smelly blanket over my body. Whitey sat down carefully on the edge of the bench.

"Here, have a swig. You need it."

The hot whiskey from the pint bottle felt rough on my throat, but I kept drinking, because after it hit my stomach, the liquor spread through my insides like kindness itself.

"You been pretty banged up. Take it easy. Rest here awhile," he said.

I looked into the shiny pug face covered with gray grizzle, into the warm black eyes, and farther up into the network of green branches high above me. "You get what you need in this life," I thought. Then I passed out.

A few hours later, Whitey was nudging me gently. "Here's somethin' fo' you to eat," he said.

He had a quart of Schlitz tucked under his arm, and he was holding on to a big meatball hero wrapped in white paper with his free hand.

Nobody had ever been that good to me, I decided. I couldn't believe how hungry I was. And the beer—at last to be mine, given freely—what a blessing.

"Please, take this," I said, offering him the few crumpled dollars I had left.

"Nah, keep yo' money," Whitey said.

"How can I ever thank you?" I asked.

"C'mon, it's nothin' you wouldn't do fo' me if I was the one who was down."

He handed me the sandwich first. I tore into it. The meatballs tasted luscious and sweet, the doughy bread even sweeter. Then, after I had finished most of the sandwich, Whitey passed me the quart. I poured that into my sore throat.

"Well, you seem to be a whole lot better now. Why don't you think about goin' home?"

"I can't," I said.

"You gotta go sometime. This be no place fo' a woman after it gets dark," Whitey said.

"I know," I said.

Damn, I hated that "no place fo' a woman." I hated how they kept us locked up inside with just the threat of those weapons of theirs, those penises. 'Rape—ha! Big deal! Is that the best you got? Big fucking deal. You know what men really can't stand? They can't stand that we can take it. I can take it, motherfuckers! Damn, look at me. I'm not even bleeding anymore,' I thought. I was about to start shaking my fist and cursing out loud but stopped myself in time when I realized Whitey was still there.

"I was hopin' you and I could leave together. See, I gotta get back to my room fo' some sleep," he said.

"Of course, of course. You shouldn't have stayed so long. I'll be fine, I promise. Don't worry," I said.

Whitey shook his head. "I don't like leavin' you out here by yourself," he said.

"Listen, I'll be fine, OK?"

"Well, all right. Here, you can have dis pint. Try to drink it slow," Whitey said.

"Thank you with all my heart." I leaned over and gave him a kiss on his cheek.

"Here take this, too. It's not the best but them boys is out to harm. So take it. Better than nothin'." He laid the whiskey down on the blanket and next to it a knife. Looked like a switchblade. I wasn't sure. I hadn't seen that many knives in my life. It was long. There was a button in the handle. I looked up to ask him about it, but he was gone. I hid the knife underneath the jacket I was using as a pillow.

I was alone with a full pint, an afternoon breeze tickling the branches of the tree overhead, a hazy, gentle late-summer sky. I was at peace. Except I had to pee. 'Every problem has a solution,' I thought. I pulled off my underpants (the toilet paper by now stuck to them) while I was still under the blanket, and then I went and stood next to the trunk of the big sycamore. I looked around until I was sure that no one—not the old people on the benches across the path, not the basketball players in the distance—was watching. I spread my legs wide underneath my skirt and let the urine flow. Back to bench, under blanket, pull on pants. Tra-la. I really felt at home now. I took a swig of whiskey. Something shifted inside my head. Even though I knew better, it felt as if the world had righted itself, suddenly, and I was where I always should have been: back on top.

Another Rescue

As the afternoon wore on, I struck up a conversation with the gods—not God, mind you, only the gods. They appeared to me more imp-like than Olympian, their tiny wreathed heads poking through the low-hanging clouds. I felt as though, in this respect, I had come down in the world. These gods (a vague mixture of Greek and Roman) were not as protective or as intimate as God and His Mother had been. They were raucous, wearying, in fact. The more I defended the earthy simplicity of my current setup, the more they touted the glories of civilization.

"Believe me," Saturn said, "it's better to contemplate a chair than a tree. And look at that skirt, what an affront!"

"Why do you think people wear clothes?" Mars asked me. "To stave off the boredom, that's why."

I was getting fed up with them, with their Old World decadence, with their very lack, if I may say so, of spirituality. I turned over on the bench and closed my eyes. Somewhere right above me a few sparrows were twittering, the sound of their two-note song muffled in the humid air. I was seized with an unexpected wave of pity for little Eddie. What would become of him? For the first time, it really hit me that his life was in danger. "Oh, but he can take care of himself," I thought. But could he? I was beginning to wonder. I heard people walking by; they were avoiding me, I could tell. Which was fine with me...wonderful to be left alone. I marveled over how far I had come, "from Park Avenue to a park bench." Where had I heard that? It's a long way to travel in one short lifetime, I thought, not without considerable pride. I was free. I drank some more whiskey and fell asleep again, feeling as if I had finally arrived.

"Janet! Janet!"

"Shh, she's over there, see?"

"All right, I see. Fred, Dr. Monroe, I've found her!"

It was Maggie, calling out through the park in her best theatrical trill, and behind her, Maggie's longtime shrink and party-going friend, Fred Schuster. Another man, pretty bald with a double chin and dressed in a three-piece suit, was tagging along after them.

Maggie was wearing a new matching flower-print skirt and top and low heels. There were yards of material in that skirt, which swirled around her as she marched over to me. It looked like she'd dressed for the occasion.

I sat up fast and took a drink. This was going to be rough.

"OK, what are you doing here?" I asked.

"Oscar told me where you were going. He told me you looked terrible," Maggie said.

Maggie was standing over me now. Up came the doctor fellows.

"Hi, Fred, I'd offer you a snort, but all I got is what you see here," I said, taking another drink.

"Thank you anyway, Janet. I'd like you to meet a friend of mine, George. George, say hello to Janet," Fred said, smiling that unctuous smile of his.

It never ceased to amaze me what a cheeky little bloodsucker Fred was in his eternal cardigans, the white of his bony shin guaranteed to reveal itself whenever he crossed his legs. A real creep. Typical of him, he was trying to fob off his colleague as a casual friend, and this was supposed to be a casual meeting of friends, I suppose. How patronizing. It was insulting.

"Hello, Janet," the George character said.

"Listen, I know why you're here. Don't pull this crap on me. I know it takes two doctors' signatures to get someone committed. Forget it, I'll go back to Sixth Street. I know when I'm beaten," I said, starting to stand.

Maggie had moved away. She was standing quietly behind the tree like a little kid playing hide and seek.

"OK, Fred and what's-your-name, you can split now. I don't need you," I said.

"Not so fast, young lady," George said. He took a few steps in my direction, hovering with the frightened bravado of an inexperienced lion tamer before he cracks the whip.

Holy shit, the faggot in the three-piece suit was trying to get physical with me. With me! I hadn't spent all this time on the street for nothing. I drained the pint.

"If that's how you want it," I said.

Then I reached under the jacket, pulled out the switchblade and pressed the button. It shot out like a snake. I stuck it next to the doctor's face.

"You better back off, unless you want one nostril," I said.

To my fierce delight, he jumped about a foot.

But Fred grabbed my wrist and started to twist it. Then George grabbed my other arm. I was shouting and kicking. They had me, though, at least for the time being.

"Somebody call the police!" Fred yelled.

A small crowd of old people and little kids had gathered.

"Help me, help me, I'm being kidnapped!" I screamed, but the crowd just stood there.

Meanwhile, Maggie had run out of the park, as it turned out, to call the police.

"If it were a man taking a snooze on a park bench on a warm afternoon, do you think anybody would be throwing him into the nuthouse? Oh yeah, and look at me: I'm dirty and smelly and I've got a crack on my head and blood on my skirt, so I must be nuts, right? When a man becomes totally violent, they throw him in the drunk tank overnight. When a woman misbehaves, gets out of line even just a little bit, they lock her away forever. Watch out boys, female at large! Woman on the loose! Whatsa matter, do I scare you? Do I threaten you?" I screamed at Fred and George. Then I spit in their smug faces.

"A woman—that is a white woman—stretches out on a park bench, and they come right down on her. Can you dig what they're doing to me?" I was addressing the crowd now. "You're not free until I'm free!" I yelled, twisting and turning in the surprisingly strong grip of the two doctors.

Maggie came sailing back then, flanked by what looked like a squadron of cops. They pushed their way through the crowd.

"All you pigs for one little defenseless chick?" I said, laughing a hollow laugh.

The knife was still in my hand. Fred had not been able to get it away from me. A cop came up and took it. Several others eased the doctors away and assumed their place. I had at least three or four of them restraining me. When I heard the ambulance, I struggled again, just to register one final protest, and then I gave up, letting the cops shove me along. Maggie was already seated on one of the narrow benches lining the back of the ambulance.

"You sons of bitches. Nobody's gonna fuck with me," I said after they pushed me inside.

The cop riding with us sat up straight. "You better simmer down, sister," he said.

But he and I both knew this last expression of my outrage was merely a formality. It was just that I did not want to remember myself riding along to my doom without even a whimper.

I focused my narrowed eyes on Maggie, who was sitting very tall, her mouth set in a hard, thin line. She looked self-righteously hell-bent on remaining in control. In control of everything, I thought. I would have liked to beat her phony composure clear out of her, to knock those thick glasses off her face and smash them.

"I thought you didn't want to have anything more to do with me," I said.

"Janet, I'm sorry." Her voice cracked. "I had to do this." She started to cry.

"Oh, shit, I don't know why you're crying. They're not putting you away. Mother, stop them, you don't know what it's like. Stop them before it's too late!" I yelled.

She turned her head.

The ambulance pulled up to a red light. Through the back window, I could see the two doctors in their Lincoln Continental tailgating us in the rush-hour traffic. Meanwhile, the two of us and the cop were all traveling for free through the streets of New York. A five-dollar cab ride at the very least. I felt pampered riding in the ambulance.

But the gods, fair-weather friends that I knew them to be, had disappeared. I was stuck inside the crush of three dimensions one more time, in a paddy wagon with the woman who had always been out to destroy me. She had hunted me down and trapped me just because I was a wild thing.

The ambulance began to move again, crawling slowly up the avenue. There was no air where we sat. My bleached-dead hair was plastered with sweat. My whole body ached. Now Maggie was crying again.

She was embarrassing me in front of the cop. 'I travel in the company of fools,' I thought. Oh well, you had to forgive her. She didn't know what she was doing. I sank back on the hard bench. Then, without warning, I burst into tears: real salt tears covering my contorted red face, the mucus running from my nose. Everything obliterated. I began to sob convulsively; I had been seized with a revelation of grief. Maggie staggered across the rocking ambulance, sat down, and put her arms around me. She held me and patted my back awkwardly, not sure what to do, as if I were someone else's strange, small child.

"There, there" was all she could think to say at first, but then, as if she had suddenly gotten the word, she added, "Don't worry. Everything's going to be all right."

We continued to ride like that, me weeping silently and peacefully on my mother's shoulder until we got to Bellevue.

Bellevue

An "old-timer"— someone with long-term sobriety—once said after hearing my story, "This disease takes you where it wants you to go."

It took me finally to Bellevue, where they—in this case the faceless, inaccessible hospital authorities—pumped me full of the newest and strongest narcoleptic, Haldol. After about two hours, I was vibrating and twitching in the unfurnished dayroom beside the other quivering outcasts, all of us staring at a restless TV picture that jumped and rotated along with us. That night, I had to sleep on a rubber sheet. The following morning, I was forced to take a cold bath in the one tub everyone had to use, but forbidden a towel because, the warden of the bath said, there were no towels to be had just then. After I bathed and dressed in front of the warden, who glared at me the whole time, I was released back to the dayroom.

A shrunken, toothless, little white woman turned crone too soon by the street approached me slyly in that human warehouse and pressed something into my hand. It was a raised, satin-faced picture of the Virgin. Her robe was a shimmering cerulean blue, her dress underneath was the color of a robin's breast, and her face peered up through a gilded halo. I made good use of my gift, praying to Mary more or less constantly for the next few hours until Maggie showed up.

She marched across the visitors' room to where I was standing in front of the big windows covered in wire mesh. I was vibrating from my morning dose of Haldol and otherwise amusing myself watching the gridlock on First Avenue. Maggie looked like she had come on serious business. She was wearing a navy-blue miracle-fiber suit and sturdy black heels, and had combed her flyaway hair back behind big gold earrings.

"Janet, why didn't you tell me about Rayfield? Don't you think I would want to know? I never would've had you put in Bellevue if I'd known!"

"Well, Mom, I thought about it, but then I was pretty sure you wouldn't believe me."

"Of course I would have believed you. Janet, nobody would make up something like that."

"So who, especially at seven in the morning, would make up being raped?"

"Oh." Maggie swallowed hard. "Oh. I'm sorry. But now what are we going to do? Poor Janet. We've got a real situation on our hands." She looked sheepish. "How am I going to get you out of here? I signed that paper, you know."

"Mother, don't give me that helpless bullshit. Call your two buddies, Fred and what's-his-name, George. Call the fucking shrinks. They put me in, they can get me out."

"Yes, yes. Of course, I'll call them right away. I'm sure it can be arranged once they know the circumstances." She paused. "We do have a little time. Betsy is waiting until Saturday to have the funeral so the children and grandchildren can make arrangements. Thoughtful as always. She's handling everything all by herself. She was the strong one in that marriage."

"All right, Mom. Cool it. The old man just died."

"Of course, you're right. You've been through a lot these past few days, Janet, too much. And I haven't been much good to you, have I? But I was trying to save your life. You do understand that, don't you?"

"Yes, yes. Anyway, nobody should have to, but people around the world go through hell and worse every day. I don't know that a choice of horrors didn't help somehow. One thing distracted me from the other and vice versa, you know? But this little Bellevue episode is a bit much to handle, even for me, Mom."

I then told her everything that was going on, including the ice-cold bath and no towel. I knew that detail would get her.

"Oh my God, it's worse than Olivia de Havilland in *The Snake Pit*! Oh Jesus, Janet, I've got to get you out of here. Just be brave. It won't be long."

"Hurry up, please. And, Mom, you have to get word to Eddie."

"How do you expect me to do that? You don't own a phone."

"Please, it's imperative. Those guys who raped me are going to kill him. It's a matter of life and death. Maybe he's safe with Evelyn on City Island, I don't know. I hope so. But if not, then what? Please. Anyway, I want him to know I'm OK. Won't you go to our house and slip a message inside?"

"No. I refuse to go down there by myself. It's too dangerous. Eddie can call me if he's so worried."

I almost asked her to get in touch with Evelyn but then thought better of it. "OK then, could you maybe just call the Monterey Bar and Grill? Tell whoever answers to have Eddie call you. Mom, please."

"All right, I can do that."

"Right now, today? Promise?"

"I promise, Janet. Don't get so excited."

Maggie did leave a message at the Monterey with old Doc himself, but she never heard back from Eddie. That night on the six o'clock local news she found out she never would. She just caught the tail end of it, the part where they showed the original footage of Donna Vickers, clearly shaken, being escorted out of her saloon, Chester's. Donna was blinking in the morning light, trying to shield her eyes from both the rising sun and the cameras. Then they showed footage of Arthur O'Rourke earlier that afternoon when he was released from the police station. He made no attempt to hide his face. He just stood there and gazed into the camera. He was tall with a drooping moustache and appeared surprisingly dignified under the circumstances, inconsolably sad. Maggie had never seen him before, but she knew the name: one of Janet's men, Arthur from the Alamo, old Arthur.

I didn't get to watch the local news, because the consensus on the floor at Bellevue was that news was boring compared with *Starsky and Hutch* reruns. The vertically rolling TV picture, even though it moved slowly down the screen, made talking heads hard to follow. Car chases, for some reason, lent themselves better to that format.

After what Maggie saw, she wasted no time getting in touch with Donna, who volunteered to come see me the following day. Visiting me in a hellhole like Bellevue didn't faze Donna. Most of her oldest friends and best customers had ended up on the flight deck at one time or other. In any case, it had happened on her watch and she wanted to be the one to tell me.

I went and stood in front of the bank of wire-mesh-covered windows. The sun poured over a sooty group of related hospital buildings across First Avenue. A few people scurried along the street below. It was afternoon, around two, and traffic was moving. I watched the free world carry on, oblivious. I turned and stared at Donna. I kept peering into her face. The big beauty mark above her lip fascinated me. Even without any makeup, her coloring was vivid and her features well defined. She was conventionally pretty. But Donna ignored this fact in order to live like a man. She had no personal vanity, as if, having chosen the life of a professional rummy, she had decided it would violate her code to pay attention to her looks. I wasn't thinking at all about what she had just told me. Instead, I was contemplating all of this when she cupped my face in her hands and said, "OK, Janet, let's sit down."

"I don't want to sit right now. I want to stay by the window."

I felt my stomach tighten up and a dull weight descend right on my solar plexus. A longing for Eddie kicked in immediately, which surprised me.

Donna thought I should know how it went down. She turned her back to the light and parked herself on the windowsill.

"I was sitting there at the bar after closing waiting for Arthur to come by for a drink."

She saw the expression on my face.

"OK, yeah, Arthur and I occasionally get it on. Never mind. I was sitting there, I don't know why in the dark, sipping my drink. I wasn't doing lines or anything, just sitting listening to the quiet. It was soothing in the dark. Then Eddie knocks on the window. Of course I let him in. Why wouldn't I? You know I loved little Eddie, Janet. You know I did."

Her voice broke a little.

"He starts waving this piece in my face. 'We're going down to the safe,' he says, 'and you're going to give me all your money.'" She sounded incredulous.

"'Eddie, what's the matter? You don't need to point that thing at me. Eddie, you and I are true friends, asshole buddies. I'd never let anything happen to you if I could help it. I'll give you whatever you need. Just put down the gun.'

"He starts shaking. He says, 'No, man, you don't understand. I can't take that chance. Let's say I do put the gun down and then you decide to change your mind about helping me—I'm fucked. The people I owe, if I don't pay them now, it's not like they're just gonna break my kneecaps. Yeah, sure, you and me used to be tight, but I can't afford to have friends anymore. That's over. Take me down to the safe *now*, capiche? Otherwise I'm going to hurt you.'

"OK, so I had no problem believing him. Janet, he was gone, out of control. His eyes were wild. I'd never seen him like that, or anyone really. I was fucking scared. But I kept talking. I figured if he could just hear a calm, reassuring tone, like a mother, you know, someone who would never hurt him, who would only help him. It's a blur now, but I remember we were in the basement, right across from the stairs in that little room where the safe is. I was still talking, telling him to put down the gun. Take everything in the safe, but for God's sake stop pointing that thing right at my temple. Eddie or no Eddie, he was like a stranger. It was driving me crazy, I was so scared. I was shaking, trying to get the combination lock to click. And then we both hear someone on the stairs. Eddie starts to back out and turn around, still holding the gun. The next thing I know, I hear a shot. Eddie collapses on the ground. That was it, Janet. Instant. It was horrible, terrible. God, I'm sorry."

Donna started hugging herself. Then she put her head down and turned her face away from me. Still looking away, she said, "At least he didn't suffer. I don't think he ever knew what hit him, if that's any consolation.

"Anyway it was Arthur, the gunny sergeant, the sharpshooter. He come by to see me and stepped inside because the door was open, heard me pleading with Eddie to put down the gun. Obviously he didn't know who I was talking to. Arthur went behind the counter and got my Saturday night special, the one I picked up in Florida, out of the drawer underneath the cash register. He knew just where I kept it. So does everybody. It isn't a secret. He went to the head of the stairs and pointed the gun down in the direction of Eddie. When Eddie backed out like that I'm sure Arthur still didn't know who it was—didn't have time to know—just a guy with a piece ripping me off. Well, I mean, you get what happened. It really was all a terrible accident, Janet.

"Poor Eddie. I gotta say it. For a smart kid, he could be incredibly stupid. None of this ever should've happened. You know, Janet, I would have given him the money, all of it in that safe, whatever he needed, no questions asked. It was just a couple of nights' worth anyhow. I loved Eddie. OK, he was crazy. Hell, I knew that. I knew he was a junkie. Who didn't? But Eddie, he was special."

The sun all of a sudden dipped and made a beeline for my eyes. It hurt. By this time Donna was patting me on the back, and then she put her arm around me, because it had finally hit me for real, and I was crying. My whole body just seemed to give out and I started to faint. Donna grabbed me, steered me to the long table and sat me down. She called over a nurse's aide.

"Get her something to drink. She's just had some very bad news."

We waited a long time for the aide to come back. Donna mostly held me while I cried. I just couldn't stop. Physically couldn't. Every time I tried to stop it was like a force backed up inside and then broke through. I gave up trying. Donna told me to let the tears come. It did feel good, the grief pouring out of me. I kept picturing little Eddie the first time I saw him sitting in the tree. I could hear him calling after me, "Janet, don't go." If only I hadn't walked out the door.

I felt that I had let him down that night and in some basic way a long time ago. Maybe I could have done something. Been stronger. Stood for something other than willful self-destruction. I felt that I just let him die. Donna was crying now, too. I think to some degree she felt the same way. It's like we were both watching Eddie kill himself, and we did nothing. In fact, we were entertained by it really. Of course, neither one of us were doing that much to take care of ourselves either. But Eddie was the most spectacular. He went higher than anyone.

Finally the aide showed up again with a young doctor in tow. The doctor had a lot of straight black hair that kept falling over his forehead. He would occasionally brush it back with his hand, almost flirtatiously, while Donna explained, with a hostile edge in her voice, that I needed to leave Bellevue and go home to my mother. First she told him my father just died. Then she told him about Eddie. He actually was familiar with the news story. I don't think a death in the family necessarily would've moved him, but all of a sudden, he linked my being locked up in Bellevue with the big news event. Maybe he thought he smelled yet another suit against the city and the beleaguered hospital, this time incurred on his watch. He could see the headlines: "Police Drag Grief-Stricken Girlfriend off to Bellevue." Anyway, he agreed with Donna right away. I was amazed. He instructed the aide to bring me some coffee while he went back to the office to call his superiors as well as my mother. I got sprung a few hours later.

"There's not a lot left to lose," I said to myself.

The Wake

The Episcopal minister hired to say a few parting words about Rayfield apologized for his brevity, but he never knew the deceased. "You're not the only one," I thought. Rayfield's offspring in particular all seemed to wear the same faintly eager look, as if, given the chance, they would have been glad to learn something about the departed. I met one half sister for the first time and also renewed my acquaintance with the three other older siblings, two of whom I barely recognized from the faded photos gathering dust in Rayfield and Betsy's spare bedroom. They were nice kin. One of them had traveled clear across the continent. They were quiet and well behaved, uniformly tall, I remember. But I was trying so hard not to drink, I couldn't concentrate. And I couldn't help but compare it with Eddie's wake the day before, which was crowded and noisy.

In fact, for a little punk con man only in his twenties who never did much of anything but beat his friends out of a couple of dollars, the crowd was large indeed. Everyone showed up: a full roster of fringe characters from below Fourteenth Street; all the resident lowlifes on City Island; and several madams led by Corinne wearing a floppy black hat. In fact she had been the first to arrive. Evelyn's family huddled together in one corner. Later Eddie's high school chums arrived, including several ex-girlfriends. Finally, a few musicians from the clubs turned up at the last minute to solemnly pay their respects.

I had never been to a wake before. Maggie was there with me. I couldn't go alone. When we first arrived, we stood hesitating just inside the door. It was still early in the day and there were rows of folding chairs, many of them as yet empty, facing a bare stage with the coffin on it. Baskets of flowers flanked the stage. Off to one side, there was a metal tree that looked like a music stand with pictures of saints hanging from it. It was all very strange. Evelyn came over. She looked like someone else in her conservative black suit with her hair up in a bun. I introduced her to my mother. They embraced. Then Evelyn held me tight. She started to cry.

"It was just his time. That's all. We've got to accept it. Do you want to say good-bye to him with me?"

She took me by the hand and led me to the coffin on the low stage. The coffin was lit from above. Evelyn shoved me gently.

"Go ahead, Janet, say good-bye."

I went up and looked in the casket. Eddie lay there, with his hands folded, in a gray suit, white shirt and striped tie. He was wearing black wing-tipped shoes. His curly hair was much darker because it was slicked down with styling gel and combed in a side part to cover the wound at his temple. He looked waxen, of course, not luminous, not touched with moonlight as in life, but he was the same shade of junkie white. The suit made him look like a small, well-groomed, and attractive young man, someone you would trust to handle your portfolio or sell you insurance. I imagined the life we might have had together if he had been that person he was portrayed as in the coffin. We would have lived in Queens, Forest Hills if we were lucky, and had babies.

"Good-bye, I love you. Where are you now?"

Evelyn came and knelt down, so I did the same. She made the sign of the cross; I did, too: up and down, then left to right. She and I bowed our heads and lifted our hands in prayer.

A short while after that, Donna came in with Arthur, who appeared to be a natural-born mourner in his elegant, dark three-piece pin-striped suit. First he came over to where I had rejoined Maggie.

"You look lovely," he said to me. (Maggie had taken me to Lord & Taylor the day before, where I had found a flattering black crepe dress and heels.) Arthur introduced himself to Maggie and offered condolences to both of us for my father. He said how difficult it must be to have to miss Eddie's funeral the next day, as I was going to my father's funeral instead. "Your heart must be torn with grief."

Then he took my hand and looked me right in the eye. "Listen, Janet. There's no point in my telling you I'm sorry. Of course I am. But I'm not going to lose a lot of sleep over what happened, because the chances are pretty good I would have to do the same thing again given the circumstances."

He kept holding my hand, giving me that doleful look he had. I wanted to scream, 'And now Eddie's dead.'

Arthur pulled a little silver flask out of his pocket and offered Maggie and then me a swig. "Grand Marnier, excellent balm for the nerves," he said.

Maggie looked slightly tempted, and I'm sure I looked very tempted, but we both politely refused. I hadn't had a drink since I'd been hauled off to Bellevue.

Arthur put his arm around my shoulders and gave me a squeeze. "I always believed in you, kid."

"Good to finally meet you," he said to Maggie before he moved away.

Then Arthur walked right over to Evelyn. I was surprised. I would have thought Eddie's killer might have kept his distance from his victim's mother; instead I saw the two of them embrace. They both seemed to be impersonating straight people as they stood together talking in their respective black suits. Evelyn would say something and he would nod. Then it looked like he would tell a story, maybe a funny Eddie story, and she would smile, a little of her former gleam appearing for an instant before the shroud of bottomless grief descended again. I remembered Arthur always did indulge Eddie like an impossible prodigal, the cross he had to bear.

I kept looking at Arthur and Evelyn, trying to make some sense of it all. Eventually I watched them go before the coffin, each one making the sign of the cross as, in one fluid motion, they knelt, bowed their heads, and prayed. Their rhythm and economy of movement impressed me. 'Catholics really know how to exit this world,' I thought.

Michael came with Ava. I wouldn't have believed Michael had it in him. He even wore a jacket over his black turtleneck and real shoes, black loafers. Ava had pulled her massive hair up into a bun.

She wore a long black skirt that accentuated her height. Michael and Ava went over to Evelyn and Arthur, who both stood up from where they were kneeling in front of the coffin. Ava knelt down right away in front of Eddie. Michael made the sign of the cross but remained standing. I watched Evelyn introduce him to Arthur. It was all so civilized. Especially Evelyn. I would have expected her to be lashing out with grief. But she was so entirely miserable, all she could do was love and forgive.

Maggie nodded respectfully to everyone. She summoned her theatrical training to play the role of the young widow's mother, as if this were an antebellum affair and the collective dignity of the local gentry was being gathered up to honor the pride of the southern countryside.

I introduced her to Evelyn's longtime boyfriend, Daniel, who smiled his benevolent, toothless smile. Then he produced a flask, which he waved at me. I could have used a drink. I hated this saying no to a drink.

Michael retreated to a corner alone, where he stood also nipping from a flask. He had pulled his black hair back in a ponytail, and he looked wonderfully forlorn. He was a frail soul, I realized, not for the first time. I was playing the familiar game with myself in which I tried every way I could to dismantle the appeal he still held for me. But whatever I came up with backfired. All his faults were treasures to me. What kind of person was I that at poor Eddie's wake, right in front of his cold body, I could be lusting after an old flame? Life makes beasts of us—it's base, this desire in the face of death. Which is precisely what had always revolted Eddie about the whole deal.

Meanwhile, Michael continued to stand there alone, managing to appear awkward and poised at the same time. God, he was tall and majestic—splendid, really. He looked like a frosty quart of beer on a hot afternoon. Finally I hit on something that allowed me to detach from my Svengali. I had heard through the grapevine he and Ava were just about through, and this had the peculiar effect of liberating me. I don't think it was gloating exactly, because I felt for Ava. It was more that I had a new understanding: Michael, the once and future king of one-night stands, could only enjoy at most one inspired weekend with a woman, after which he felt obliged to spend the next two to ten years letting her down easy. Seeing Ava across the room, her body drooping with grief and depression, I could remember the chronic pain of enduring Michael's protracted rejection. I remembered it was like watching someone gracefully disentangle himself from a messy web. Except I was the web.

Michael could not have brought himself to approach anyone, but once I took Maggie over to him, he responded with his characteristic diffident charm. He took Maggie's hand, shook it, and nodded his head slightly at the same time.

"Your daughter is a true love of mine," he said.

"One of them, I understand," Maggie said, ever the cynic on this subject.

"Yes, but it's a very small club, and I have a feeling there won't be any more new members."

"Don't be ridiculous, you're still a very handsome young man. In fact, you look more sensitive and artistic than I would have thought. Anyway, hunker down, kid, because love keeps at you for a long time, and it's a bloody nuisance."

Michael smiled. "Thank you. I can take heart now."

The way they were romancing each other with their wry disillusion. They were both so full of crap. I wished Eddie were there to tell them so.

Epilogue

Evelyn never sold another piece of tail again. Instead, she opened a no-frills packaging store off Main Street on City Island. It was a forerunner to Mail Boxes Etc. She liked it because the inventory required a minimum of upkeep. I also heard she never left City Island if she could help it.

Meanwhile, I joined an outpatient clinic downtown.

"I wouldn't have given a plug nickel for your sobriety," Laura, my alcoholism counselor, told me. "In swaggers this punk in rags with matted hair—manic and unreachable is what I thought."

Nevertheless, Laura must have suspected something, because, to keep me occupied, she composed for me a long reading list. That got my attention. I discovered later that my counselor had herself written several well-received plays, one of which made it to Broadway in the late fifties. Laura was a writer and an intellectual. But more important, she was a sober drunk.

No matter which acute crisis I brought to her—and there was nothing else but in the weeks that followed—Laura would circle a name and address in the meeting book and say, "Go to this meeting."

"The landlord's trying to evict me" or "I just lost another waitressing gig!" I'd say.

Real life or death stuff.

"Go to a meeting," Laura would always reply with stony composure.

At first, I hated those church-basement meetings. I hated those creepy, smiling faces so painfully visible under the harsh fluorescent lights. I sat cringing and hiding in the back of the room. But then one day, WE CAME TO BELIEVE A POWER GREATER THAN OURSELVES COULD RESTORE US TO SANITY" leapt out at me from the scroll on the wall where it hung. 'That's a remarkable claim,' I thought, 'sanity.' I was reminded of those times during my psychotic episodes when the handwriting on the wall had read GET WELL. Sanity. Imagine the possibility even of such a state. Sanity beckoned like a grail, and I began to attend those meetings every day. But a part of me still believed for months that in doing so I was caving in. Surrender is never easy precisely because it feels like defeat. Laura suggested I go on welfare. "You're unemployable right now" is how she put it.

The welfare office on West Fourteenth Street is a curious place for someone brought up on Park Avenue. I sat hour after vacant hour on one of the numberless hard chairs that stretched row on row like bleachers against the wall of the main room. I did some thinking. On all sides, other women sat packed in with screaming babies, their arms outstretched in the usually vain attempt to retrieve restless, wandering toddlers. Here and there solitary men waited quietly. A few of these men might have been classified as fit enough to work, but for the most part they were a forlorn, sickly bunch in obvious need. I realized sitting there I would never know what it is like to be born poor. If I spent the rest of my life depriving myself, I would not be able to entirely stifle hope or even opportunity.

After I finally succeeded in making the welfare roll, Laura suggested I move back in with my mother, with Maggie, one last time. "You can't take care of yourself yet" was how she put it.

Maggie and I made amends. She became a model mother, and I, an exemplary daughter. Every evening I would return from my AA meeting, and there would be a hot meal waiting. She did my laundry. She bought me a down pillow and a new pink comforter for the chaste single bed in my old pink-and-cherry-red bedroom.

Then I went back to school. When I found out I could get a lot of loans and grants, I decided to go uptown after all and "hustle the intellectuals," as the madam Corinne had suggested in another lifetime. I sat up front, hung on every word, and took copious notes. So it was, still too damaged and afraid to love the living, I wholly embraced the distant and the long dead. I began to understand that a relentless series of tests of survival in the street is not the only education worth having. The hot blast of the life I was running from did serve me well in one respect—it propelled me to study.

Since then, I've stopped running. The past is here with me. I respect it, even fear it a little. Otherwise I tell myself I no longer need be afraid—either of me or the rest of this mystery.

About the Author

Janet Capron is a writer based in New York City. She holds an MFA in creative writing from Columbia University. *Blue Money* is her first book.